TARA Then and Now, Here and There

Archives and Practices of the Experimental Design Bureau in Vilnius 1960s–1980s

Spector Books

Karolina Jakaitė, Deimantė Jasiulevičiūtė (eds.)

Contents

Dedicated to the artists of the Tara bureau

Foreword
On the Tara bureau and its ABCs

Tara and Tariukas

This book welcomes you with a sketch for *Tariukas* by Vladas Lisaitis. He was meant to be a character who travels around the world and dreams of reaching the moon. This is a great analogy for the artists of the Tara bureau whose own dreams, like *Tariukas* himself, were both aspirational yet unrealized. The word "Tariukas" is a Lithuanian diminutive form of a masculine name. In this case, the name is linked to the Tara bureau. The word "tara" is international in its origin, and refers to the packaging of materials, products, or other items ready for consumption, storage, or transportation. Most likely that it came to the Tara bureau "alphabet" from the Russian language, where Tara also means all types of packaging.

The character of *Tariukas* and the stories of the Tara bureau take us back to the 1960s, the 1970s, and the 1980s. The Tara bureau was established in 1964 and was most active until the restoration of Independence of Lithuania in 1990. "Tara" was the word used by the artist-constructors who worked there to refer to the Soviet era's most important graphic design institution in Vilnius – the Experimental Package Design Bureau. For the bureau's designers, which included artists with various degrees and an unusually high number of women, "Tara" became a generic key word for their workplace, as the full name of the institution was bureaucratically long and changed several times throughout the bureau's existence.

Then and Now

During the Soviet occupation, the bureau was tasked with carrying out various propaganda duties. As a result, when Lithuania regained independence and privatization began, the bureau's archives were considered too Soviet and were not preserved. This loss has made it particularly difficult to research the Tara bureau and the graphic design of the period.

Here and There

The Bureau's activities took place during the Cold War, a time when the Iron Curtain prevented people in the Eastern Bloc from traveling freely to the West. However, the bureau held a unique status tied to

Soviet efforts to compete with the West in various fields. As a result, some of the packaging and promotional materials created by the bureau's artists were showcased at Soviet "export" exhibitions in both Eastern Bloc and Western countries. In the West, these products often went unnoticed due to the propaganda embedded in their content, which did not resonate with Western audiences.

The loss of the bureau's archives is another challenge which has caused many events, names, and works to fade into oblivion. Most of the visual examples in this book are sourced from private collections. From today's perspective, this exploration reveals many intriguing, yet sensitive and painful topics that remain far from fully explored. Although this is the first comprehensive study of its kind, it marks only the beginning of further research.

Glossary and its ABCs

We designed this book as an experiment in graphic design, introducing a playful way of exploring the Tara bureau's samples through thematic ABC chapters and Glossary navigation. Throughout the book, Glossary keywords are inserted with markings reminiscent of scanned packaging, enabling navigation between *Then* and *Now*, *Here* and *There*. This approach provides a contextual introduction to the period of the Tara bureau as well as the intentions and practices of its artists. When creating the Glossary, we searched for reflections of identity, signs of time, and other codes of meaning. The attempts to explore these surviving examples from a contemporary perspective involve recreating small segments at a time, investigating the biographies of individual artists or fragments of individual works by using the essential *zoom-in* method which is discussed in our conversation. The fragmentary nature of the Tara bureau's archive, reflected by the incompleteness of the Glossary, is encoded in its very identity.

We would like to thank the many people and institutions that supported and contributed to our initiative. Most of the visual examples published in this book come from the private archives of the artists who worked in the bureau, as well as their relatives: Juozas Gelguda, Monika Jonaitienė, Vladas Lisaitis, Petrutė Masiulionytė, Kęstutis Ramonas, Laimutė Ramonienė, Vincentas Sakas, Raisa Šmuriginaitė, Kęstutis Šveikauskas and others. This book is dedicated to them – the artists of the Tara bureau and to their bright remembrance, in particular to the 100th birth anniversary of Kęstutis Gvalda (1925–2011).

Karolina Jakaitė and Deimantė Jasiulevičiūtė

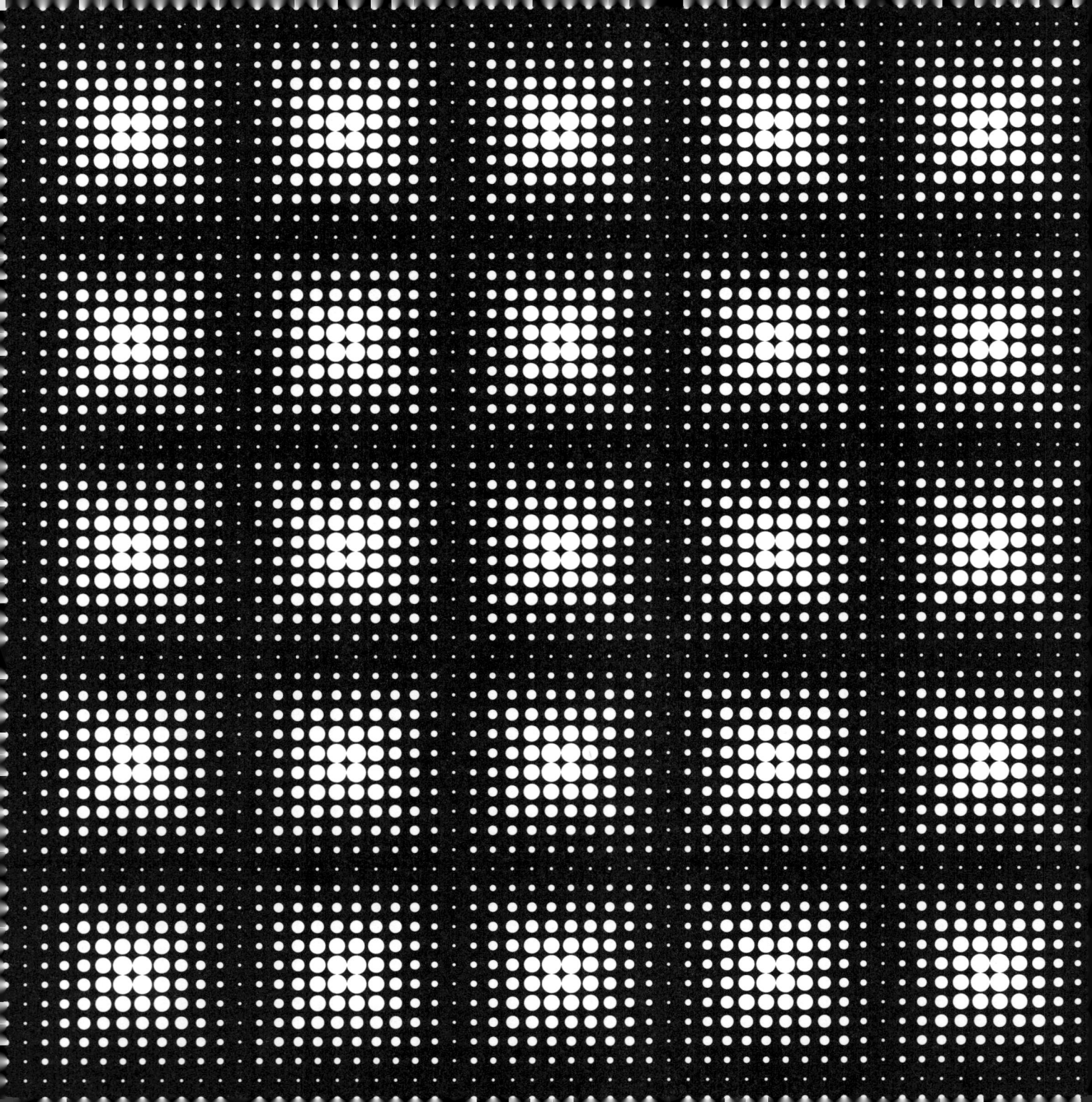

a is for archive: anonymous, (un)important, and rediscovered artefacts

Karolina Jakaitė

1

The beginning was related to my PhD research and thesis *Lithuanian graphic design in the 1950s–1970s: between National and International* (supervised by Assoc. Prof. Dr. Lolita Jablonskienė, [manuscript], Vilnius Academy of Arts, 2012).

2

David Crowley, *Writing about Heroes,* https://faktografia.com/2012/06/09/writing-about-heroes/.

Looking back after years of reflection on the artists of the Tara bureau[1] and trying to piece together the stories of the artefacts in the archive, I kept coming back to David Crowley's writings, and his important reflections on how and why the history of graphic design might be written differently, something he expresses in his unfinished essay *Writing about Heroes*. Here Crowley raises the question of whether the history of design could be written "without designers"

> *Anonymous production is, of course, of the principle definitions of ephemera, a category often associated with print history. But the problem with ephemera is its marginal status. Ephemeral does not just mean short-lived: it also suggests unimportant.*[2]

I will try to discuss the key words and related insights in this quote separately and apply them case by case to the context of the Tara bureau. First of all, the term *short-lived*. Almost all of the artefacts created by the Tara bureau's artists – be it packaging for all sorts of things, boxes of sweets, labels, posters, advertising leaflets, or simply factory brochures – are the most transient and short-lived examples of graphic design which are now tagged on social media with the hashtag *#Ephemera*. It is common behaviour to throw away the packaging of a product or an edible item once it is unpacked and its contents are consumed. If it is an illustrated promotional message, we might leaf through it, read it, and put it away. However, objects created several or more decades ago, become examples of graphic design history, witnesses of a certain period of time or even heritage objects. In the case of the Tara archive, we are dealing with artefacts created between the 1960s and 1980s, in Soviet-occupied Lithuania, where attempts were being made to establish a socialist order, while design had a slightly different function than the one we usually encounter in the context of Western design history. Even then, however, not everything always went as planned or as we might imagine. That is why the stories of Tara's artefacts are usually related to many derivative narratives, paradoxes, and inversions of conventional meaning.

To get a little deeper into the idea of transiency, it should be noted that there are areas of graphic design that tend to have more staying power. Posters are a good example of this, because even though they contain texts intended to commemorate one-day occasions or specific historical events that become outdated, they nevertheless become part of a "record" of the past, and as a result, survive for a longer time period. Posters are more likely to become collectors' items, be described in books, displayed in specialized exhibitions, or discussed in terms of their original stylistics and the style of their creators. Brand logos also deserve a mention in the context of discussing transiency. Even at that time, knowing the superficiality, absurdity, incapacity and uncertainty of the Soviet system, the artists of the Tara bureau created logos with great creative zeal. To this day, their creations are still fascinating for their abstract, symbolic, and *non-Soviet* nature. Because of these qualities, perhaps the latter especially, Antanas Kazakauskas (1937–2019), a Lithuanian master of graphic design from the same period, who had little direct connection with Tara, was also fascinated by the logos created by the Tara bureau's artists and very playfully incorporated some of them in the catalogue for the 1968 Soviet London Export Exhibition.[3] This layout could be considered a kind of tribute to the unknown, un-named Lithuanian graphic designers of the time, all of whom were working at the Tara bureau and were friends and colleagues of Kazakauskas.

3
See Karolina Jakaitė, *Šaltojo karo kapsulė: lietuvių dizainas Londone 1968*, Vilnius: Lapas, 2019, Karolina Jakaitė, *ANTANAS KAZAKAUSKAS. Everything is programmed*, Vilnius: Vilnius Graphic Art Centre, Vilnius Academy of Arts, 2022.

Antanas Kazakauskas, layout from the catalogue *Lithuania London '68*, published in English, 1968

a is for archive

Brand logos of companies and factories were created with a longer shelf-life in mind, because they were often enlarged and mounted on building façades or placed in their interiors. Despite this fact, most of them were forgotten rather quickly even during the Soviet years, almost immediately after the collapse of the planned economy, and eventually most of them disappeared completely with the fall of the occupation. However, it is worth noting that some of them, although not many, managed to survive to the present day as witnesses to history and clues to those "different times". For example, through the window of my apartment in Vilnius I can still see the Sigma sign designed by the Tara bureau artist Pranas Markevičius (b. 1937) or recall the very recently used brand logo "Sp" (press) by Kęstutis Šveikauskas (1928–2008).

Text by V. Jurevičius about the Tara bureau exhibition "Signs and Posters", published in the evening newspaper *Vakarinės naujienos*, 27 June 1984. The photograph shows "Sigma" logo modifications designed by Pranas Markevičius

ŽENKLAI IR PLAKATAI

Baigiantis mokslo metams Lietuvos TSR kultūros darbuotojų tobulinimosi institute surengta Vilniaus taros ir įpakavimo gamybinio susivienijimo eksperimentinio meninio konstravimo biuro pramoninės grafikos paroda. Joje — šimtas emblemų, prekių ženklų, dvi dešimtys reklaminių plakatų.

Grafiški K. Gvaldos, P. Markevičiaus, K. Šveikausko ženklai parodai suteikia dalykiškumo, rimtumo, o E. Lisiauskienės, V. Lisino, A. Žilinskaitės reklaminiai komercinių renginių, mugių, amatų dienų plakatai — spalvingumo, gyvumo. Instituto klausytojams paroda yra ir naudinga, ir įdomi. Ji apima laiką nuo EMKB įkūrimo iki šių dienų.

Keturiolikos biuro atstovų darbai ne tik supažindina lankytojus su taikomosios grafikos galimybėmis pramonėje ir prekyboje, bet ir atspindi EMKB kolektyvo kūrybines galimybes per dvidešimt jo egzistavimo metų.

V. JUREVIČIUS

NUOTRAUKOJE: „Sigmos" gamybinio susivienijimo gamyklų prekių ženklų modifikacijos. Dailininkas P. Markevičius.

Kęstutis Šveikauskas, mini photographs of the logo "Sąjunginė spauda" (Union Press), 1978, personal archive of Kęstutis Gvalda

a is for archive

Even though we are talking about work that is usually anonymous, it is not for nothing that I insist on mentioning the names of the artists whenever possible. They are very important to me both as personalities, with whom I have had an opportunity to frequently interact in my quest to discover more about their inspiration and creative processes, but also as witnesses who stubbornly preserved the history and salvaged parts of the archive of the Tara bureau. I also have to acknowledge that these are in many cases *personalized* stories, which often make seemingly simple artefacts of graphic design speak in a different – empathetic and sensitive – way. This is why, when writing about the graphic design stories of the Tara bureau, I make sure to include the designers, mention their names, and quote their personal testimonies.

One of the first and most important of these witnesses was Kęstutis Gvalda (1925–2011), whom I met in 2008 and communicated with quite intensively until his passing. During our very first interview, he referred to the Tara bureau as "a miracle" and began to tell me enthusiastically about the system that somehow worked really well in the gloomy Soviet years, making it possible to implement a graphic design commission from an idea to a specific product in one place. Carrying out all the research and creating a company's visual style, from brand logo, to signboard design and branded clothing. The Tara bureau's artists created posters, packaging, labels, and layouts for a wide range of promotional publications. The bureau was quite a large institution with multiple departments, a nearby printing house, a library and a methodological room, where just like in a museum, examples of the best projects were kept.

Here I would like to insert an excerpt from another important eyewitness account of how this bureau came into being. The initiative to set up such a specialized bureau came in the early 1960s. It was related to the modernization processes, the growth of production, the increasing range of goods, the Soviet "art for everyday life" programme, and the objectives of the Cold War. The first head of the bureau, Antanas Morkevičius (1928–2018), described this period in his memoir, in a chapter codenamed "Between Heaven and Earth":

At that time, a lot of importance was given to increasing the export of various goods, which needed to be packaged in an artistic and modern way and, specifically, accompanied by a large amount of

documentation (brochures, instructions, posters, etc.) and advertising material in various foreign languages. This is why already by
the end of 1961 I was given the task of setting up the Experimental
Package Design Bureau.[4]

4
Antanas Morkevičius, "Tarp dangaus
ir žemės" (Between Heaven and Earth),
in: *Lietuvos medienos pramonė:
nuo ištakų iki 2000 metų*, Vilnius:
Homo Liber, 2001, 132.

5
May 14, 1964, Proposals for the
establishment of the Pilot Bureau for
Container and Packaging Constructing
at the National Economy Council,
Lithuanian Central State Archives,
Fund R-239, List 4, File 140, Sheet 235.

6
Another interesting coincidence:
the bureau's library subscribed
to numerous foreign specialized
magazines, including the Zürich-based
TARA, several copies of which were
preserved by Vladas Lisaitis.

Most interestingly, one of the reasons he mentions is related to foreign
countries and the export of goods, and it is exactly the artefacts
intended for export that were analysed at length in the process of this
research. Morkevičius mentions the year 1961, and in archival documents I have found a record from 1963, when the Packaging Design
Department was established at the Central Design and Constructing
Bureau of the Council of National Economy of the Lithuanian SSR and
8 artist-constructors[5] – the term used for the designers of the time
– were employed. The official date of the bureau's establishment is
August 11, 1964, by the decision of the Council of National Economy.
It became the most important institution for the creation, production,
and dissemination of Lithuanian graphic design in the 1960s–1980s.
It is worth mentioning that during its most productive period
(1964–1984), the bureau employed more than 50 artist-constructors.
The name of the bureau itself was changed several times, so the abbreviation "Tara",[6] used among the artists, became the key word which
helps us unravel the bureau's stories in the present day.

Cover of the Tara bureau catalogue,
designed by Kostas Katkus, 1970

I would like to go back to Kęstutis Gvalda's quote "the bureau
was like a miracle". Only later, after many years of research into the

7

More former deportees and artists who were otherwise disobedient to the occupation regime worked at the bureau.

history of Tara and studying the biographies of individual authors, was I able to decipher the additional meaning of this quote. Gvalda was a former deportee[7] who had lived in Stalin's gulag in Siberia for more than 10 years, and at that time it was difficult for people with such an experience not only to find a job, but simply to fit into society. Therefore, when he managed to get a job at the Tara bureau right after graduation, a new phase of his life began. During this difficult period of his life, he found not only a workplace, like-minded colleagues and friends, but also an opportunity to realize his creative ideas.

Kęstutis Gvalda in Stalin's gulag in Krasnoyarsk Krai, Siberia, circa 1950s, personal archive of Regina Pranskevičienė

In all his interviews, Gvalda spoke mainly about the positive aspects of the bureau's activities: very creative artists, great works developed, exhibitions attended, awards won, but in that very first interview he also mentioned something that came into conflict with the uplifting and visionary "miracle". "Tara" was like a "swear word". First of all, perhaps because, after all, – to quote Gvalda's contemporary, poster master Juozas Galkus, who had worked in the Artistic Committee of the bureau – most artists of that time "wanted first and foremost to be real artists, to create pure art, to participate in exhibitions, to amaze their colleagues by their discoveries, to be known and famous".[8] But when they undertook commissions for applied

8

Author's interview with Juozas Galkus, Vilnius, 8 October 2021.

a is for archive

graphics, they knew that they would have to deal with production, that their work would often remain anonymous and their authorship would disappear. Therefore, such activity was often considered a kind of "creative setback".

This "swear word" also refers to the marginality and the feeling of being *unimportant*, which David Crowley mentions in his essay. However, in the case of Tara, there were more meanings attached to the unimportant. It is necessary to mention here, that in the Soviet system, advertising commissions posed a number of additional challenges and uncertainties, since the declared visions of the government were very different from reality: people lacked basic items and goods, their quality was often very questionable, and artists had to create a large number of representational exhibition projects that did not necessarily make it into production. Therefore, in some cases artists themselves considered the commissions for applied graphics to be more of a "side job" and did not necessarily include the examples of graphic design in their solo exhibition lists and catalogues, with perhaps the exception of the previously mentioned isolated areas of posters and brand logos, which graphic designers tended to categorize as artistic work. That was how applied graphics often found itself on the "margins", "behind the scenes" or "on the fringes" of the creative field. Most of the mentioned Tara artists, were and are little known or completely unknown in the Lithuanian art and design field.

When projects gained success, there was also a sense of pride in that the products created by artists sold better, that the specially designed packaging looked more aesthetically pleasing, featuring original shapes and compositions. The Tara bureau was home to a collective of artists who believed in creative projects. And I would say that it is not for nothing that the longest-lasting name of the bureau – Experimental Artistic Constructing Bureau[9] – had the word "artistic" in it, as it was the artistic and aesthetic value in particular that was very important to the artists working there. Sometimes it seems appropriate to quote Latvian design researcher Kristīne Budže who claimed that we are talking about a time "when design was in the hands of artists".[10] And artists, naturally, find exhibitions particularly important. The poster of one of the last and largest exhibitions organized by the Tara bureau – the 1984 Republican Exhibition of Applied Graphic Art – features an enlarged hand, a motif of a paper roll, and an eye. This poster, created by the long-time Tara artist Vladas Lisaitis (b. 1939), is like one of the most mysterious testimonies

9
In Lithuanian *Eksperimentinis meninio konstravimo biuras* and its abbreviation *EMKB*.

10
Kristīne Budže, "When Design was in the Hands of Artists. Interview with Džemma Skulme", in *Just on Time. Design Stories about Latvia*, eds. Kristīne Budže, Inese Baranovska, Riga: Latvian National Museum of Art, 2018, 52–56.

a is for archive

regarding the Tara bureau. Its metaphorical messages can be interpreted in many ways, but for me they speak of the fact that all graphic design objects, even the smallest ones, are created by human hands, with love for people, looking deeply inwards with eyes wide open.

Vladas Lisaitis, sketches for the poster of *The Republican Exhibition of Applied Graphics*, 1984, personal archive of Vladas Lisaitis

The applied graphics projects displayed in exhibitions, in real life, usually differed significantly from the artists' ideas. When creating modern brand marks, designing colourful advertising posters, publications, and packaging for a wide variety of goods they often would not even get to see, they treated all of it as creative tasks and sought to create examples of interesting and often bold artistic language while trying to keep up with global trends. However, those projects were not always interesting to Soviet companies or their managers, not to mention their inefficiency in the context of a planned economy. The same goes for the disappointments that accompanied entries to international exhibitions, according to Gvalda's testimony: "Moscow blocked our logos for a long time", telling the story of how the central Soviet institutions and various commissions in charge, specifically refused to send Lithuanian-made logos and posters to the Brno International Biennial of Graphic Design and other exhibitions. When Gvalda realized this, he undertook the curatorial missions himself.

Vladas Lisaitis holding printed sheets of design proposals next to one of the factories, circa 1980s, personal archive of Vladas Lisaitis

Another important aspect concerns realization. Deviations and discrepancies were inevitable in the execution of print-related commissions. The Tara bureau had a large production base, but it was the polygraphy-related restrictions "this can't be done!", "that won't work!" and the poor printing quality that caused constant frustration to the artists. However, there were exceptions to this rule commissions for exhibitions or for export were sometimes printed by foreign printers, on better paper, and with inks of exceptional quality.

Here I would like to introduce an extended account of a visual nature, describing several export exhibitions and the expositions presented there. Not only were the most beautiful samples of Tara packaging and exceptional souvenir objects selected for these exhibitions, but also the exhibition architects who designed them often chose logos created by the bureau's designers to be featured as the main artistic accents. It was these highly creative logos that were displayed at the Baltic Food Exhibitions that travelled to all three Baltic capitals Vilnius, Riga, and Tallinn in 1966. The same year, at the Leipzig Fair where the Soviet republics of Lithuania and Estonia were invited to participate, an enlarged Kęstutis Ramonas' logo of the Tara bureau itself was also displayed. However, during the installation of the Leipzig exhibition it was hung upside down. It was probably a human error, haste, or simple carelessness on the part of the mounters, but from a contemporary perspective, it could also be interpreted as a metaphor for *discrepancy* or as a symbol of some kind of misunderstanding. Another coincidence may also prove fateful: all official correspondence documents gave the address of the Tara bureau at 12 *Paribio* (meaning "Periphery") Street in Vilnius. The bureau was located on the territory of the cardboard-lithography factory, next to the *Pergalė* confectionery factory. Although the buildings of the factory and of the Tara bureau in particular are long gone, the name of the street has survived to this day. In Lithuanian, the meaning of the word sounds like a programmed code for "periphery" or "margins".

Logo of the Tara bureau (upside-down) and next to it – a display of food production of the Soviet Lithuania Republic at the 1966 Leipzig Spring Fair, 1966. Architect Albinas Purys, photograph from Lithuanian Central State Archives

The many contradictions in Tara's stories are seemingly connected by another important keyword: experiment. It was embedded in the name of the Tara bureau and other institutions of the time. In the Soviet system, it carried the meaning of certain progress, giving a company the chance to obtain more advanced equipment, quality materials, and receive special commissions. However, through today's perspective, more aspects of this experimentation reveal themselves. Artists working in the field of applied graphics experimented all the time. They eagerly learned from foreign samples seen in magazines, while facing the reality of many inconsistencies and system cracks, having to constantly maneuver between unique projects and manufacturing defects, professional mastery and deficit, implemented and unimplemented ideas. Typical of this disparity was the cartoon "Tariukas on the Moon",[11] which featured a cheerful character, *Tariukas*, who not only travelled around the world, but even went to the Moon to promote the new projects of the Tara bureau! This unrealized project not only reflects the then visions and aesthetics of the cosmic age and the goals of the Cold War, but also speaks of the creators' ambitions

11
In the late 1960s–early 1970s the cartoon was produced by the bureau's employees artists Vladas Lisaitis and Kęstutis Šveikauskas, Karolina Jakaitė and Deimantė Jasiulevičiūtė interview with Vladas Lisaitis, "Design Foundation", Vilnius, 11 November 2021.

a is for archive

which were often directed to the "broad" world beyond the Soviet reality. In this context, we can interpret the bureau itself as a kind of experiment, the ambitious founding goals of which in many cases remained unfulfilled – merely aspirational, utopian ambitions.

The Tara bureau's logos and packaging at the Baltic Food Exhibition, circa 1960s, photograph by Vytautas Zaranka, Lithuanian Archives of Literature and Art

On an ending note, let's once again discuss the *unimportant* and the problematics of the Soviet past in the present-day context. It should be mentioned that most of the researched advertising samples are on a list of "written off" publications, meaning that they were discarded as worthless and no longer needed, therefore would have been simply lost. Another important fact is that already in the late 1980s, after the privatization of the Tara bureau's premises began, the specialized library and materials of the methodological office were being lost. Kestutis Gvalda managed to preserve a small, yet important portion of archival material from the Tara bureau. The present-day research was based on artistic research methods and interviews in collaboration with the designers of the Tara bureau themselves. An empathetic and personalized approach made it possible to view the artefacts of the occupation period from a different angle, to extract the lost names of creators and disentangle the chronicles of their complex biographies from the rigid fear, the lies, and the vows of silence. Today, the rediscovered artefacts of the Tara archive speak not only of the processes of Lithuania's intermittent graphic design history, but also of the signs of time, the sensitive narratives and the stories of identity recorded in those otherwise insignificant objects.

a is for archive

East German visitors are viewing the display of Soviet Lithuanian souvenirs and packaging by the Tara bureau in Erfurt at the 'Litauen 70', 1970, architect Albinas Purys, photograph from Lithuanian Central State Archives

a is for archive

Eksperimentinis meninio konstravimo biuras

EKSPERIMENTINIS
TAROS IR ĮPAKAVIMO
KONSTRAVIMO BIURAS

b is for bureau:
artist-constructors and their practices

The bureau first opened its doors in 1964, on the grounds of the newly constructed Cardboard and Lithography Plant at 12 *Paribio* Street in Vilnius, near the *Pergalė* Confectionery Factory. Initial plans called for a small staff to work in the non-production design unit, that consisted of a department head, a senior architect, five so-called category one designers, four category two designers, and a senior technician. The scope of the bureau's operations grew quickly and the design team expanded. In the first year and a half of operations, an additional twelve artist-constructors were hired, and by 1969 their number had grown to nearly fifty.

    For a general idea of the size of the bureau, data from 1972 records that 485 employees worked at the bureau, of which 130 were related to constructing-design work. The artists who worked at the bureau were trained in different fields. Many of these artists were graduates of the LSSR State Art Institute (now Vilnius Academy of Arts), but *artist-constructor* positions were also filled by artists with backgrounds in painting, set design, frescoes and mosaics, ceramics, and textiles. For the thirty or so designers who spent their entire careers at the bureau and worked for more than 25 years, the Tara had become more than a workplace, it was their whole life.

Iliustravo patys dailininkai

[A]rtist-constructors   [W]omen-designers

Artist-constructors employed at the Experimental Package Design Bureau, 1970s

b is for bureau: artist-constructors and their practices

As a new graphic design institution, the bureau focused on the creation of its own representational image. A competition was held in 1965 to design a logo and style for the bureau. The winner was a young designer named Kęstutis Ramonas, who linked the first letters of two key words ("Tara", for container, and "Įpakavimas" for packaging) to create a powerful and memorable logo to be used on all bureau's promotional materials.

b is for bureau: artist-constructors and their practices

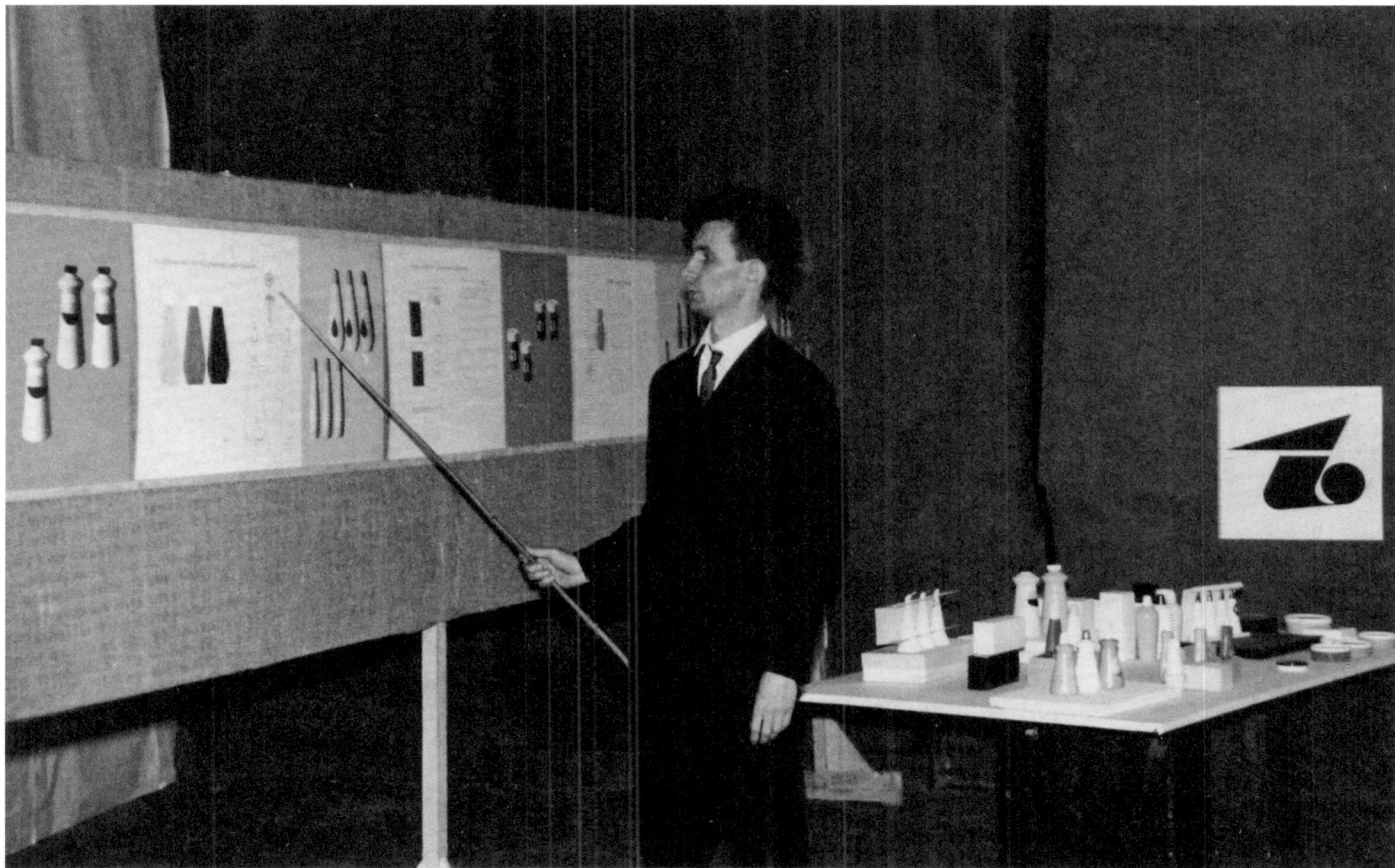

[A]bstract advertising   [D]esign   [E]xperimentation   [J]ury

Kestutis Ramonas was one of the very first graduates of the newly established Department of Artistic Constructing of Industrial Products at the Vilnius Art Institute (now Design Department at the Vilnius Academy of Arts). In 1965, Ramonas defended his thesis under the supervision of Professor Feliksas Daukantas (1915–1995). The graduation project included new forms of containers and packaging for household chemicals. They were manufactured at *Plasta* for the purposes of this project, but never went into actual production.

b s for bureau: artist-constructors and their practices

[E]xperimentation   [I]maginary design   [L]ithuanian   [V]isionary

[A]bstract advertising   [E]xperimentation   [L"]ithuanian   [U]topia   [V]isionary

b is for bureau: artist-constructors and their practices

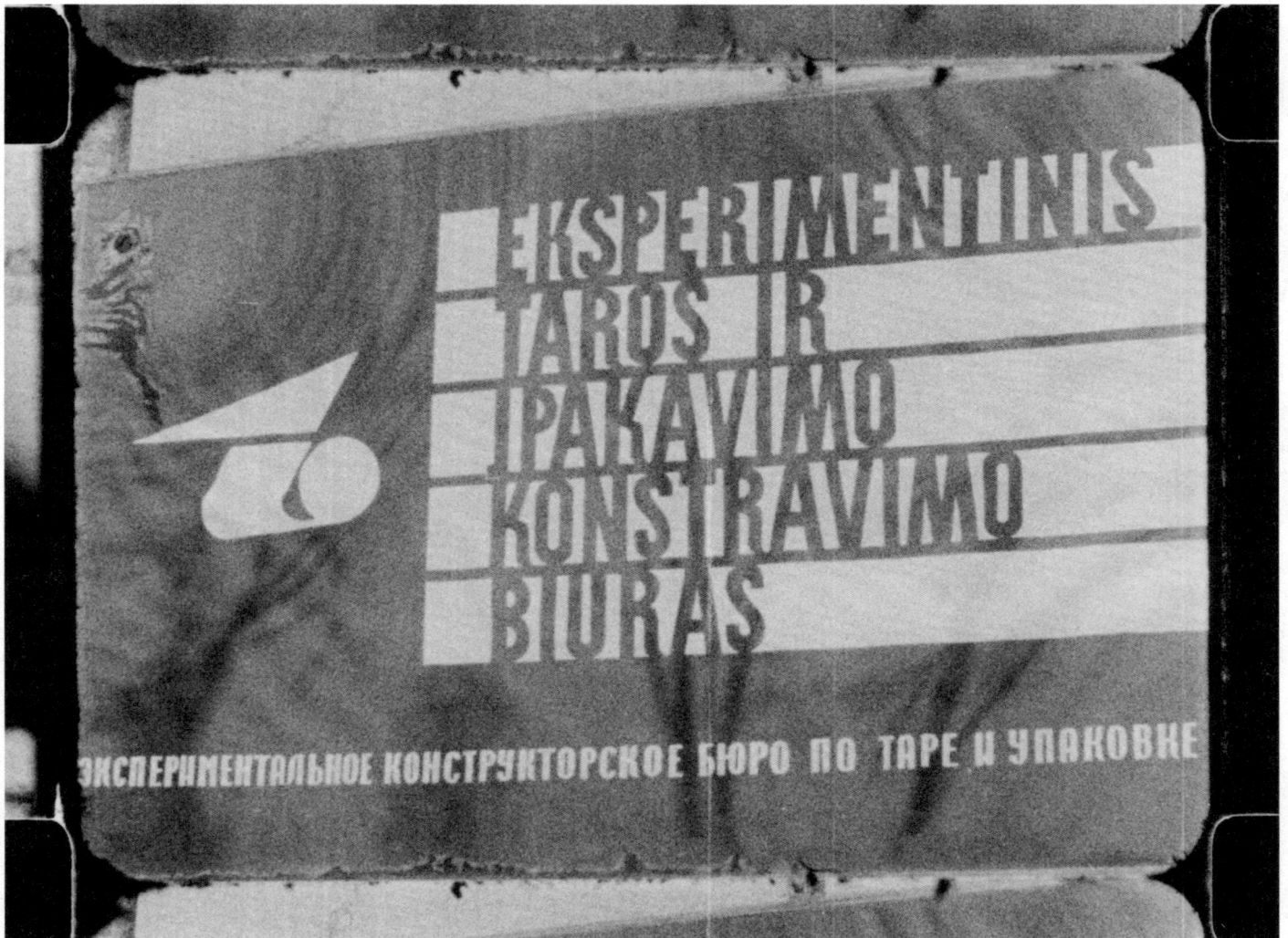

[A]rtist-constructors   [E]xperimentation   [F]açade   [M]odernisation

b is for bureau: artist-constructors and their practices

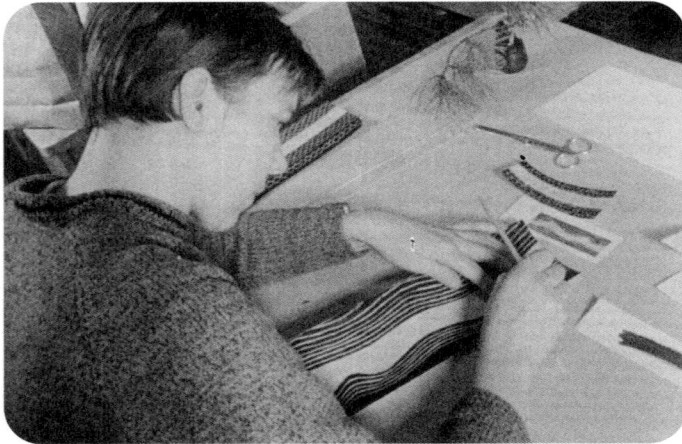
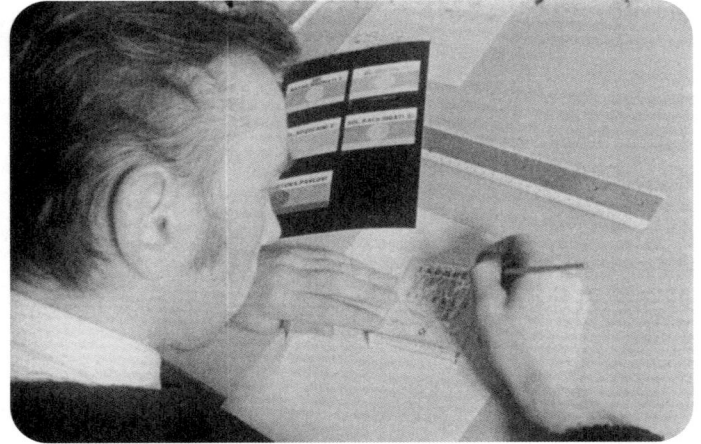

b is for bureau: artist-constructors and their practices

[A]rtist-constructors   [F]açade   [G]ray   [h.]andmade   [J]ury

8

| PROJEKTAS | ↑ h 4 cm ↓ | Zmt |

UŽSAKOVAS Žuvininkystės ckis „Pajūris", Šventoji
Рыбное хозяйство „Пагорис" Шентой

AUTORIUS Svalda Kęstutis, Stasto

MENO TARYBOS ĮVERTINIMAS
PROTOKOLO Nr.
DATA 1968

SKYRIUS	UŽSAKYMO Nr.	NEGATYVO Nr.	MET. KAB. FONDŲ Nr.	ATIDUOTA UŽSAKOVUI	GAMINA

PASTABOS СВИДЕТЕЛЬСТВО № 43837 Класс 29
Зарегистрирован на имя Рыбного хозяйства „Пагорис", Шентой Литовской сер.
Заявлено 30 августа 1971 г.
Срок действия по 30 августа 1981 г.
Товарн: рыбная продукция холодного и горячего копчения (зт. Откры-
тия, изобретения, промышленные образцы, товарные знаки, М, 1973 № 40 стр. 172)
Опубликовано 1 октября 1973 г.

[H]andmade   [I]maginary design   [J]ury   [S]low   [W]estern

[A]rtist-constructors   [F]açade   [F]ear

The bureau also set up a special methodology laboratory, a small but unique type of graphic design museum for the collection of archival documentation and examples of graphic design projects. Bureau's designers and artists had access to a special library and its collection of the latest publications from the Soviet Bloc as well as an impressive collection of Western advertising and packaging periodicals, books, and albums. The most valuable samples stored there, were unfortunately lost during the time of the privatization of the bureau, but luckily a small part was salvaged by Kęstutis Gvalda.

b is for bureau: artist-constructors and their practices

[G]ray   [F]açade   [V]isionary

b is for bureau: artist-constructors and their practices

PLK

Артикул № 05224
Ширина см 140+2
Кол-во метров
Длина куска
Сорт I
Сделано в СССР

1966

«ВИЛЬНЯ»
«СПАРТАК»
«МАСТИС»
«СКЛЯВА»
«НЕКЛОН»
«ВЕРПСТАС»

ОКТЯБРЬ 31 | НОЯБРЬ | ДЕКАБРЬ

ИЮЛЬ | АВГУСТ | СЕНТЯБРЬ

АПРЕЛЬ | МАЙ | ИЮНЬ

ЯНВАРЬ 31 | ФЕВРАЛЬ | МАРТ

LIET. TSR LŪT LPV
PANEVĖŽIO LIN
KOMBINATAS
PANEVĖŽYS, SANDĖLIŲ

УАП СНХ ЛИТ. ССР
ПАНЕВЕЖСИССКИ
ЛЬНОКОМБИНАТ
г. ПАНЕВЕЖИС УЛ. САНДЕЛ

PLK

GAMINIO PAVADINIMAS
НАЗВАНИЕ ИЗДЕЛИЯ

ARTIKULAS NR
АРТИКУЛ №

RŪŠIS
СОРТ

PLOTIS CM
ШИРИНА В СМ

KAINA I-MOS RŪŠIES M
ЦЕНА I-ОГО СОРТА

STANDARTAS
СТАНДАРТ

IŠLEIDIMO DATA
ДАТА ВЫПУСКА

BROKUOTOJO NR
№ БРОКОВЩИКА

ATKARPŲ KIEKIS GABALE IR GABALO ILGIS
КОЛИЧЕСТВО ОТРЕЗКОВ В КУСКЕ И ДЛИНА КУСКА

GABALO NR
№ КУСКА

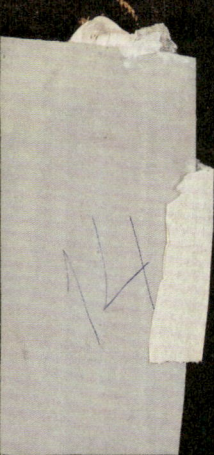

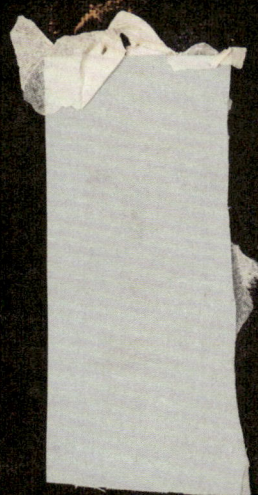

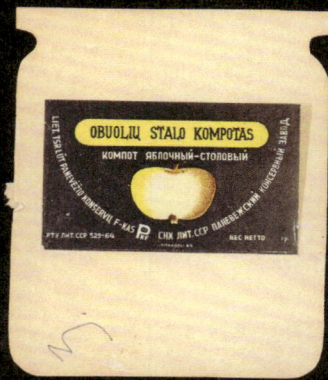

LTSR LŠT VIENAUS VYNO · IN DESTINĖS GAMYKLA
Dar po Viena
0,51
40°
2,50 Rb.
ДАР ПО ВИЕНА
СНХ ЛКТ. ССР ВИЛЬНЮССКИЙ ВИНО-ВОДОЧНЫЙ ЗАВОД

LTSR LŠT VIENAUS VYNO · IN DESTINĖS GAMYKLA
Dar po Viena
0,51
40°
2,50 Rb.
ДАР ПО ВИЕНА
СНХ ЛКТ. ССР ВИЛЬНЮССКИЙ ВИНО-ВОДОЧНЫЙ

LTSR LŠT VIENAUS VYNO · IN DESTINĖS GAMYKLA
Dar po Viena
0,51
40°
2,50 Rb.
ДАР ПО ВИЕНА
СНХ ЛКТ. ССР ВИЛЬНЮССКИЙ ВИНО-ВОДОЧНЫЙ ЗАВОД

LTSR LŠT VIENAUS VYNO · IN DESTINĖS GAMYKLA
Dar po Viena
0,51
40°
2,50 Rb.
ДАР ПО ВИЕНА
СНХ ЛКТ. ССР ВИЛЬНЮССКИЙ ВИНО-ВОДОЧНЫЙ

0,51
40°
ДАР П

PIPIRINĖ ПЕРЦОВКА
0,51 2 Rb. 30°

PIPIRINĖ ПЕРЦОВКА
0,51 2 Rb. 30°

PIPIRINĖ ПЕРЦОВКА
0,51 2 Rb. 30°

PI

non[Q]uality   [S]low

The bureau had a large industrial facility, consisting of numerous divisions, including: printing, cardboard and photomechanical units, an experimental printing process laboratory, the first imported flexographic printing machines in Lithuania, letterpress printing machines, offset printing, Rotaprint machines, machines that could print on polyethylene film and laminated paper, punching machines, and other complex printing equipment. Though this list of capabilities may appear impressive, there were limitations and the often inferior quality of printed materials remained a constant source of disappointment for designers.

b is for bureau: artist-constructors and their practices

Photomechanical bar and its manager Pranas Jonaitis (1937–2014), circa 1970s

b is for bureau: artist-constructors and their practices

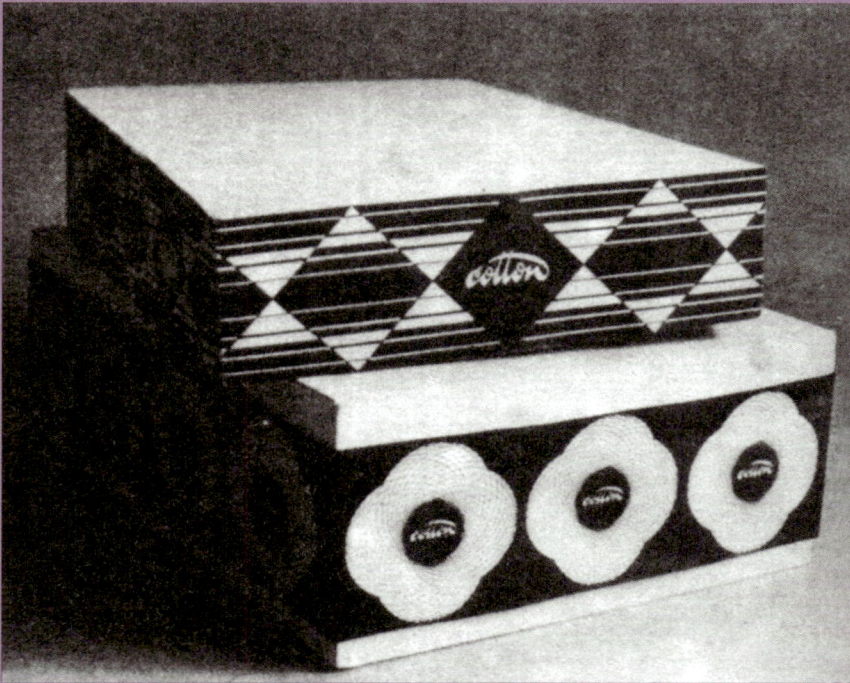

[A]bstract advertising   [E]xperimentation   [G]ray   [O]p-Art   [W]estern   [Z]ooming in

Cotton was one of the many textile factories in the interwar Kaunas. It was nationalised during the Soviet occupation, but the name of the factory survived. Laimutė Ramonienė (b. 1935) while designing the logo in the 1960s preserved some recognizable elements of the interwar design. Monika Jonaitienė (1935–1999), another Tara bureau's designer, created many experimental packaging and labels for *Cotton* in the late 1960s.

b is for bureau: artist-constructors and their practices

cotton

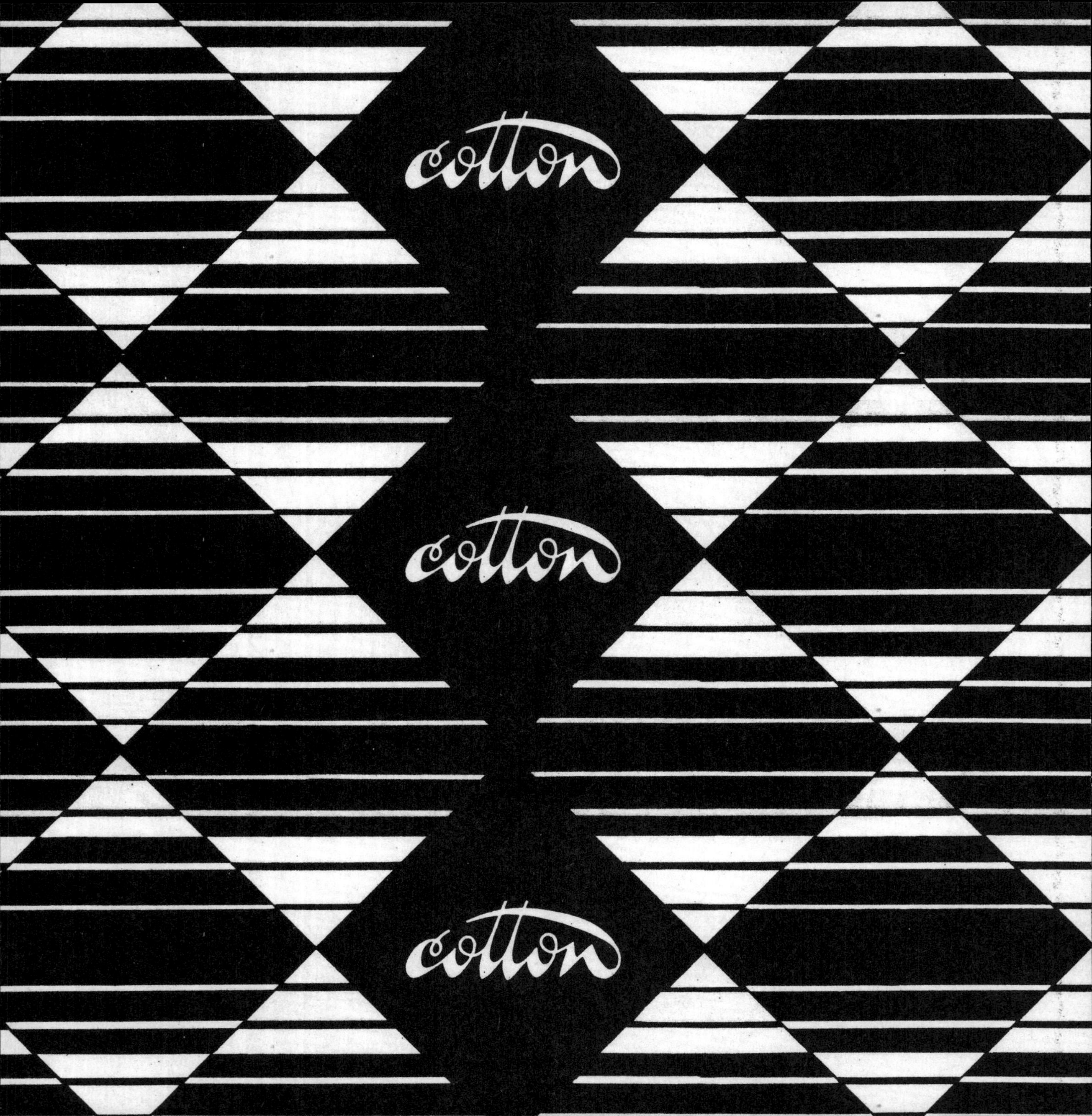
cotton
cotton
cotton

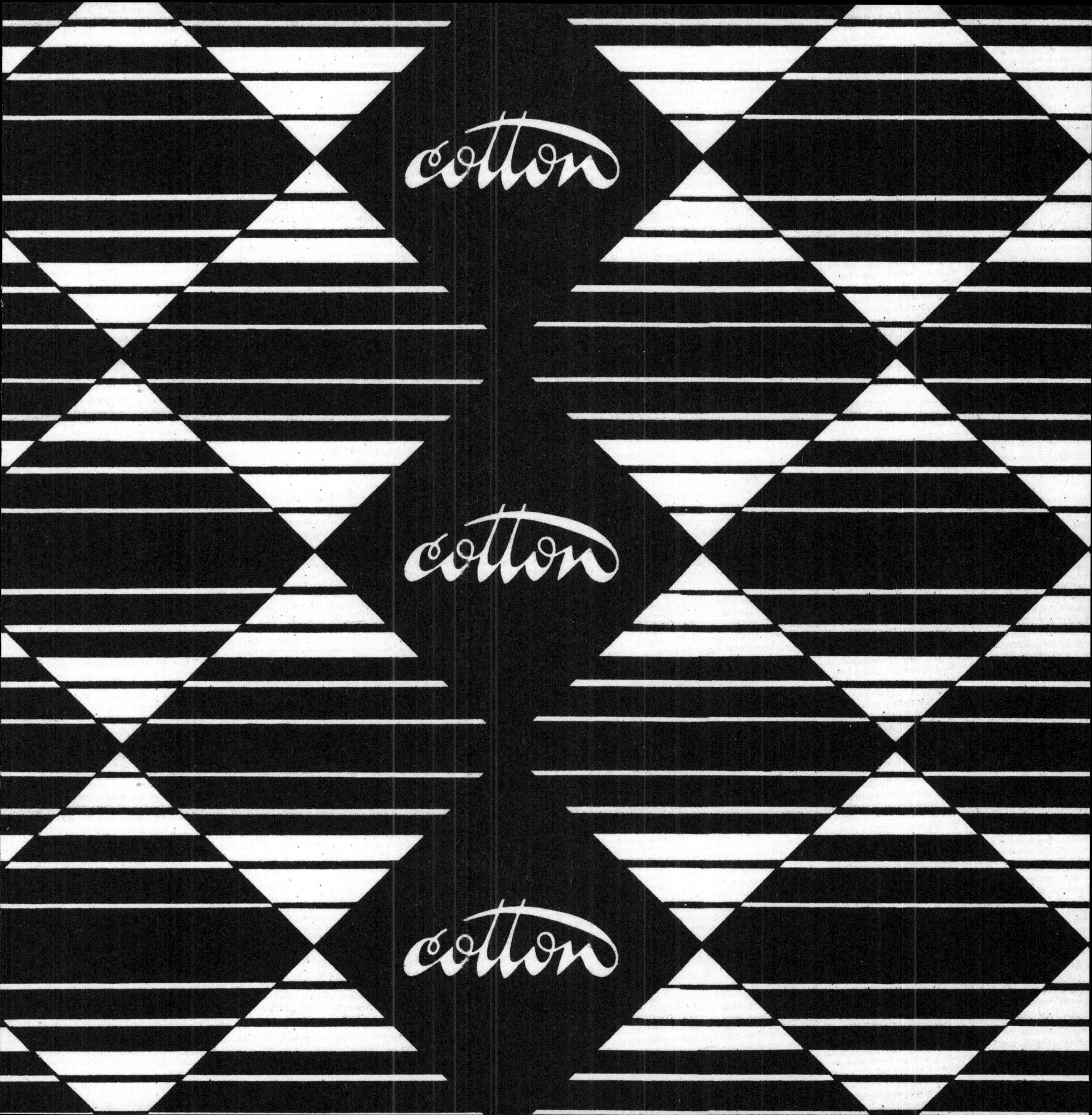
cotton
cotton
cotton

AINIS • PILOTAS • SALDAINIS •F

KOND. F-KAS „PERGALĖ" VILNIUS   LIET. TSR MPM KOND. F-KAS „PER

МПП ЛИТ. ССР КОНД. Ф-КА „ПЯРГЯЛЕ"   КОНД. Ф-КА „ПЯРГЯЛЕ" ВИЛЬНЮС

ETA • ПИЛОТ • КОНФЕТА

SALDAINIS · **RUDENS SODAS** · SALDAIN

LIET. TSR MPM KOND. F-KAS „PERGALĖ" VILNIUS · LIET. TSR

МПП ЛИТ. ССР КОНД. Ф-КА „ПЯРГАЛЕ" ВИЛЬНЮС · ВИЛЬНЮС

ОСЕННИЙ САД · КОНФЕТА · САД

 SALDAINIS *Kregždutė*  КОНФЕТА *Ласточка*  SALDAINIS

TAIKA"   SALDAINIS „TAIKA"   SALDAINIS „TAIKA"

PERGALĖ", VILNIUS   LIETUVOS TSR MPM KOND. F·KAS „P

МПП ЛИТОВСКОЙ ССР   СР КОНД. Ф-КА „ПЯРГАЛЕ", г. ВИЛЬНЮС

КОН   „ТАЙКА" КОНФЕТА   КОНФЕТА „ТАЙКА"

b is for bureau: artist-constructors and their practices

Designs for confectionary items, specifically candy and chocolate boxes, were among the products that received the most attention from clients and consumers alike. The confectionary packaging revealed several trends in graphic design of the 1960s, of which the most prominent was the use of folkloric motifs – a common feature found throughout all Lithuanian graphic design of this period. Folklore was embraced in graphic design both as a thematic subject and as part of a fluid language of design elements, ranging from the use of folk-art illustrations to modern decoration.

b is for bureau: artist-constructors and their practices

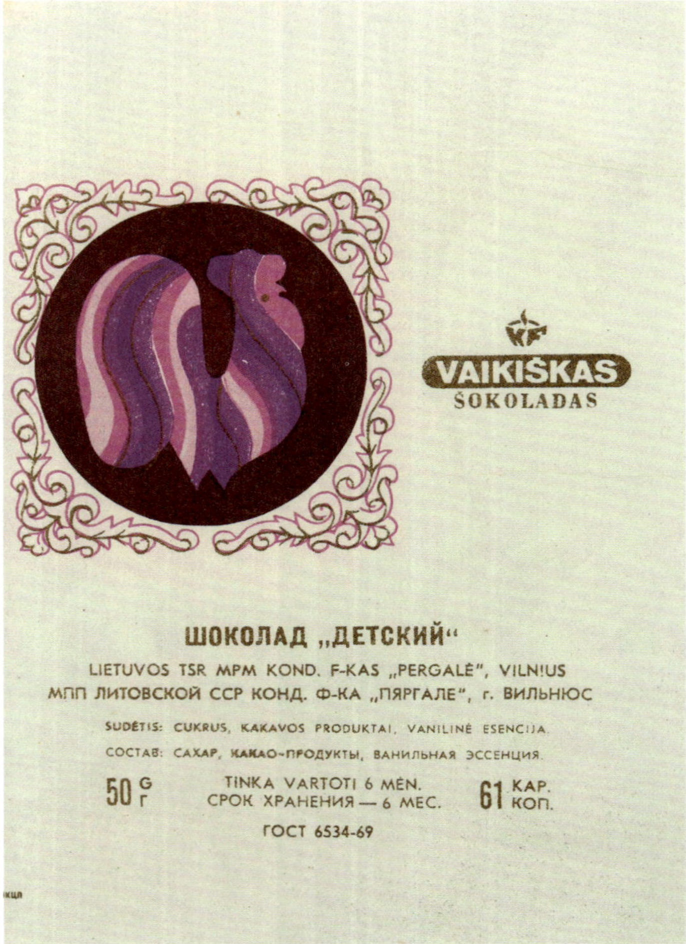

VAIKIŠKAS
ŠOKOLADAS

ШОКОЛАД „ДЕТСКИЙ"

LIETUVOS TSR MPM KOND. F-KAS „PERGALĖ", VILNIUS
МПП ЛИТОВСКОЙ ССР КОНД. Ф-КА „ПЯРГАЛЕ", г. ВИЛЬНЮС

SUDĖTIS: CUKRUS, KAKAVOS PRODUKTAI, VANILINĖ ESENCIJA.

СОСТАВ: САХАР, КАКАО-ПРОДУКТЫ, ВАНИЛЬНАЯ ЭССЕНЦИЯ.

50 G г   TINKA VARTOTI 6 MĖN.   61 КАР.
           СРОК ХРАНЕНИЯ — 6 МЕС.   КОП.
                ГОСТ 6534-69

[E]xperimentation   [L]ithuanian

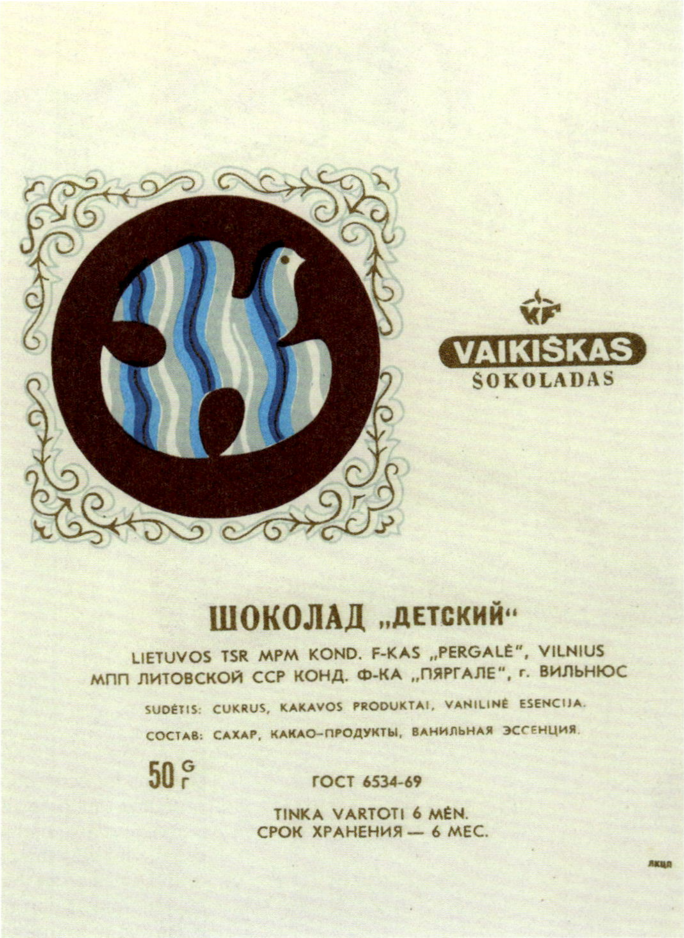

VAIKIŠKAS
ŠOKOLADAS

ШОКОЛАД „ДЕТСКИЙ"

LIETUVOS TSR MPM KOND. F-KAS „PERGALĖ", VILNIUS
МПП ЛИТОВСКОЙ ССР КОНД. Ф-КА „ПЯРГАЛЕ", г. ВИЛЬНЮС

SUDĖTIS: CUKRUS, KAKAVOS PRODUKTAI, VANILINĖ ESENCIJA.

СОСТАВ: САХАР, КАКАО-ПРОДУКТЫ, ВАНИЛЬНАЯ ЭССЕНЦИЯ.

50 G г   ГОСТ 6534-69

TINKA VARTOTI 6 MĖN.
СРОК ХРАНЕНИЯ — 6 МЕС.

b is for bureau: artist-constructors and their practices

ШОКОЛАД · ВАНИЛЬНЫЙ ·

ŠOKOLADAS ·VANILINIS·

KOND F-KAS „PERGALĖ", VILNIUS
КОНД. Ф-КА „ПЯРГАЛЕ", г. ВИЛЬНЮС
SUDĖTIS : KAKAVOS PRODUKTAI, CUKRUS, VANILINAS

KARAMELĖ

КАРАМЕЛЬ «ПУШИС»

Pušis

Neskubėdama plukdo savo vandenis į Baltiją Dangė. Upės krantai ir tiltai — mėgiama klaipėdiečių susitikimų, poilsio vieta.

Klaipėdos konditeriai įsitikinę, kad skanaudami jų firminę malonaus gaivinančio citrinos skonio, baltą, mėlynom juostelėm sluoksniuotą kriauklytės formos karamelę, Jūs panorėsite dar ne kartą prie Dangės atvažiuoti.

Quietly flows the river Dangė into the Baltic Sea. A lot of the residents in Klaipėda use its banks and bridges as places for meetings and rest.

The Klaipėda confectioners are sure that once you taste refreshing boiled candies "Dangė" you will be reminded of the port and town on the banks of Dangė once again.

Shell-shaped sweets with highly refreshing lemon flavour are of white colour interlaid with blue sugar mass stripes.

Gintarėlis

IRISAS

ИРИС «ТУЗИК»

Tuzikas

KARAMELĖ

КАРАМЕЛЬ «ДАНГЕ»

KARAMELĖ

КАРАМЕЛЬ «БАНГА»

Banga

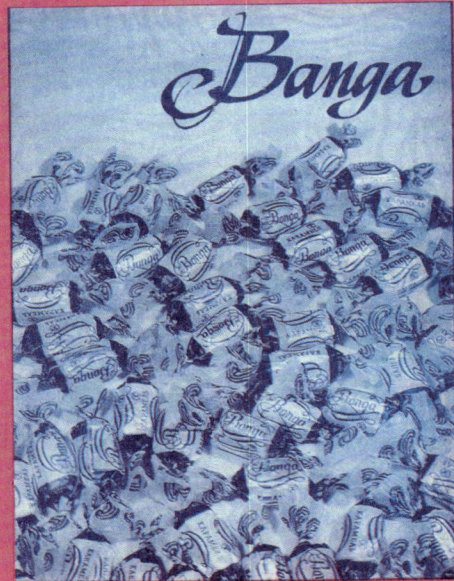

KARAMELĖ

КАРАМЕЛЬ «КЛУМПАКОЙИС»

Klumpakojis

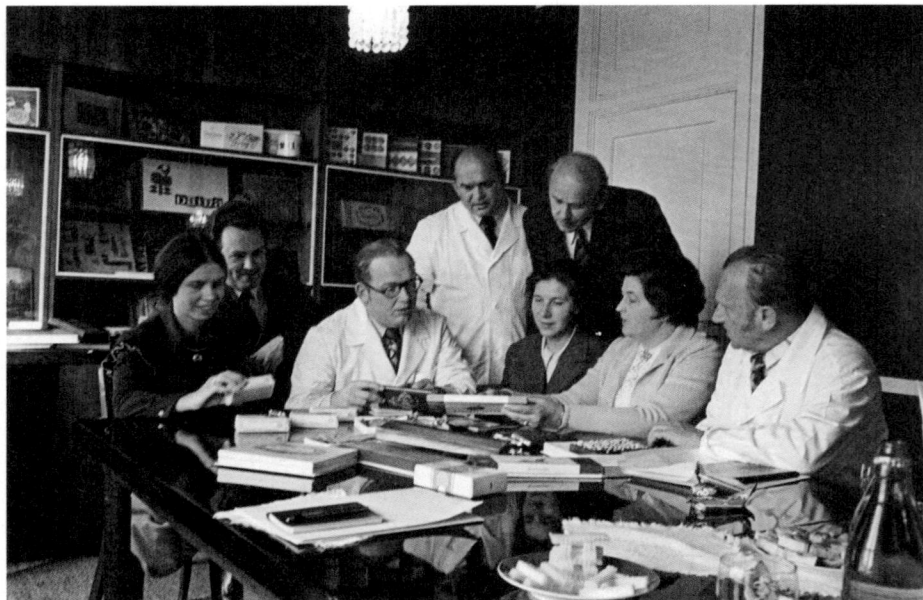

[C]ensorship   [F]açade   [J]ury   [S]oviet

Representatives of the confectionary companies' association of the German
Democratic Republic are visiting the confectionery factory "Pergalé", 1976,
Lithuanian Central State Archives

b is for bureau: artist-constructors and their practices

b is for bureau: artist-constructors and their practices

PALYDOVAI

Saldainiai Pirmokas

Rudens Sodas

SALDAINIAI

ƒ

PAUKŠČIŲ PIENAS

SALDAINIAI

OBELĖLĖ

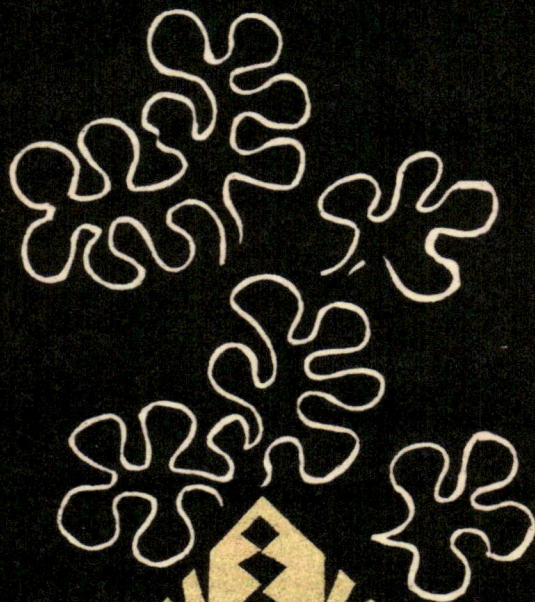

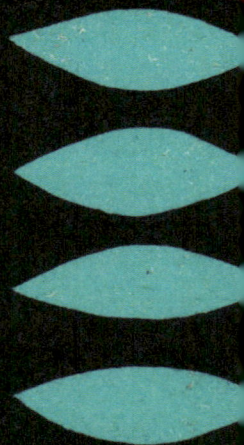

KAIP GI GRAŽUS GRAŽ

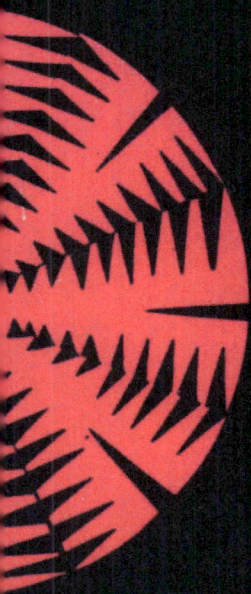

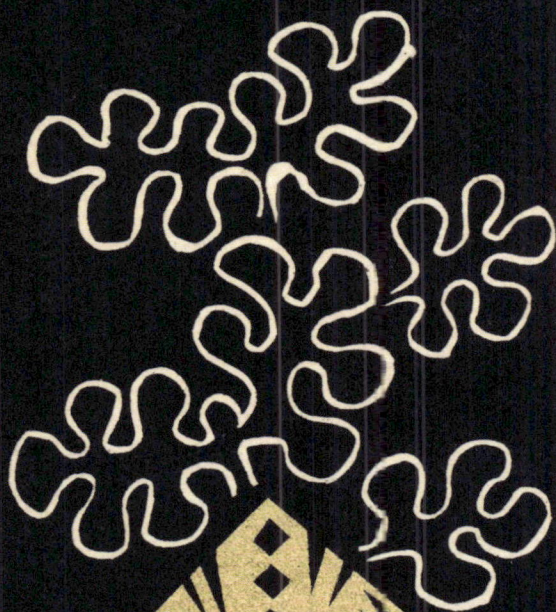

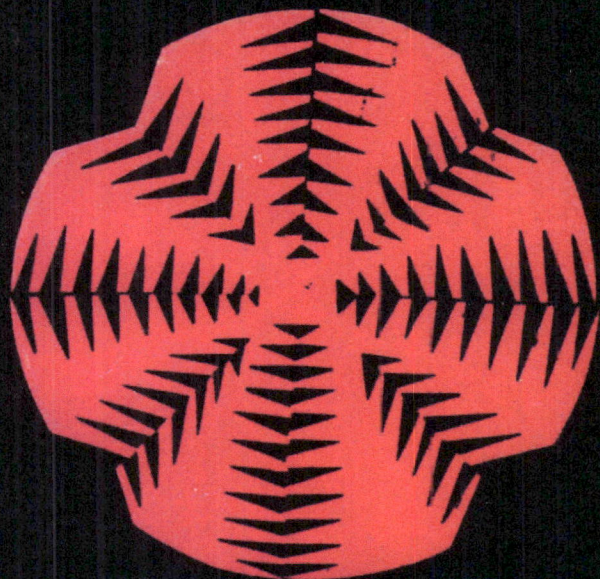

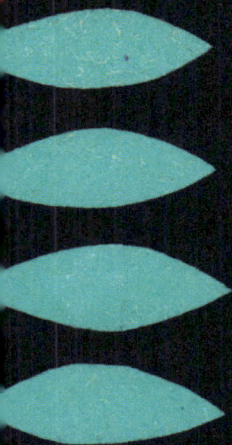

IS RŪTELIŲ DARŽELIS

Pergalė

saldainiai „Vyšnia su vitaminu C"

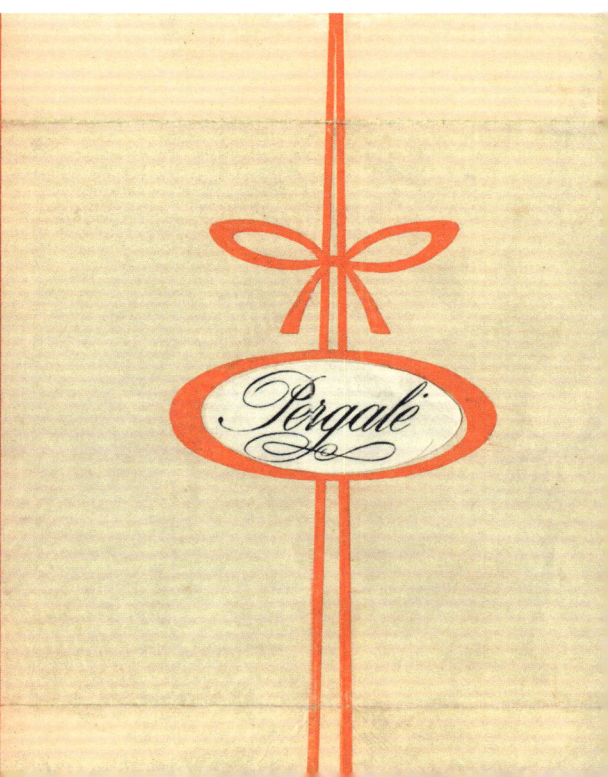

Dovana

SUVENYRAI

1973

LIETUVOS TSR VIETINĖS PRAMONĖS MINISTERIJA
МИНИСТЕРСТВО МЕСТНОЙ ПРОМЫШЛЕННОСТИ ЛИТОВСКОЙ ССР

Dovana

LTSR
Vietinės pramonės ministerija
EKSPERIMENTINIS MENINIO
KONSTRAVIMO BIURAS

PLATINTI
Leidinio m. _4036_
Užsakymo m. _____

Sudarytojas _____
Redaktorius _____
Vyr. redaktorius _____
Moksl. redaktorius _____
Vyr. dailininkas _____
Techn. redaktorius _____

TVIRTINU PLATINTI
Skyriaus vedėjas _____
19__ m. _____ mėn. __ d.

MENO VERSLŲ DIRBINIŲ IR SUVENYRŲ GAMYBOS ĮMONIŲ
SUSIVIENIJIMAS „DOVANA"

ОБЪЕДИНЕНИЕ ПРЕДПРИЯТИЙ ПО ПРОИЗВОДСТВУ ИЗДЕЛИЙ ХУДОЖЕСТВЕННЫХ
ПРОМЫСЛОВ И СУВЕНИРОВ „ДОВАНА"

[A]bstract advertising   [E]xperimentation   [L]ithuanian   [N]ational   [O]p-Art

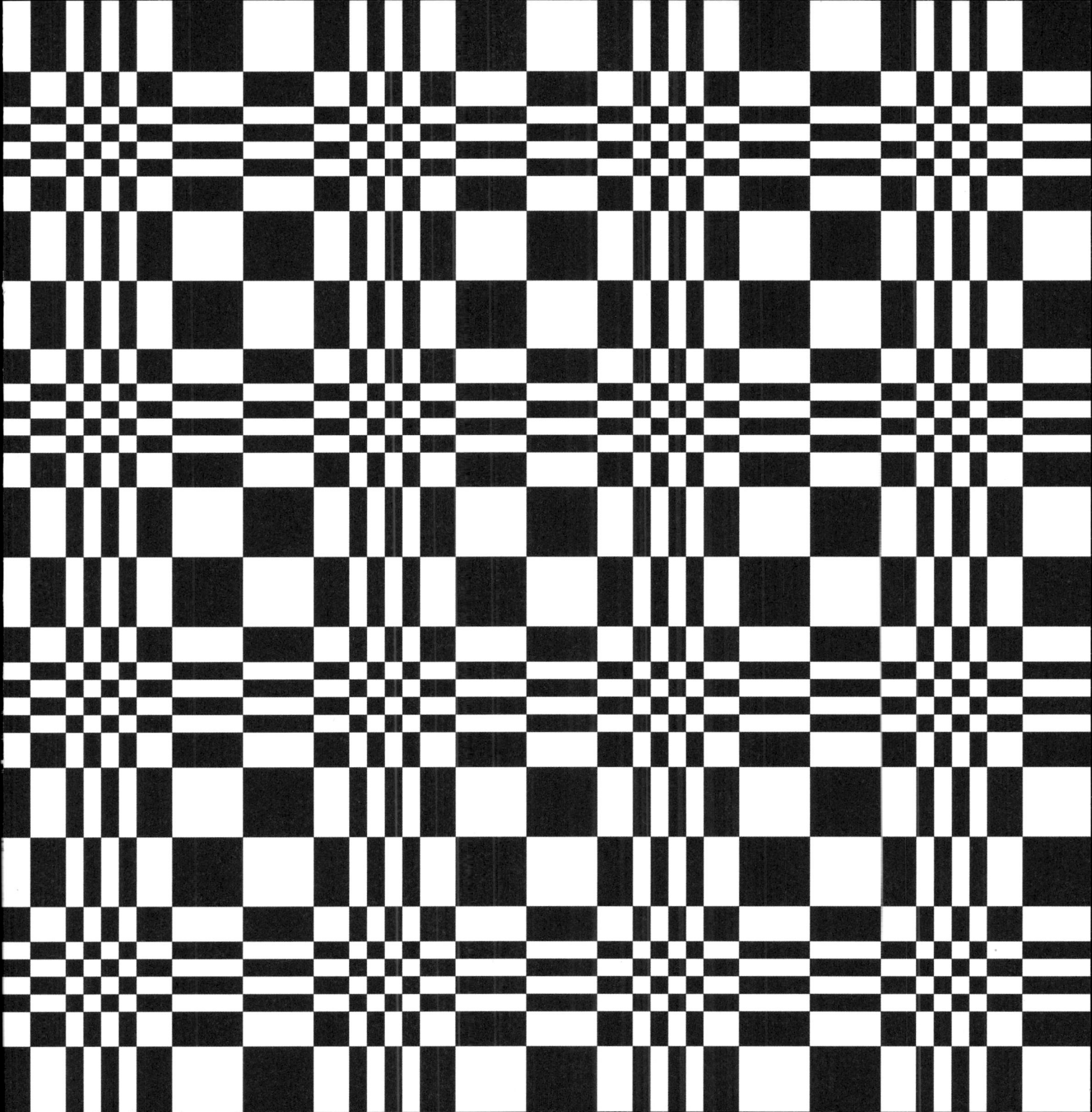

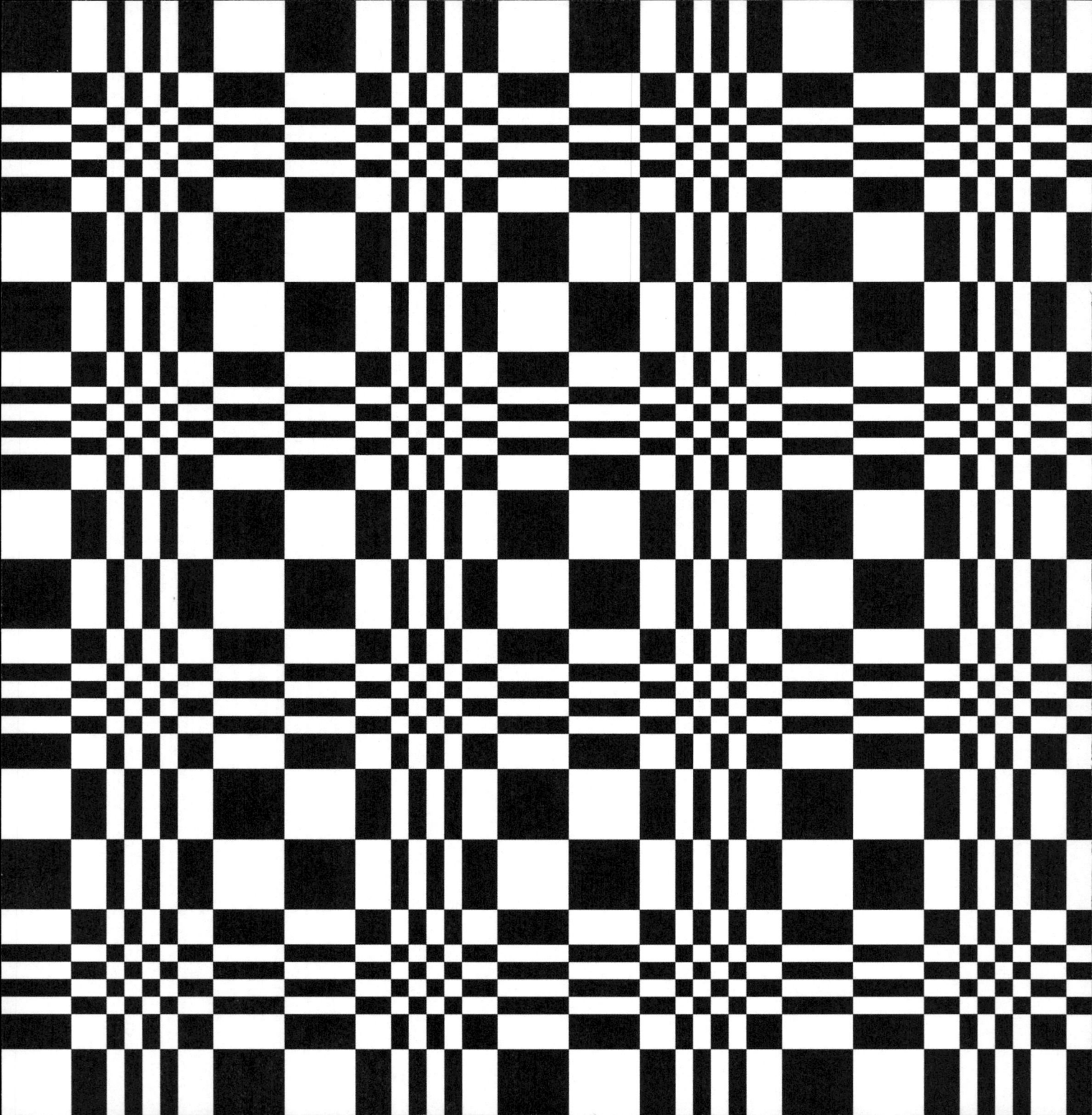

e is for exhibitions:
visionary projects
and utopian aspirations

The Tara bureau fostered a tradition of holding exhibitions since its genesis. This occurred most often during the bureau's anniversaries with the aim of presenting its projects to the public. Such specialized graphic art exhibitions took place in Vilnius in 1967, 1968, 1969, 1974, 1979 and the last one in Kaunas in 1984.

The most experimental, most aesthetic, innovative, often one-of-a-kind showcase projects were presented at the exhibitons, most of which never made it into the products and into the press. For the artists who worked at the bureau, exhibitions were very important, because those were special occasions during which they presented themselves to the art community and could reveal their personal style and artistic vision. In retrospect we could say those were utopian aspirations, since most of them remained unrealized. From today's perspective, this is best indicated by the comments people left in visitors books.

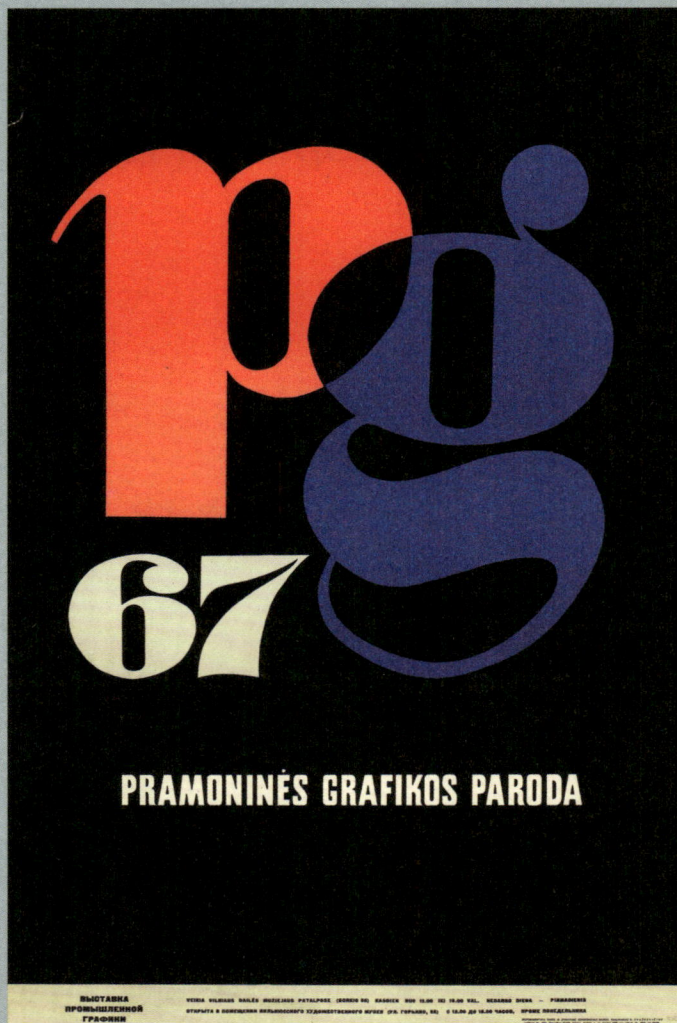

The first exhibition that was specialized in graphic design, was held in 1967. It took place at the Lithuanian Art Museum from December 18, 1967, to February 1, 1968. The poster – "pg", a Lithuanian abbreviation for "industrial graphics" – was designed by Romualdas Svaškevičius, head of the artistic department of the bureau, better known as Jurgis Raslanas (1926–2001).

In preparation for the exhibition, a comprehensive catalogue that was illustrated by the artists themselves was published. The publication was black and white, richly illustrated, containing annotated illustrations of creations from the 1960's and presenting short biographies of all 39 artists, including personal photographs and featuring one creator per page. The copy preserved by Kęstutis Gvalda is the only surviving copy of this catalogue.

e is for exhibitions: visionary projects and utopian aspirations

KATALOGAS

pramoninės grafikos parodos

1967

Eksperimentinis taros ir įpakavimo
konstravimo biuras

Vilnius, 1967

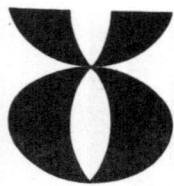
66

67

68

69

70

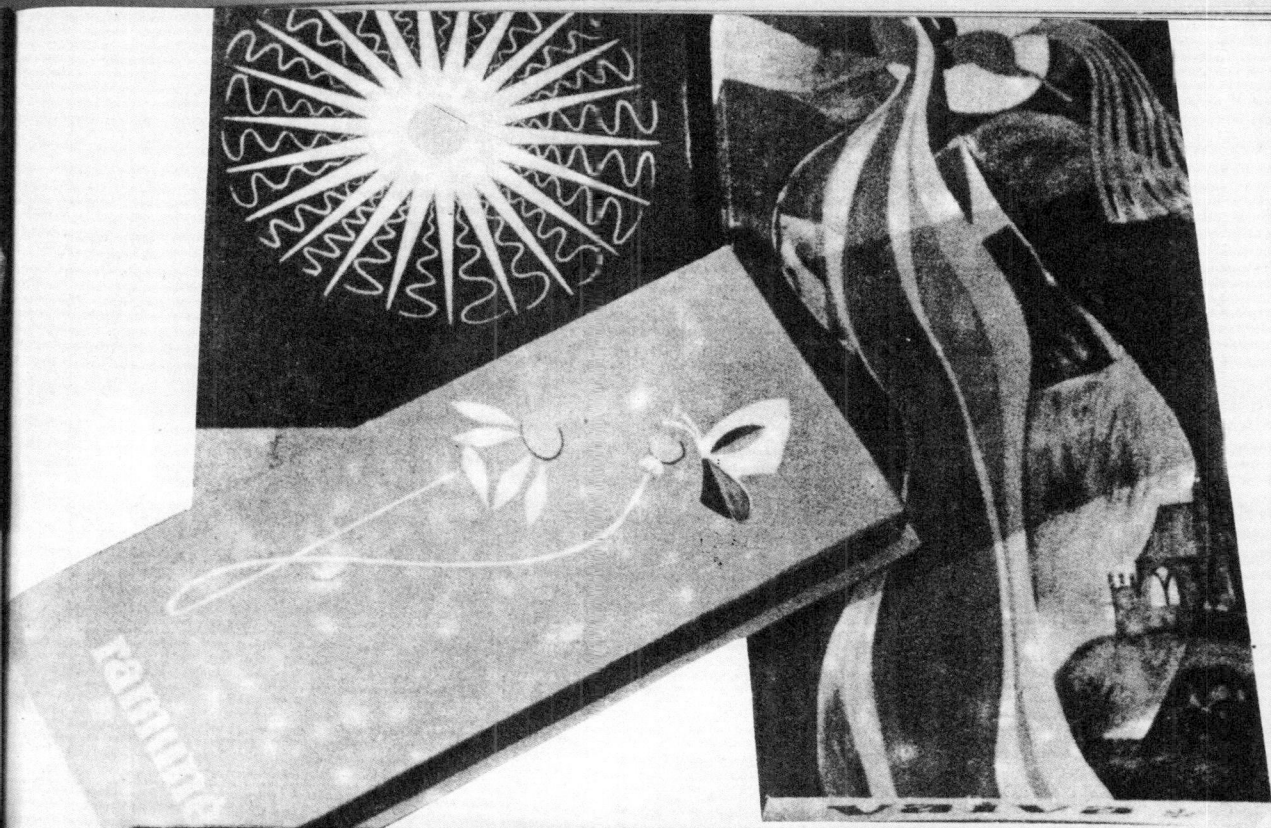

VAI KUR BUVAI,
DIEDUK MANO?

—VILNIUJ BUVAU,
DŪSIA MANO...

SALDAINIAI „SU RAIDELIAIS"

55

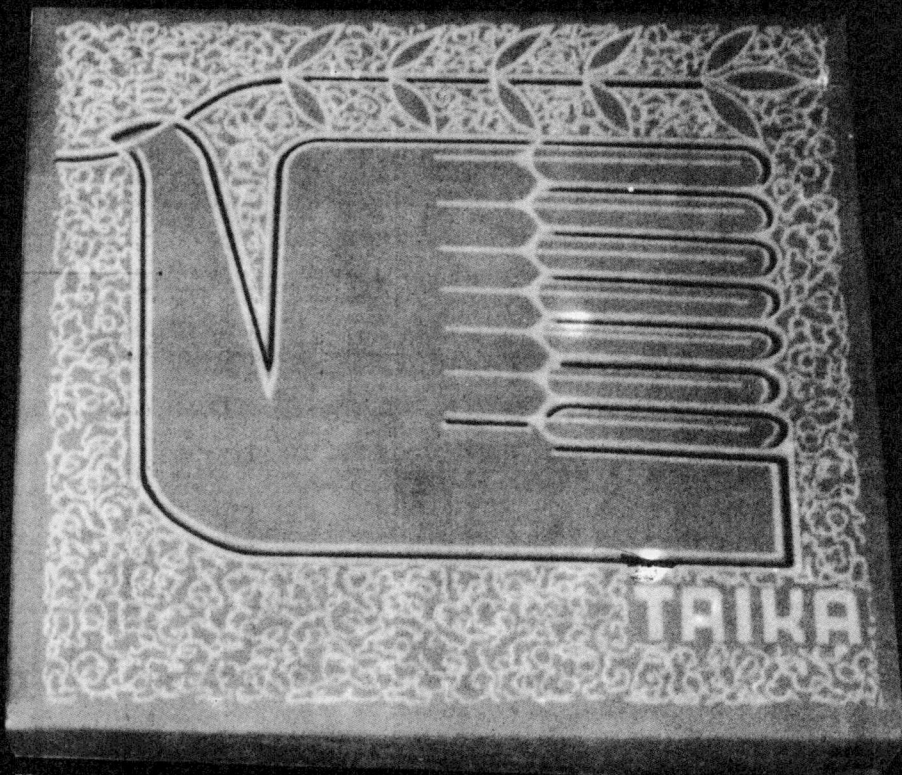

TAIKA

56

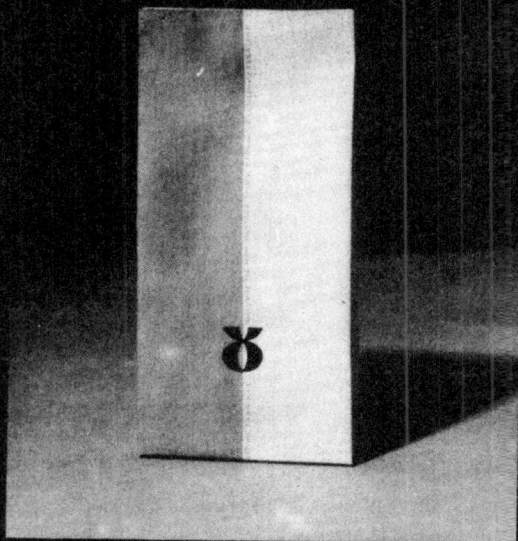

126

RAMBYNO SŪRIS

ПЛАСТИЛИН

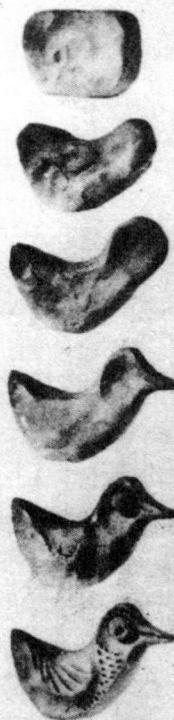

„klaipėda"

132

131

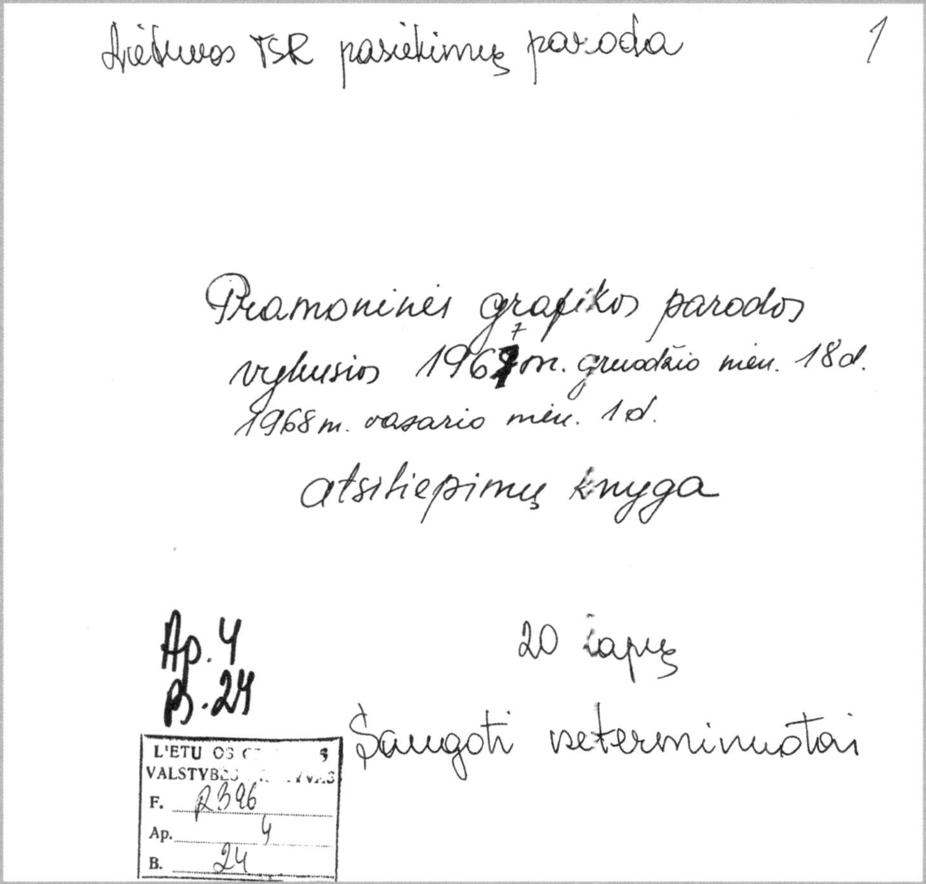

Lietuvos TSR pasiekimų paroda   1

Pramoninės grafikos parodos
vykusios 1967m. gruodžio mėn. 18d.
1968m. vasario mėn. 1d.

atsiliepimų knyga

Ap. 4
B. 24

20 lapų

Saugoti neterminuotai

LIETU OS C...
VALSTYB... ...VAS
F. R396
Ap. 4
B. 24

[V]isitors' reviews   [U]topia

No surviving photographs of the first exhibition ever came to the surface. However, the comments left in the visitor's book of this exhibition are stored to this day in the Lithuanian Central State Archives.

Gerardas Bagdonavičius (1901–1986), a master of Lithuanian graphic design who is considered one of the pioneers in that field and became famous in the interwar period for his stylish advertisements and folk style furniture sets, visited the exhibition and wrote down his impressions in bold calligraphic font in the aforementioned review book. His evaluations used highly sophisticated professional terms, expressing admiration and praise for the artists. In his words we now recognize the echoes of independent interwar Lithuania, and understand why he urged the directors to implement these projects by the Tara bureau and print the reviews publicly. He would have been disappointed as these utopian aspirations were never realised.

e is for exhibitions: visionary projects and utopian aspirations

PRAMONINĖS PARODOS

1967 - 68 XII-I

REZULTATAI PAČIOS AUKŠČIAUSIOS KOKYBĖS!

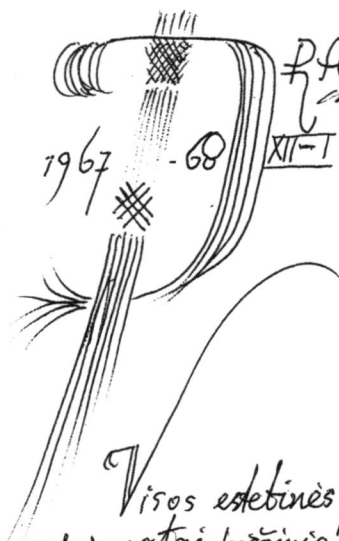

Visos estetinės pramoninės grafikos parodos visi, įvairūs eksponatai piešinio, spalvos, tono, kompozicijos įvairių branžių ypatybės rodo vaizdžiausiai, kad mūsų grafikos-kūrėjai išsamiai suprato ir sugebėjo realizuoti jiems skirtus atsakomingus ir būtinius eksponatų paskirties uždavinius ypatingai aiškiai labai nūdieniom formom, pažangiojo taikomojo meno stiliais, nepaprastai vykusiai tuo pat laiku riešdami mūsų tradicinio meno pavidalus su šios dienos pažangios grafikos estetika, tuo pat laiku gražiai prisiderindami prie vartotojų įvairių reikalavimų prekei ir jos supakavimo apyforminimui ir, svarbiausiai, ne išleidžiant iš akių visumos psichologiško prekės apypavidalinimo emocingumo!

December, 1967 – January, 1968

RESULTS OF THE INDUSTRIAL EXHIBITION ARE OF THE HIGHEST QUALITY!

All the various exhibits of the aesthetic industrial graphic design exhibition demonstrate most vividly in terms of drawing, colour, tone, composition, and features of the various branches, that our graphic designers have thoroughly understood and realized the responsible and practical tasks of the exhibits' purpose with the utmost clarity. State-of-the-art forms, in the style of advanced applied art are combining the shapes of our traditional art with the aesthetics of today's advanced graphic art. At the same time these designs adapt beautifully to consumers' various demands for the product and its packaging; all this without ever losing sight of the emotionality of the product as a whole!

e is for exhibitions: visionary projects and utopian aspirations

MAKE SURE TO RELEASE LARGE SEPARATE PUBLICATION
PACKAGING!
[...]

In addition to all this, the designs impress with their neatnes
them feature a suitably joyful warm mood, a harmoniously
a presentable appearance, quite suitable even for souvenirs
practical packages for CARRYING (unfortunately, new to us

The envelopes for the gramophone records are also e
they are EXTREMELY STYLISH, conveying HISTORICAL EPO
composers The only thing is that the Bach No. 2 envelope s
but rather in the Baroque style, even if it is a tapestry, becau
Gothic period. Composition No. 1 is quite in tune with the e
excellent old Vilnius-style solutions, modernizations of folk a
of successful, original, extraordinarily fine works!

Logos of companies and factories feature an enchanting, hy
symbolic-emblematic quality! The exhibition is captivating,
Such a joy!
Incredible modern creative, mesmerizing POSTERS!

I can't give a better review of the exhibition than the honorable artist Bagdonavičius
Gerardas, although I would very much like to... Thank you!

A. K. Kazlauskas
Master of folk art

Shame on you, master! [entry by another visitor]

Very mediocre exhibition. We still have far to go to keep up with foreign countries...

You know nothing [entry by another visitor]

Would be wonderful to see everything we see in the exhibition in shop windows as well!

Don't be blind and you will
Eyes alone won't help you! [entry by another visitor]

Polygraphy will spoil everything anyway

Bravo [entry by another visitor]!!!

e is for exhibitions: visionary projects and utopian aspirations

The exhibition made a good impression. Thank you!
The trio:
Judita, Jūra ėlė, Daivulė

It's very nice seeing all this, but why is this beauty so rarely seen in shops?
6 January 1968

A pleasant exhibition. Most importantly, good taste prevails.
Actor
7 January 1968

I liked the exhibition very much. Its national tone is particularly charming. It is also pleasing that some of the exhibits I have already seen on the shelves in shops.
Unfortunately, not all of them!
7 January 1968

e is for exhibitions: visionary projects and utopian aspirations

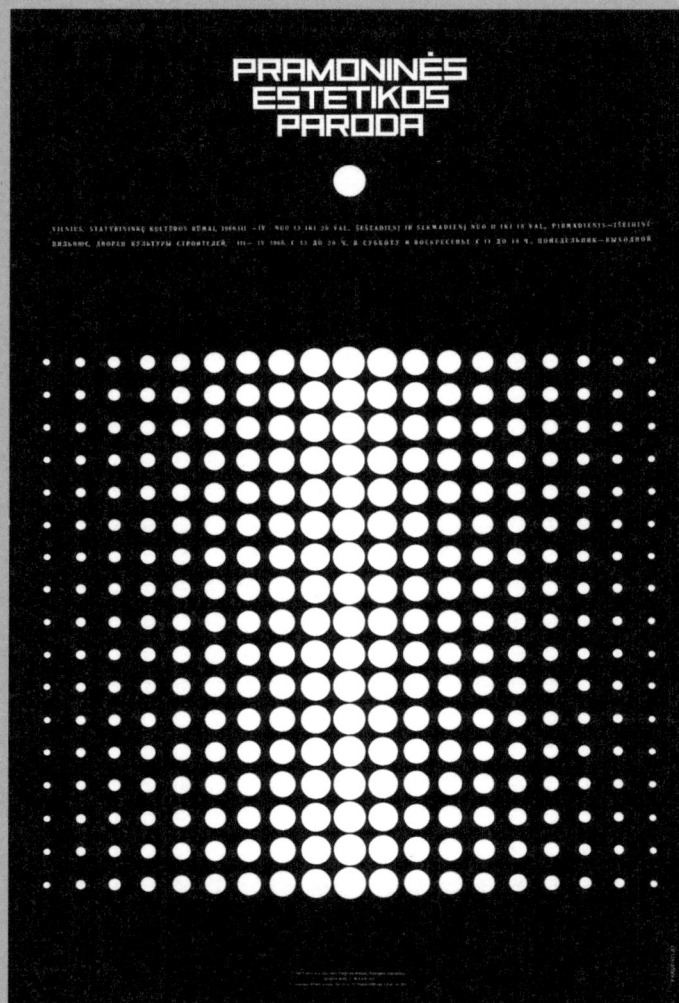

In 1968 "Exhibition of Industrial Aesthetics" was held in Vilnius, where the projects designed by Tara bureau were also exhibited. The poster for this exhibition was designed by Vytautas Kaušinis (1930–2009), one of the finest poster artists of his time, who continues to stand out with his minimalistic, often Op-Art design and conceptual solutions.

In the Soviet era in general, instead of the English word "design", other word combinations were favoured to describe exhibitions or texts devoted to design. Popular terms included industrial aesthetics, applied graphics or artistic constructing. This was done intentionally to avoid capitalistic terms such as "design" and "designers". At this exhibition however, one of the hanging slogans proclaimed: "The designer is an intermediary between the producer and the consumer".

e is for exhibitions: visionary projects and utopian aspirations

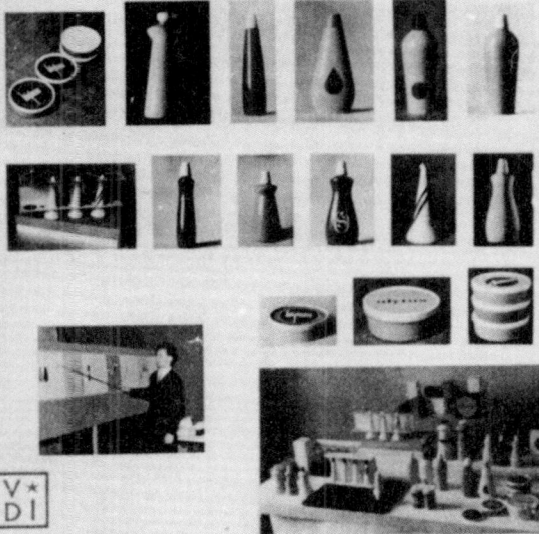

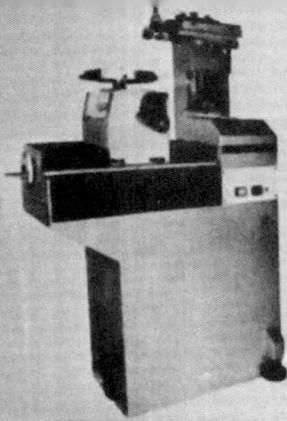

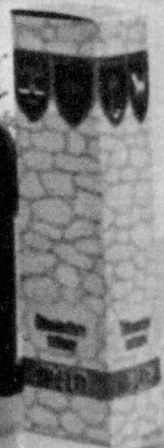

[A]bstract advertising   [D]esign   [E]xperimentation   [Z]ooming in

Among the ¯ara exhibits we see one of the earliest covers of the chocolate packaging *Asorti* (Assorted), which was exhibited many times. It was designed by Vaidilutė Grušeckaitė (1937–2021), whose packaging designs were known for meticulous photographic detail and a minimalist approach.

e is for exhibitions: visionary projects and utopian aspirations

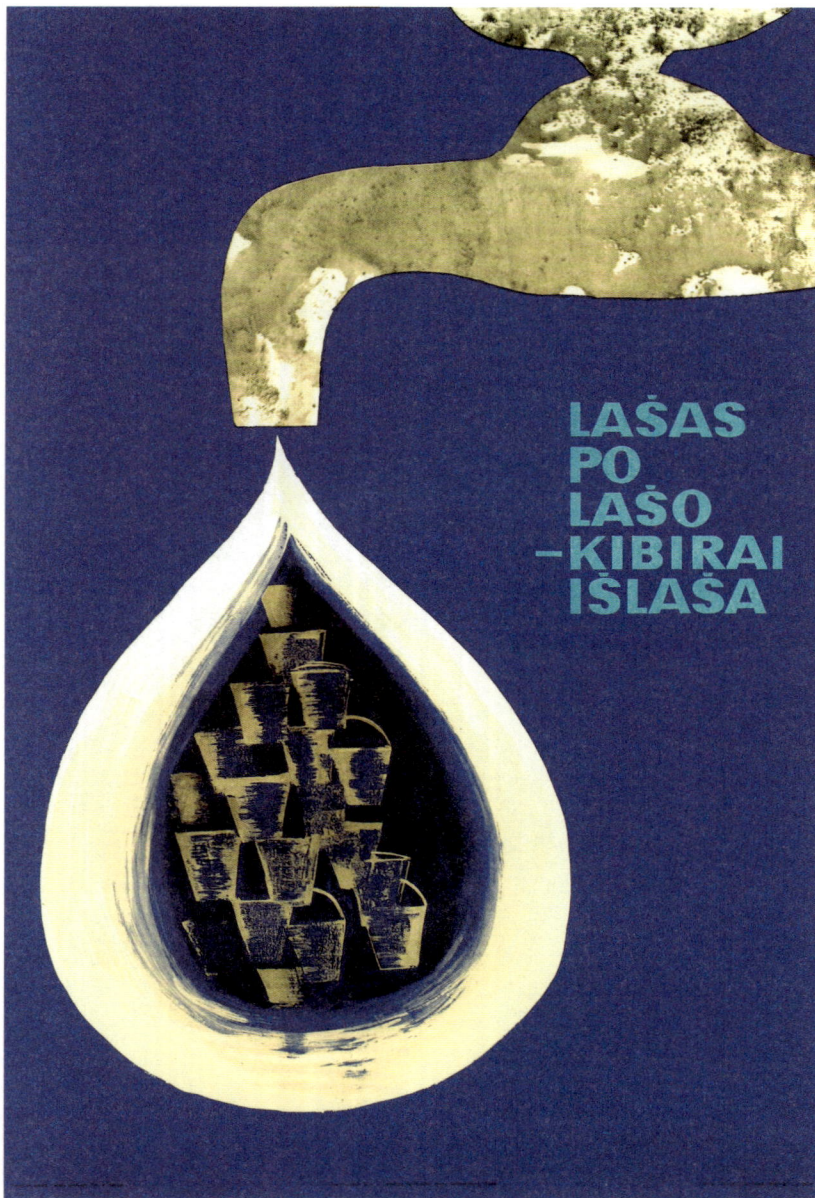

Among the Tara exhibits we also see the poster by Kęstutis Gvalda "Drop after drop – buckets are lost". It is a very layered poster – in today's terms – on the subject of sustainability. In the context of the Soviet era, this topic sounds paradoxical, especially with regard to the declarative statements and slogans of the government, while in reality the natural resources were being carelessly exhausted. However, having Gvalda's personal story in mind, his life-long true existential frugality, this poster can be seen as extremely sensitive, authentic and emotionally impactful.

e is for exhibitions: visionary projects and utopian aspirations

1974

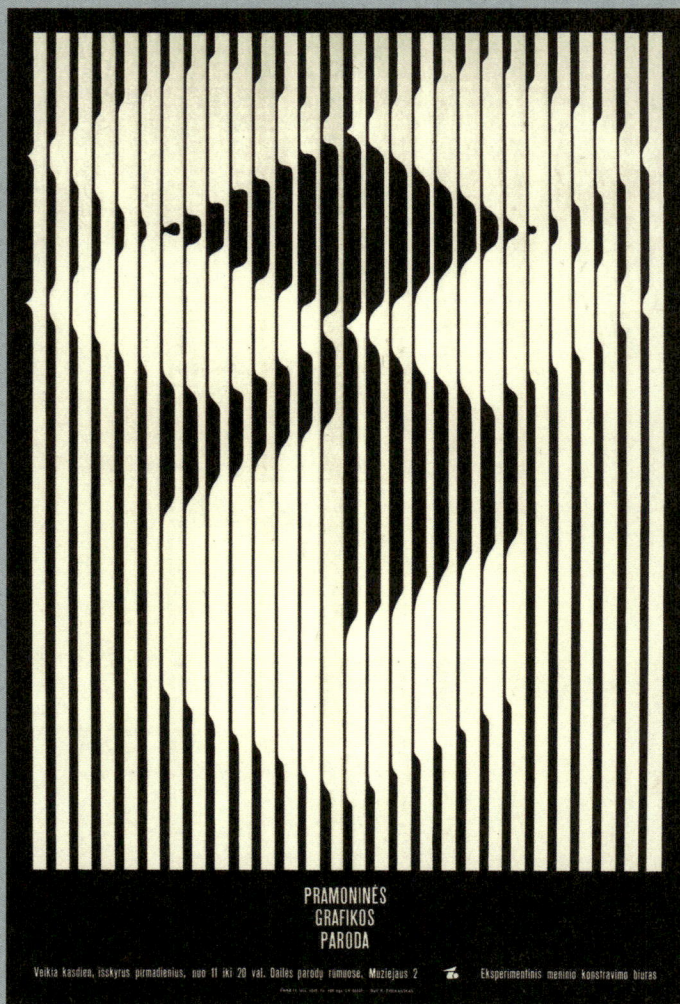

PRAMONINĖS
GRAFIKOS
PARODA

Veikia kasdien, išskyrus pirmadienius, nuo 11 iki 20 val. Dailės parodų rūmuose, Muziejaus 2   Eksperimentinis meninio konstravimo biuras

The "Exhibition of Applied Graphics" was organized at Vilnius Exhibition Hall (later the Contemporary Art Center, now the Lithuanian Artists' Union Gallery) in 1974. It was dedicated to the 10-year anniversary of the Tara bureau. The poster and the entire visual style of this exhibition was designed by the outstanding artist Kęstutis Šveikauskas (1928–2008), and the exhibition design was created by the architect Vladas Vizgirda.

e is for exhibitions: visionary projects and utopian aspirations

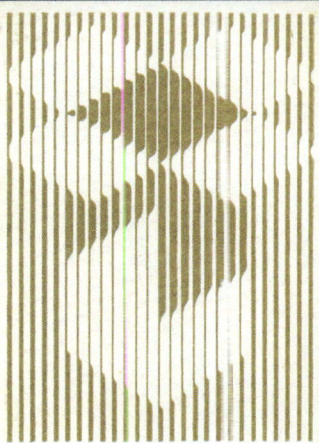

PRAMONINĖS GRAFIKOS PARODA

Eksperimentinio meninio konstravimo biuro dailininkai konstruktoriai projektuoja plakatus, teisinės apsaugos ženklus, diplomus ir garbės raštus, katalogus, prospektus, bukletus ir kitus reklaminės literatūros leidinius, etiketes, koloretes, banderoles bei vartotojišką tarą iš popieriaus, kartono, polimerinių medžiagų ir stiklo. Nuo 1964 metų Biuro specialistai sukūrė daugiau kaip 100 plakatų, apie 500 teisinės apsaugos ženklų, 1890 reklaminės literatūros leidinių ir 18.100 vartotojiškos taros projektų.

Jų darbai buvo eksponuojami Londone, Monrealio, Osakos, Santjago (Čilė), Leipcigo, Poznanės, Zagrebo, Prahos, Sofijos, Erfurto parodose, apdovanoti Visasąjunginės liaudies ūkio pasiekimų parodos medaliais, premijuoti sąjunginėse ir respublikinėse apžiūrose.

Ši Pramoninės grafikos paroda — kukli gausaus Biuro dailininkų kolektyvo kūrybinio darbo ataskaita.

Kęstutis Gvalda's work as a whole, along with his artistic and public activities were insepara-ble from the Tara bureau. From his official biography we knew that he entered the Faculty of Graphic Arts at the Art Institute in 1946, receiving his diploma in 1965. However, that 19-year gap concealed the experience of his deportation. From today's updated biography, we know that he was deported to Stalin's gulag for more than 10 years as a second-year student, where he managed to finish art school and worked as a postman among other odd jobs. Most of the objects and artefacts presented in this book are from the Gvalda collection. In the backdrop of his painful experience of Soviet repressions, his tireless optimism is revealed by his dedication to preserving Tara's archive and carefully cataloguing in envelopes and boxes all the precious materials he could find.

A personal exhibition of posters by Kęstutis Gvalda was held at the "Lietuva" cinema theatre (now the MO Museum in Vilnius) in 1977 on the occasion of the artist's 50th anniver-sary. After the exhibition, most of the exhibited posters were stored in Gvalda's room. Some of them have been preserved to this day.

e is for exhibitions: visionary projects and utopian aspirations

[A]bstract advertising   [R]eklama

MOKSLO PASLAPTYS—MOKSLO POPULIARINIMO LEIDINIUOSE

e is for exhibitions: visionary projects and utopian aspirations

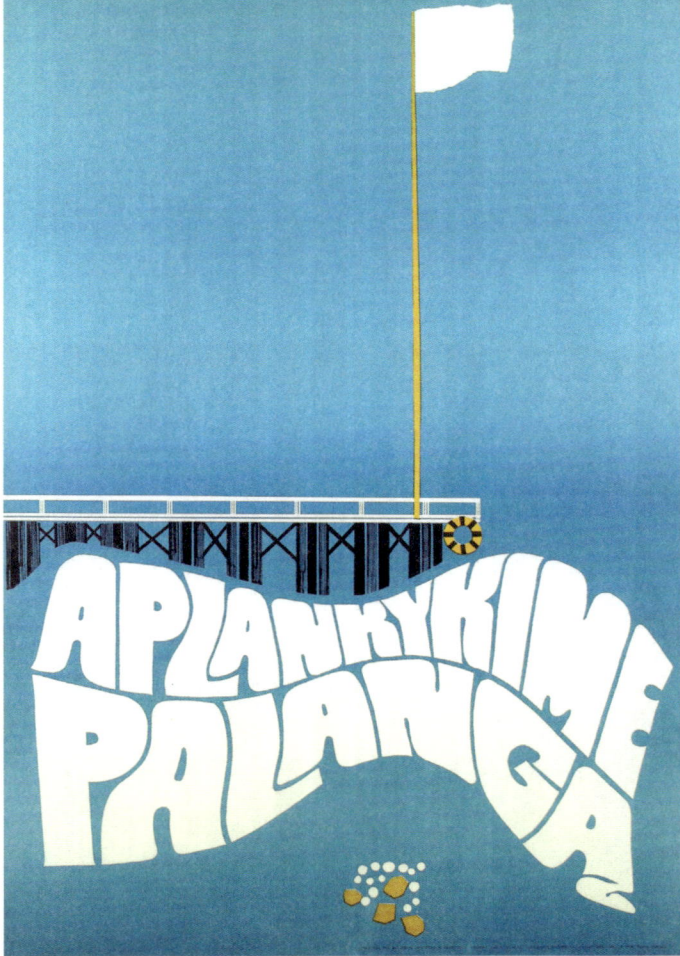

[P]ropaganda   [T]ypography

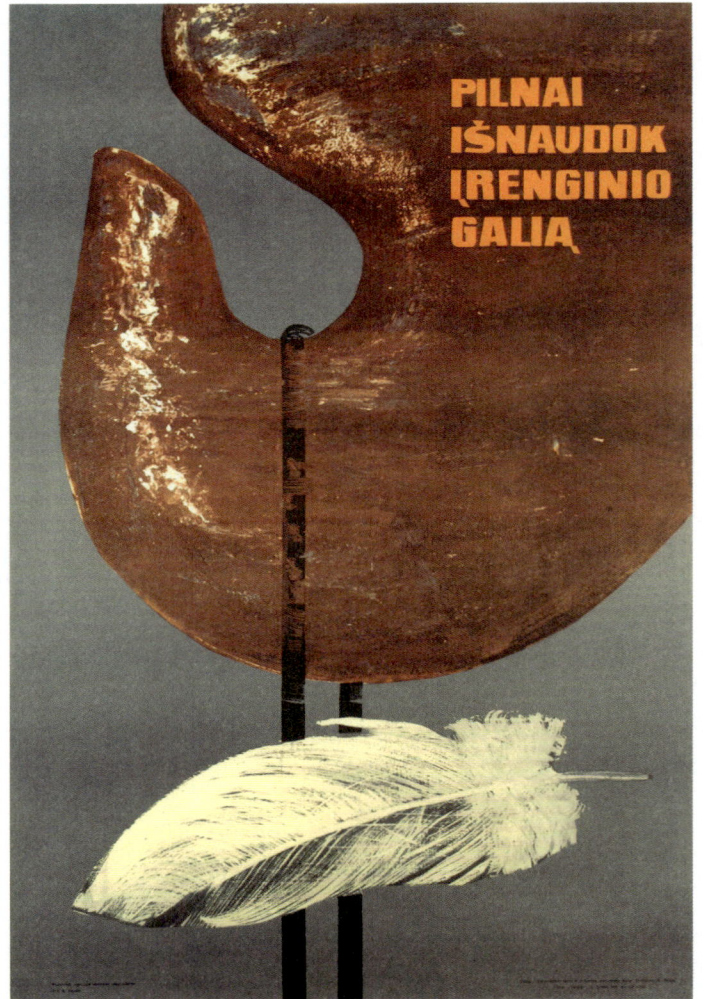

PILNAI
IŠNAUDOK
ĮRENGINIO
GALIĄ

e is for exhibitions: visionary projects and utopian aspirations

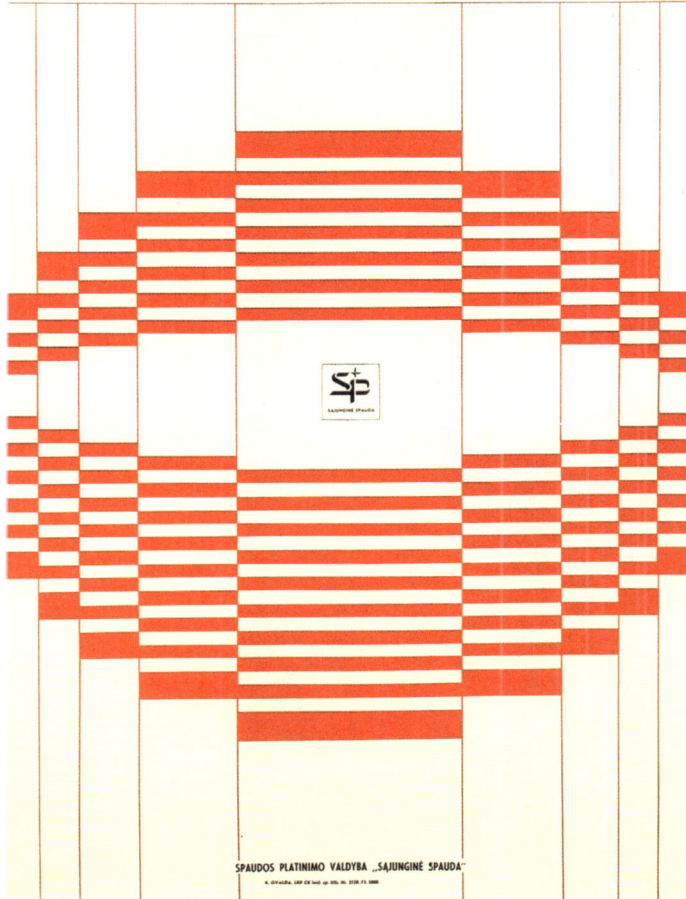

SĄJUNGINĖS SPAUDOS KIOSKUOSE IR PARDUOTUVĖSE
–LAIKRAŠČIAI, ŽURNALAI, FILATELIJOS PREKĖS

SPAUDOS PLATINIMO VALDYBA „SĄJUNGINĖ SPAUDA"

[I]deology   [M]achinery

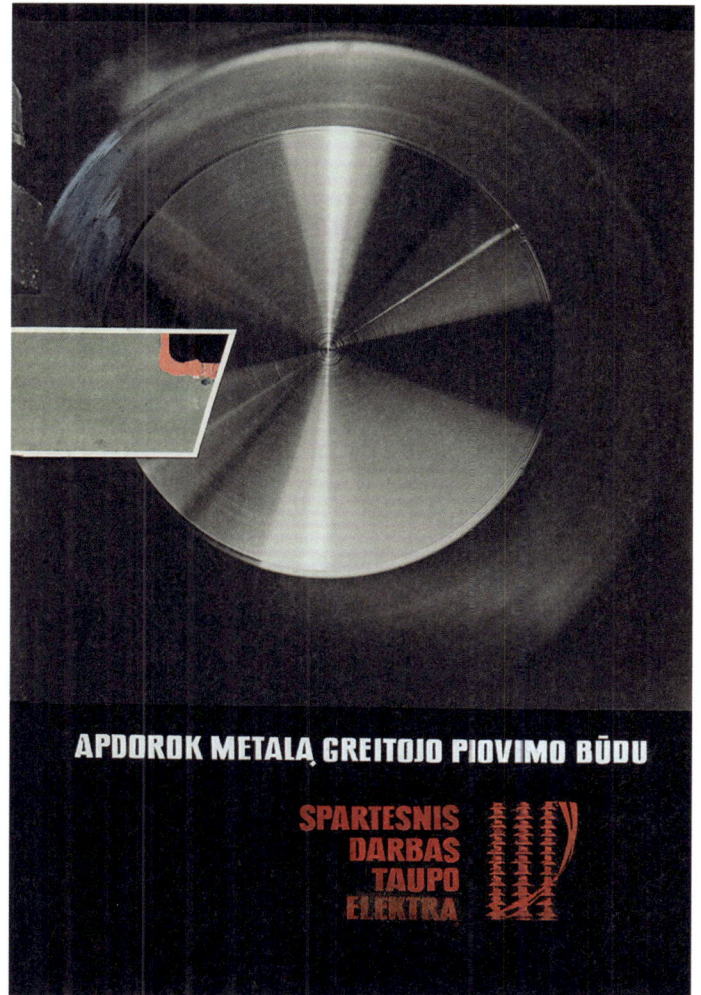

APDOROK METALĄ GREITOJO PIOVIMO BŪDU

SPARTESNIS
DARBAS
TAUPO
ELEKTRĄ

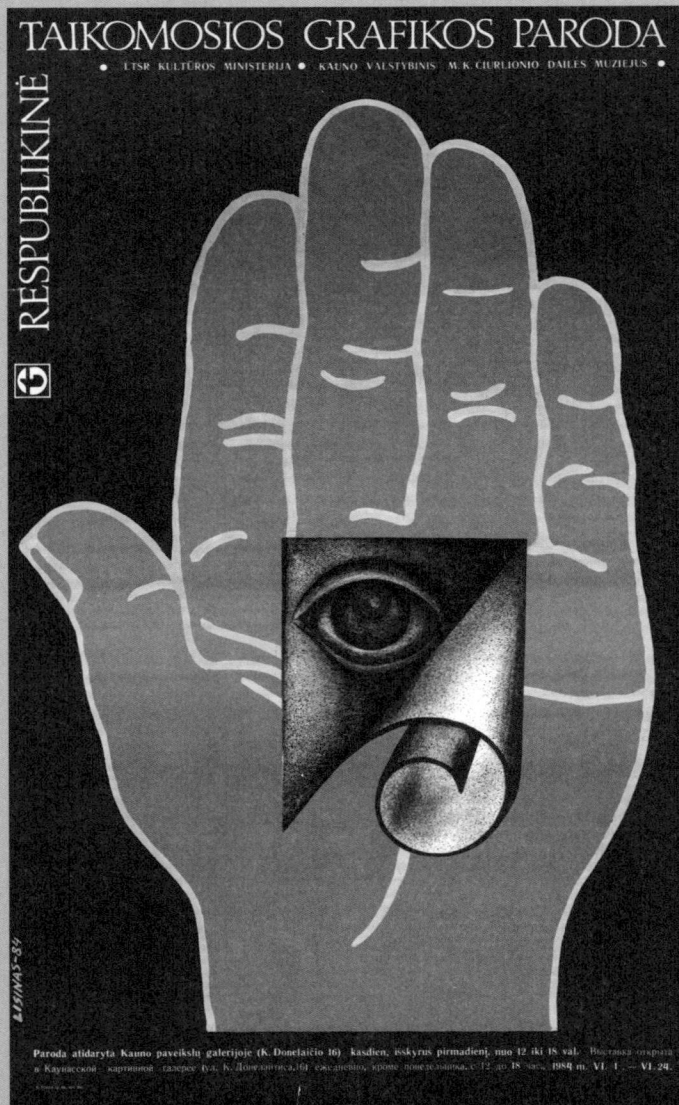

In 1984, to commemorate the 20th anniversary of the Tara bureau, a Republican Exhibition of Applied Graphics was held at the Kaunas Picture Gallery (now part of the M. K. Čiurlionis National Museum of Art). This exposition was initiated by Kęstutis Gvalda. It was one of his life's most important projects. The poster was designed by Vladas Lisaitis and had many sketches, which were preserved in his personal archive.

e is for exhibitions: visionary projects and utopian aspirations

The Kaunas exhibition was the first to cover the whole republic and to gather not only the bureau's artists, but also creators from all around Lithuania. Two hundred artists contributed with over 2,000 exhibits. The exhibition was a retrospective of two decades of artistic work.

e is for exhibitions: visionary projects and utopian aspirations

[A]rtist-constructors   [G]ray   [V]isionary

e is for exhib tions: visionary projects and utopian aspirations

TAIKOMOSIOS GRAFIKOS PARODA

e is for exhibitions: visionary projects and utopian aspirations

TAIKOMOS
GRAFIKOS
PARODA

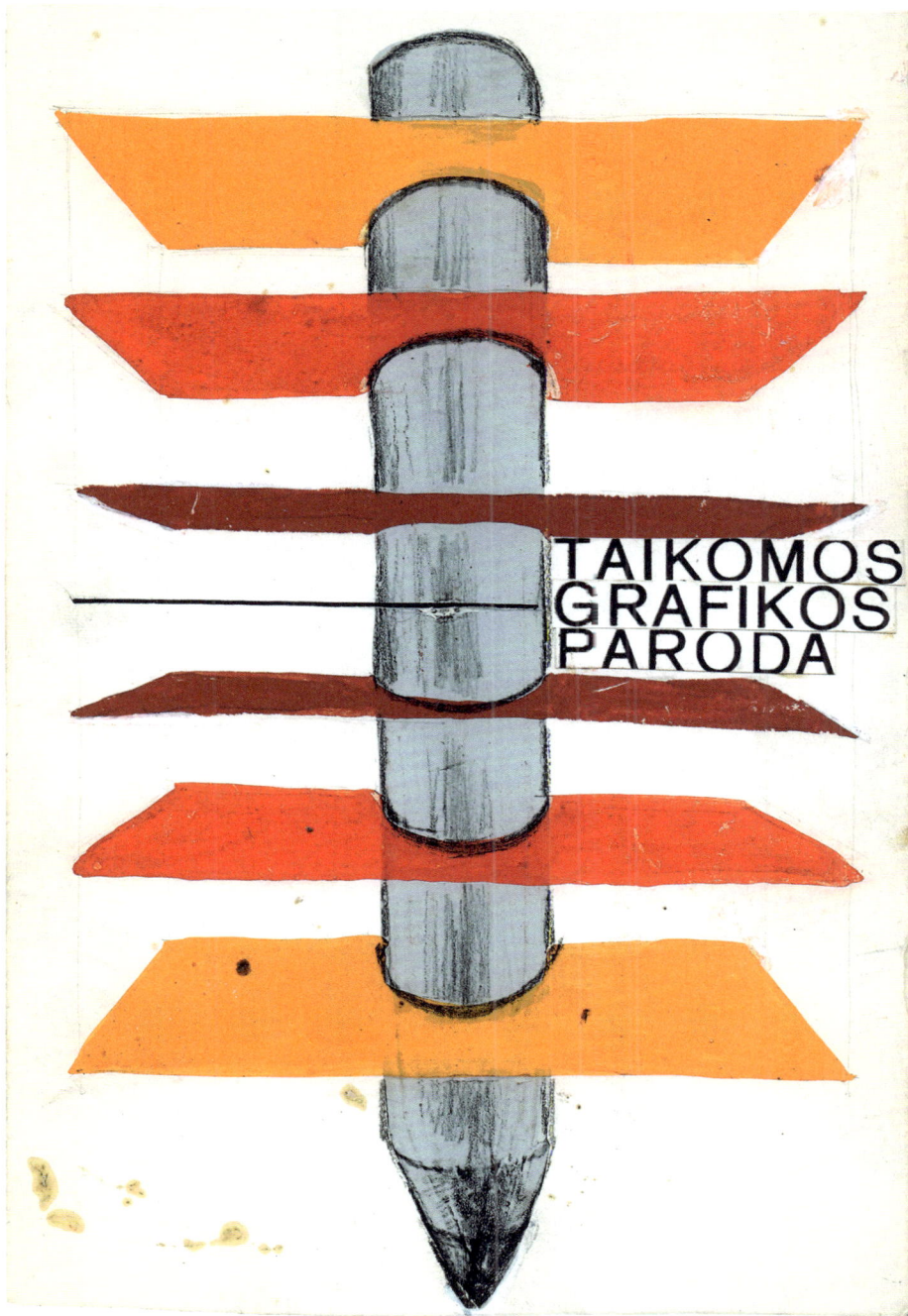

[E]xperimentation   [H]andmade   [S]low

[A]rtist-constructors   [P]lay   [W]omen-designers

An exhibition by four women who worked at the Tara bureau was organized at Vilnius Exhibition Hall in 1984. At that time, the artists Marė Trečiokaitė (b. 1939), Petrutė Masiulionytė (b. 1940), Almona Gudaitienė (1942–2024) and Lidija Glinskienė (1938–2014) presented samples of their designs, mainly packaging for confectionery products and toys.

e is for exhibitions: visionary projects and utopian aspirations

MARÉ TREČIOKAITÉ

1965 m. baigė Vilniaus valstybinį dailės institutą. Dirba Eksperimentiniame
meninio konstravimo biure. Bendradarbiauja „Vagos", „Minties" lei-
dyklose, Prekybos ir pramonės rūmuose.
Yra sukūrusi kompleksinių įpakavimų „Verpsto", „Jiesios" fabrikams,
apie 40 dėžučių saldainiams, etikečių
gėrimams, suvenyrinių įpakavimų ta-
bako gaminiams. Saldainių dėžutė
„Legenda" atžymėta TSRS LŪPP bron-
zos medaliu.
Dailininkės darbai buvo eksponuo-
ti respublikinėse, sąjunginėse bei užsienio parodose.

DARBŲ SĄRAŠAS

1.	Saldainių dėžutė „Avio"	13.	„	„Operos ir baleto teatro 60-mečiui"
2.	„	„Su kovo 8-ąja"	14.	„	„Premjera" (2 variantai)
3.	„	„Bananiniai"	15.	„	„Pjovėja"
4.	„	„Kauno asorti"	16.	„	„Kauno rotušė"
5.	„	„Laimės žiburys"	17.	„	„Pergalė"
6.	„	„Taika"	18.	Dėžutė „Jiesios" I-ko porcelia-nui įpakuoti (servizui)
7.	„	„Legenda"	19.	„	(vazelei)
8.	„	„Sveikinu"	20.	Etiketė alui „Utenos alus"
9.	„	„Milda"	21.	Etiketė „Šalmėtinis likeris"
10.	„	„Jubiliejus"	22.	Etiketė gėrimui „Sajanai"
11.	„	„Nemuno kraštas"	23.	Pakelis cigaretėms „Regata"
12.	„	„Šiaulių suvenyras"		

taikomosios grafikos paroda

LTSR DAILININKŲ SĄJUNGA, LTSR DAILĖS FONDAS,
EKSPERIMENTINIS MENINIO KONSTRAVIMO BIURAS

PARODOS BUKLETAS
DAILININKĖ P. MASIULENYTĖ
FOTONUOTRAUKOS K. BUDRECKAS
ATS. REDAKTORIUS O. SKARINKAITĖ

Duota rinkti   Pasirašyta spausdinti 1984.12.28
        LV 16007. Formatas   Popierius kreidinis
     Spauda   sgl. sp. l.   sgl. spelu. atsp.
Tiražas 300 egz. Užsak. Nr.   Nemokamai
        Išleido Eksperimentinis meninio konstravimo biuras.
Vilnius, Paribio 17, spausdino Taros ir įpakavimo GS „Vilnis"

VILNIUS, 1984

LIDIJA GLINSKIENĖ

1963 m. baigė Vilniaus valstybinį dailės institutą. Dirba Eksperimentiniame meninio konstravimo biure.

Dailininkė dalyvauja respublikinėse bei sąjunginėse parodose. Be įpakavimo vaikų žaislams yra sukūrusi iliustracijų, plakatų. Darbai buvo eksponuojami parodose Varšuvoje, Bratislavoje, Paryžiuje, Bolonėje. Už knygų apipavidalinimą, plakatus, pramoninės grafikos darbus yra apdovanota diplomais.

ALMONA GUDAITIENĖ

1967 m. baigė Vilniaus valstybinio dailės instituto grafikos fakultetą. Parodose dalyvauja nuo 1969 m. Dirba taikomosios grafikos, plakato, ekslibriso srityse.

Dailininkė dalyvavo kuriant kompleksinius įpakavimus suvenyrams ir žaislams. Darbai buvo eksponuojami respublikinėse bei tarptautinėse parodose. Parodoje „Dailininkai pramonei" apdovanota diplomu.

PETRUTĖ MASIULENYTĖ

1966 m. baigė Kauno St. Žuko taikomosios dailės technikumą. Dirba Eksperimentiniame meninio konstravimo biure, bendradarbiauja „Minties" leidykloje.

Autorė yra sukūrusi firminių ženklų, daug įvairių, jų tarpe kompleksinių, įpakavimų. Dalyvauja konkursuose, turi darbų, atžymėtų diplomais. Dailininkės darbai eksponuojami respublikinėse, sąjunginėse bei užsienio parodose (Vienoje, Solonikuose, Diuseldorfe, Kopenhagoje).

DARBŲ SĄRAŠAS

ĮPAKAVIMAI ŽAISLAMS

1. Gaisrinė mašina
2. Pienovežis
3. Tiltų statymo mašina
4. Tralas
5. Garvežys su dviem platformomis
6. Medinis konstruktorius
7. Keleivinis traukinys
8. Keleivinis traukinys
9. Sunkvežimis
10. Cementovežis
11. Automobilis
12. Automobilis
13. Automobilis
14. Medinis konstruktorius
15. Žaidimas „Kelias į kempingą"
16. Domino „Eismo ženklai"

DĖŽUTĖ „SALDAINIŲ DOVANĖLES"

17—21. Naujametinės dovanėlės
22—23. Olimpinės
24. Naujametinis maišelis saldainiams
25—26. Bačkonio suvenyrai

DARBŲ SĄRAŠAS

1. Žaidimas „Mokausi skaityti"
2. Pešto rinkinys vaikams
3. Saldainių dėžė „Šventinė dovanėlė" I
4. Saldainių dėžė „Šventinė dovanėlė" II
5. Saldainių dėžė „Šventinė dovanėlė" III
6. Dėžė „Saviėrė" raketinė mašina"
7. Dėžė „Kelių statybos mašina"
8. Dėžė „Abėcėlės sukutis"
9. Dėžė „Žaidimas su žiedais"
10. Dėžė „Automašina „Hoperis"
11. Dėžė „Traktorius su varikliu"
12. Dėžė „Virtuvė"
13. Vyniojamas popierius žaislams
14. Dekolės 1, 2, 3, 4
15. Dėžė „Katinas"

DARBŲ SĄRAŠAS

1. Saldainių dėžutė „Saldainių rinkinys"
2. „ „Nerija"
3. „ „Olimpiada-80"
4. „ „Su švente"
5. „ „TSR 40-čiui"
6. „ „Dražė Pieniška"
7. „ „Dražė „Citrina su vit. C"
8. „ „Dražė „Juodieji serbentai"
9. „ „Jaunatvė"
10. „ „Suvenyrinė"
11. „ „Saldainiai"
12. „ „Kara-Kum"
13. „ „Senasis rūsys"
14. „ „Saldainių rinkinys"
15. Saldainių popieriukas „Gėlių puokštė"
16. „ „Nomeda"
17. „ „Planeta"
18. „ „Subatėlė"
19. „ „Daiva"
20. Dėžutė žvakei „Kauno rotušė"
21. Etiketė „Naminis obuolių džemas"
22. „ „Juodųjų serbentų džemas"
23. „ „Naminis slyvų džemas"
24. Dėžutė loto žaidimui „Miškų ir pievų gėlės"
25. Etiketė „Vanilinis šokoladas"
26. „ „Šokoladas „Likėnai"

l is for logos and labels:
advertising for different industries

During the 10 years of its operation, the Tara bureau designed 500 logos for different factories and enterprises. The personal libraries and archives of the creators confirm that the designers of the Tara bureau were thoroughly acquainted with Western literature and the history of brand marks and they had been focusing on the most contemporary trends. A paradoxical situation: even though the logos were created for very Soviet institutions, their symbolism, abstractness and purity seemed to disconnect them from the Soviet system.

Labels and leaflets – the smallest examples of graphic design projects – were very regularly redesigned or updated, or reprinted after supplies of one series had been exhausted, changing paper types, formats, typefaces, or colors. Tens of thousands of labels were produced over the course of several decades. When artist-constructors of the Tara bureau entered the advertising field in the mid-1960s, however, label designs became noticeably more professional – more bright and colorful, with better coordinated colors, more variation in composition, and the use of more modern typefaces. At the initiative of its designers, the bureau began producing thematic label series with more unified styles displaying the creative styles of a given designer.

Girulių vaikų
Stovykla
„Gintarėlis"

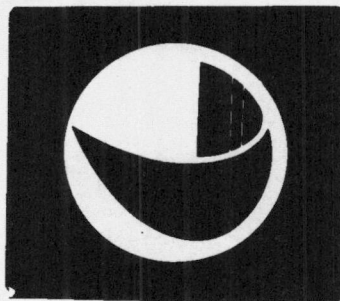

KLAIPEDA

GINTARO KRANTAS
PIONIERIŲ STOVYKLA

Nem
1975

kuršių nerija

Šilutės Vaikų
Salos
Stovykla
Valdyba N3
1987

NERINGA

1955 m,

Gusevo trikotažo —
—galanterijos f-kus

N. Jelinčionienė

17

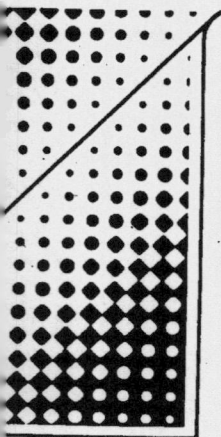

jūrų laivininkystės
ramai "Vėtrungė"

K. Ramonas

praktika

1576

nevėžis

rasa

Siuvimo f. „Nevėžis"

K. Ramonas

l is for logos and labels: advertising for different industries

I is for logos and labels: advertising for different industries

6. Jehučioni
Šimeno
kulnokas

LIETUVA

5

buit aptarnavimo kombinat-
„Jaunystė"

26   27   28   29   30   31

34   35   36   37   38

41   42   43   44   45   46

49   50   51   52   53   54

57   58   59   60   61   62

65   66   67   68   69   68

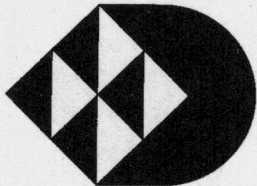

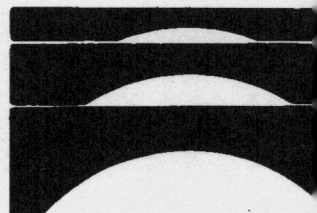

Kometalinio ūkio projektavimo instituto techninė informacija.

K. Ramonas
1976

Svaja

"Kultūros barai"
žurnalas

K. Ramonas

pfasta

BALTIJA

Kalon

Lietuvos
kino-
studija
Kaunas
1968

Tulpė

KAS
Autorius?

[X]unknown

SILVA

GMK

1975 kretingos
buitinio gyventojų
aptarnavimo
kombinatas

4

12

GILDIJA

9

[L]ithuanian   [M]odernisation

KAUNO AUDINIAI

Kauno Audiniai

[E]xport   [P]ropaganda

l is for logos and labels: advertising for different industries

Tualetinis Muilas

ТУАЛЕТНОЕ МЫЛО

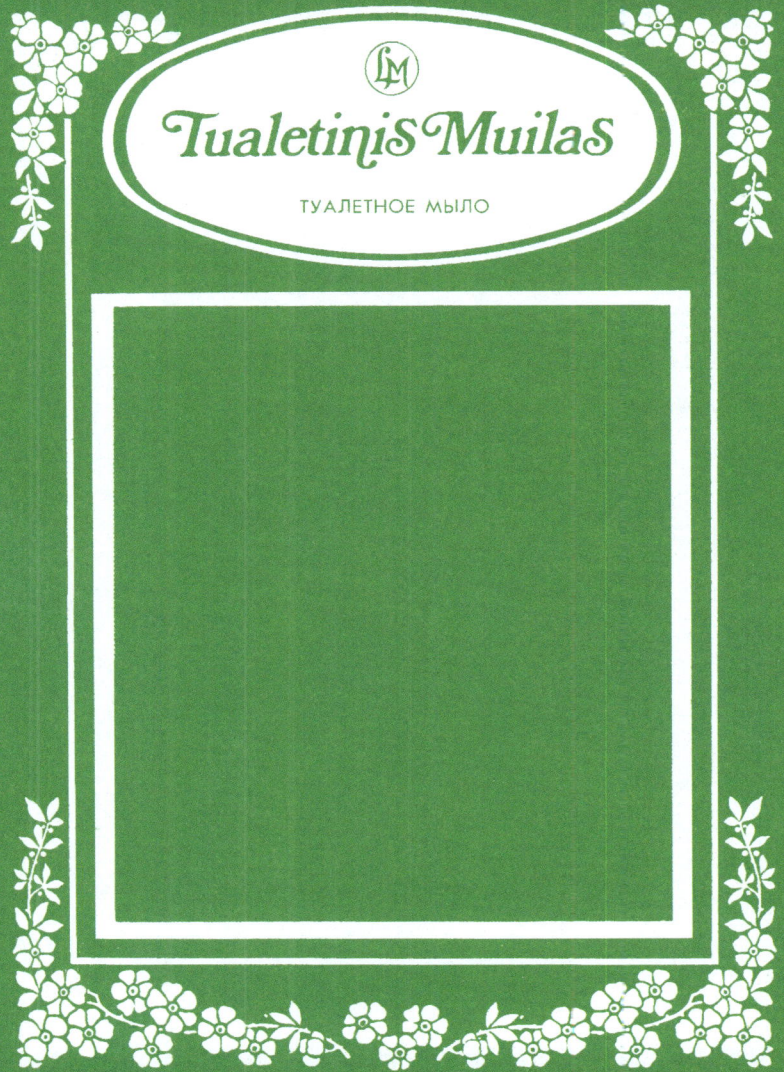

[G]ray   [K]itsch   [R]eklama   non[Q]uality   [T]ypography

I is for logos and labels: advertising for different industries

tualetinis muilas
Aksominis

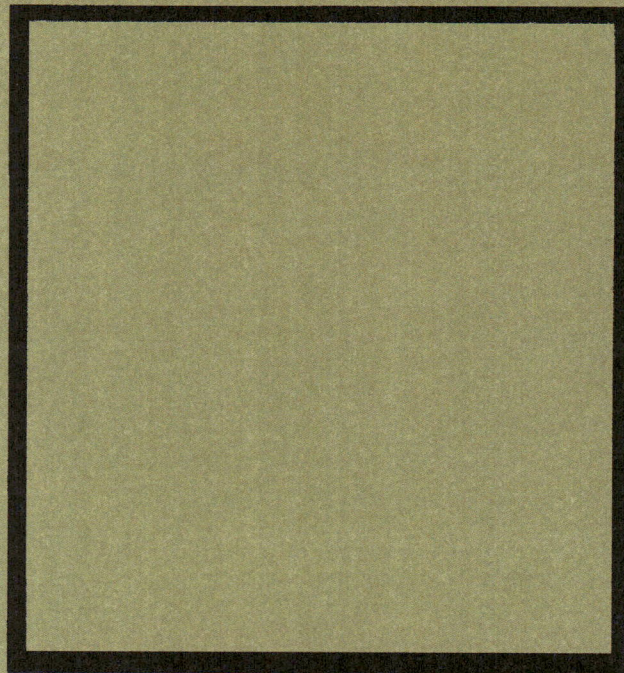

[G]ray   [L]ithuanian   [R]eklama

l is for logos and labels: advertising for different industries

LIESAS
KEFYRAS
ОБЕЗЖИРЕННЫЙ
КЕФИР

СОКАМ

DIETINĖS
PASUKOS

ДИЕТИЧЕСКАЯ ПАХТА

MĖGĖJŲ
sviestas

VA
SŪ

КРЕ

**liesa
varškė**

ОБЕЗЖИРЕННЫЙ
ТВОРОГ

ČIŲ

s

СЫР

LEDAI
SU VAISIŲ-UOGŲ
SULTIMIS
IR SIRUPAIS

GĖRIMAS

Vilnis

НАПИТОК «ВИЛЬНИС»

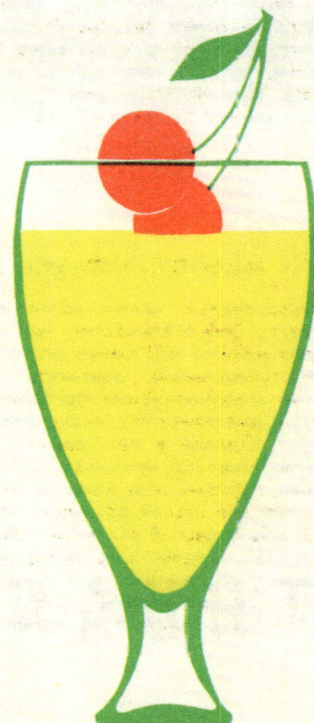

PIENO PRAMONĖ

LITHUANIAN MILK INDUSTRY

I is for logos and labels: advertising for different industries

[L]ithuanian   [M]odernisation

l is for logos and labels: advertising for different industries

LIETUVOS TSR MPM   **KAUNO ALAUS IR B/G KOMBINATAS**

MINERALINIS VANDUO

CHEMINĖ SUDĖTIS:
(gramais litre)
Anijonai
Chloras	3,9—4,8
Sulfatas	0,7—1,1
Hidrokarbonatas	0,31—0,34
Jodas	0,006218
Bromas	0,0069

RTS 440—63

CHEMINĖ SUDĖTIS:
(gramais litre)
Katijonai
Natris ir Kalis	1,5—2,5
Kalcis	0,63—0,69
Magnis	0,2—0,4
Litis	0,0002
Geležis	0,0004—0,002

Bendras ištirpusių druskų kiekis 8,7 g litre.

VYTAUTAS

Gali būti natūraliai iškritusių druskų nuosėdų. Butelius laikyti paguldytus vėsioje vietoje.

1 2 3 4 5 6 7 8 9 10 11 12

„GIEDR‹

LIETUVOS TSR MPM   **KAUNO ALAUS IR B/G KOMBINATAS**

MINERALINIS VANDUO

CHEMINĖ SUDĖTIS:
(gramais litre)
KATIJONAI
Natris ir kalis	0,47
Kalcis	0,14
Magnis	0,17

RTS 440—63

CHEMINĖ SUDĖTIS:
(gramais litre)
ANIJONAI
Chloras	1,12
Sulfatas	0,29
Hidrokarbonatas	0,23

Bendras ištirpusių druskų kiekis 2,4 g litre.

BIRUTĖ

1 2 3 4 5 6 7 8 9 10 11 12

„GIEDRA"

l is for logos and labels: advertising for different industries

non[Q]uality   [S]oviet   [T]ypography

l is for logos and labels: advertising for different industries

m is for macaroni and pizza

Paul Gangloff

1
Ursula K. Le Guin, "The Carrier Bag Theory of Fiction" in: *Dancing at the Edge of the World*, Grove Press, 1989.

In her essay, "The Carrier Bag Theory of Fiction",[1] Ursula K. Le Guin convincingly tells why a bottle makes a better central character of a story than a hero. She argues that a bottle (or any sort of container) may be the oldest form of culture.

> Not just the bottle of gin or wine, but bottle in its older sense of container in general, a thing that holds something else.

> (…) A leaf a gourd shell a net a bag a sling a sack a bottle a pot a box a container. A holder. A recipient.

> The first cultural device was probably a recipient… Many theorizers feel that the earliest cultural inventions must have been a container to hold gathered products and some kind of sling or net carrier.

2
Kęstutis Gvalda, a long-time employee of Tara, quoted in Karolina Jakaitė, "The Process of Graphic Design Projects: the Establishment and Practice of an Experimental Design Bureau", MO Museum, Vilnius, article published online in 2016, https://www.mmcentras.lt/cultural-history/cultural-history/design/19541979-was-there-such-a-thing-as-soviet-lithuanian-design/the-process-of-graphic-design-projects-the-establishment-and-practice-of-an-experimental-design-bureau/79137.

3
Ibid.

4
Ibid.

Without going that far back in time, I want to explore this idea of Le Guin and look at containers designed by Tara to see what story they are the central characters of.

"Tara" was the nickname given to the Experimental Package Design Bureau, a bureau established in 1964 upon approval of the Soviet Lithuanian Council of Ministers State Academic Research Works Coordinating Committee. "Tara" literally means "container" and that was something the artists working for the bureau disliked. They felt no pride in designing food containers and other packaging. The name "Tara" itself was synonymous with an inferior kind of job, one experienced as a compromise of artistic integrity and even "a humiliation."[2] "Tara (…) the name itself was horrible – students laughed at it."[3] Yet, artists took the jobs for the income it would provide. "Everyone wanted to eat."[4] Working for Tara meant engaging in a Soviet state propaganda and its bureaucratic apparatus with a commission judging whether designs would enter production or not. Yet the artists often worked from home. The image of a team working collectively, as shown in group photographs, was more of a staged setup than the actual reality. Everyone was rather free to work how they liked. If something akin to freelancing existed in a Soviet state, this might have been it.

The bureau had an ethical position towards the design of containers. As the interface between the product and its consumer, the container not only protects, conceals, and preserves the contents, it also informs the consumer. It can be seducing, deceiving, even manipulating, "trying to push a product by any means possible."[5] However, for Tara "the purpose of a socialist advertising was to provide objective and correct information about a product, its characteristics, and utility; it was meant to "suggest and advise", not to push."[6]

I am looking at flattened boxes of pasta designed by Raisa Šmuriginaitė (1931–2019) and printed in Lithuania sometime in the 1970's. There are seven of them plus a mockup design. It's a series; the same elements repeat – bold colored frames, the name of the pasta in large type, the pasta's precise sort, variety, taste or shape, with nutritional facts and other info in a smaller type. The color palettes are as follows:

olive green, red and brown
sand, spring green and chestnut
pale pink, orange and vermillion
bright yellow, red and brown
orange, red and brown
army green, bottle green and greenish brown
orange and bright yellow.

The design of these containers of *makaronai* is entirely typographic with a couple of stylized drawings, one of short noodles and one of elbow macaroni. The latter, on the box of *Ragučiai*, is dynamic – as if the macaronis would rotate around an axis formed by the central macaroni in an evocation of modern and rationalized food production. The drawing is not coldly mechanical. It could be a wood carving. It is hand drawn and slightly irregular and has something folksy and ornamental about it that connects it with a more ancient imagery. Raisa Šmuriginaitė paired the woodcut-like images with a typeface looking like Octopuss, a typeface designed in 1970 by Colin Brignal for the British rubdown typography company Letraset. Such a packaging

5
Ibid.

6
Ibid.

m is for macaroni and pizza

NETO
HETTO

500 g
г

MAKARONŲ GAMINIAI

Mokykliniai

"ШКОЛЬНЫЕ"

МАКАРОННЫЕ ИЗДЕЛИЯ

VIRIMO BŪDAS:

Į 1/2 STIKLINĖS PIENO IR 1/3 STIKLINĖS VANDENS ĮDĖTI ARBATINĮ
ŠAUKŠTELĮ CUKRAUS IR ŽIUPSNELĮ DRUSKOS. UŽVIRTI. SUPYLUS
VALGOMĄJĮ ŠAUKŠTĄ (15 G) MAKARONŲ, PAMAIŠANT VIRTI 5 MIN.
IŠVIRTĄ KOŠĘ PASKANINTI SVIESTU.
"MOKYKLINIAI" MAKARONŲ GAMINIAI REKOMENDUOJAMI ĮVAI-
RAUS AMŽIAUS VAIKŲ MAITINIMUI (GARNYRAMS IR PIENIŠKOMS
SRIUBOMS).

LAIKYTI UŽDARYTAME PAKELYJE, SAUSOJE VIETOJE

TINKA VARTOTI 6 MĖN.

100	G BALTYMŲ	G, ANGLIAVANDENIŲ	G, RIEBALŲ	3 G,
	Г БЕЛКОВ 16	Г, УГЛЕВОДОВ 67,6	Г, ЖИР	

MIN. MEDŽIAGOS	G,	368 KCAL	TAME SKAIČIUJE:
МИН. ВЕЩЕСТВА 0,4	Г,	368 ККАЛ	В ТОМ ЧИСЛЕ:

KALCIO	MG	FOSFORO	MG	GELEŽIES	MG
КАЛЬЦИЙ 49,7	МГ	ФОСФОР 132,3	МГ	ЖЕЛЕЗО 1,6	МГ

REKOMENDUOTA TSRS MMA MITYBOS INSTITUTO
РЕКОМЕНДОВАНО ИНСТИТУТОМ ПИТАНИЯ АМН СССР

m is for macaroni and pizza

m is for macaroni and pizza

design for the socialist *makaronai*, I would argue, was not just a matter of "providing objective and correct information about a product," but of creating (or expressing) a desire that was perhaps not just a consumer desire for macaroni. It might have been a desire for a colorful, cool, psychedelic and abundant socialist culture.

The modernization and industrialization of food production was part of the Soviet revolutionary project being rapidly forced upon people in the Baltic States during and after WWII. As the Soviet Ministry of Food Manufacture stated in its 1939 "Book of tasty and healthy food", "our most important tasks are to awaken the population to new tastes, to create new demand, to educate to new needs, to create desires for new products, for new assortments."[7] To feed the people but also to "release the housewives from hard work in the kitchen as well as enable fast and effortless preparation of meals for every working person without having any specific knowledge in cookery."[8]

The party wanted to increase its control on food and centralized its production to this end. Reforms made Lithuanian farms non-viable and reorganized production on an industrial scale across countries of the Soviet bloc (contemporary capitalist agro-industry does the same; it makes small farms non-viable). Despite the promises of abundance that accompanied this modernization, shortages remained, as admitted in between the lines of the USSR program for provision of food products: "In five years public demand will be met not only for bread, a wide assortment of bread, pastry and noodle products, potatoes and sugar, but also for such products as cereals, confectioneries, margarine, eggs and fish, while the supply of meat, milk, vegetable oil, fruit and vegetable produce will be increased."[9]

Tara's packaging designs were made in the context of this shortage of foodstuffs. The designs of the containers formed a decor of abundance and modernity that concealed the struggle to produce the food they were meant to contain. (The goods we consume do something similar; they conceal the labor that was necessary to produce them.) If there was no food in the boxes, to design objective information was to create an illusion. This façade of modernism was prolonged on the level of the design bureau itself. The designers of Tara can be seen in a photograph wearing white coats and working in an office that seems to be setup for the precision work of a laboratory. In practice, they would not be in such an office and even less likely to be wearing lab coats, but in reality worked from their own ateliers or homes.

7
Ministry of Food Manufacture. "Book of tasty and healthy food", Moscow, 1939. Quoted in Indrė Klimaitė, *On Continuous and Systematic Nutrition Improvement*, Maastricht: Jan Van Eyck Academie, 2013, p. 27.

8
Ibid, p. 41.

9
The USSR program for provision of food products till 1990 and the means of its realization: transcript from 1982, in K. Vyšniauskas. Public catering at factory, Mintis, Vilnius 1984, in Indrė Klimaitė, *On Continuous and Systematic Nutrition Improvement*, p. 168.

m is for macaroni and pizza

The international fairs were another part of the façade. These exhibitions displayed an image of prosperity and refinement of a modernity that had nothing to envy from the capitalist economies of the West. For the fairs, the designs of Tara were printed abroad, in Italy or France, to achieve a result that could not be reached on the presses of Lithuanian printers who suffered constant material shortages. Like inverted versions of the Trojan horse, these containers without contents were meant to deceive, something which seems to have worked excessively well, as it provoked the response "We don't need your products, but we'd gladly take your packaging."[10]

If the designs of Tara tell something about the efforts and illusions of the particular time and place of their making, one might ask what story do the containers of our contemporary food have to tell. I have no insider knowledge of packaging designed for corporate clients. The container designs I could talk about are those of DIY products: labels for bottles and cans of beer by Felicia von Zweigbergk for her own Butcher's Tears, printed by riso print shop De Stencilkelder in Amsterdam and the hot sauce labels by Our Polite Society for Alexander Krone's Desmadre Salsa Picante. Working with DIY products that have enjoyed some success over the past years, these designers circumvent the ambivalent relationship with corporate clients. The DIY idea is to make something without the state and without the corporate capital, and in its radical forms, to make something against the state and against the capitalist corporations. Butcher's Tears or Desmadre Salsa Picante function more as excuses to organize social events than products for profit or nutrition. They are not unlike Christoph Keller's schnaps bottle labels that were reproduced alongside an interview between Sarah Crowner, Stuart Bailey and the publisher-turned-land-owner-and-schnaps-distiller,[11] in which a parallel is drawn between publishing art books and making schnaps, in relation to dilettantism and to "creating a context which doesn't exist already – a space, aura, position, community, or however you want to describe it."[12]

Leaving the fields of DIY alcoholic beverages and hot sauces (that are halfway between foodstuff and poison), we can look at a series of works by graphic designer David Bennewith that use mass produced containers as material and as format. The works are engraved by laser onto boxes of Dr Oetker Ristorante frozen pizza that Bennewith has been collecting since 2017. Historically, frozen pizzas have their origins in military food that was designed to be kept over a long period of time and prepared

10
Comment about the Lithuanian pavilion in Paris in 1977 by Kęstutis Gvalda, in Karolina Jakaitė, *The Process of Graphic Design Projects: the Establishment and Practice of an Experimental Design Bureau*, MO Museum, Vilnius, article published online in 2016, https://www.mmcentras.lt/cultural-history/cultural-history/design/19541979-was-there-such-a-thing-as-soviet-lithuanian-design/the-process-of-graphic-design-projects-the-establishment-and-practice-of-an-experimental-design-bureau/79137.

11
"Right to Burn", An interview with Christoph Keller by Stuart Bailey and Sarah Crowner, in *Dot Dot Dot* 14, 2007. Available as PDF at www.dextersinister.org/library.html?id=108.

12
Ibid.

m is for macaroni and pizza

PIRMOS RŪŠIES MAKARONAI

Ragučiai

РОЖКИ
СОРТ ПЕРВЫЙ

МАКАРОННЫЕ ИЗДЕЛИЯ

NETO NETTO
600 g/г

VIRIMO BŪDAS: MAKARONUS SUPILTI Į VERDANTĮ PASŪDYTĄ VANDENĮ ARBA SULTI-NĮ IR VIRTI 8—10 MIN. RUOŠIANT ANTRUOSIUS PATIEKALUS, IŠVIR-TUS MAKARONUS (SVERSTI) IR REFUKĄ IR PERPILTI ŠALTU VANDENIU. 100 G RAGUČIŲ — NE MAŽIAU KAIP 3 STIKLINES VANDENS IR 1/3 AR-BATINIO ŠAUKŠTELIO DRUSKOS.

PAGAMINIMO DATA / ДАТА ВЫРАБОТКИ

PAKUOTOJO № / № УКЛАДЧИКА

МПП ЛИТОВСКОЙ ССР КЛАЙПЕДСКИЙ ХЛЕБОКОМБИНАТ

KAINA: JUOSTA
ЦЕНА: ПОЯС
I — 27 кр. коп.
II — 30 кр. коп.
III — 33 кр. коп.

AUKŠČIAUSIOS RŪŠIES

Lakštiniai

ЛАПША
СОРТ ВЫСШИЙ

МАКАРОННЫЕ ИЗДЕЛИЯ

VIRIMO BŪDAS: LAKŠTINIUS SUPILTI Į VERDANTĮ PASŪDYTĄ VANDENĮ ARBA SUL-TINĮ IR VIRTI 10—15 MIN. RUOŠIANT ANTRUOSIUS PATIEKALUS, IŠ-VIRTUS LAKŠTINIUS (SVERSTI) IR REFUKĄ IR PERPILTI ŠALTU VANDE-NIU. 100 G LAKŠTINIŲ — NE MAŽIAU KAIP 3 STIKLINES VANDENS IR ¼ ARBATINIO ŠAUKŠTELIO DRUSKOS.

PAGAMINIMO DATA / ДАТА ИЗГОТОВЛЕНИЯ

PAKUOTOJO № / № УПАКОВЩИКА

МПП ЛИТОВСКОЙ ССР · КЛАЙПЕДСКИЙ ХЛЕБОКОМБИНАТ

MAKARONAI

Ypatingieji

AUKŠČIAUSIOS RŪŠIES
SU KIAUŠINIAIS
ОСОБЫЕ

ИЗДЕЛИЯ МАКАРОННЫЕ

I	JUOSTA ПОЯС	41	КАР. КОП.
II	JUOSTA ПОЯС	45	КАР. КОП.
III	JUOSTA ПОЯС	50	КАР. КОП.

LIETUVOS TSR MPM
KLAIPĖDOS DUONOS KOMBINATAS
МИНПИЩЕПРОМ ЛИТОВСКОЙ ССР
КЛАЙПЕДСКИЙ ХЛЕБОКОМБИНАТ

: Į 1/2 STIKLINĖS PIENO IR 1/3 STIKLINĖS VANDENS ĮRTI ARBATINĮ ŠAUKŠTELĮ CUKRAUS IR ŽIUPSNELĮ DRUSKOS, UŽ-RINTI, ĮBĖRUS VALGOMĄJĮ ŠAUKŠTĄ (15 G) MAKARONŲ, PAMAI-NT VIRTI MIN. IŠVIRTĄ KOŠĘ PASKANINTI SVIESTU. OKYKLINIAI" MAKARONŲ GAMINIAI REKOMENDUOJAMI ĮVAI-US AMŽIAUS VAIKŲ MAITINIMUI (GARNYRAMS IR ĮSKOMS IUBOMS). IKYTI UŽDARAME PAKELYJE OJE VIETOJE.

m is for macaroni and pizza

13
"Many frozen food products had their origins in military-developed foods designed for storage longevity and ease of preparation in the battle field, during World War II." https://en.wikipedia.org/wiki/Convenience_food.

14
The Dr Oetker company is a family-owned business founded by pharmacist Dr August Oetker who created a recipe for baking powder in 1891. During WWII, the company was run by Rudolf-August Oetker (the founder's grandson) who was a member of the Waffen SS. Nowadays the Dr Oetker Ristorante is a mass product par excellence: "every day, around 2.3 million pizzas come off the production line at [their] two German factories in Wittlich and Wittenberg." www.oetker.com.

15
Louise Beaumont, senior brand manager at Dr Oetker Ristorante, quoted in *New Look for Dr Oetker Ristorante*, www.packaginginsights.com/news/new-look-for-dr-oetker-ristorante.html. The following citations in this paragraph are from the same source.

quickly on the battlefield.[13] The company producing that particular brand is named after Dr August Oetker, a pharmacist who commercialized baking powder. During the World War II, the company supported the Nazi regime by providing pudding and manufacturing weapons.[14]

Like Raisa Šmuriginaitė's design for the *makaronai*, the container design of the Ristorante is based on one model with different colors for each topping: green for Margherita, pink for Prosciutto, etc. The color element is manifested in a thin banner under the large lettering "Ristorante," in which the topping is indicated in reversed type. This is to allow the Ristorante to be "easily identified within the freezer" as senior brand manager Louise Beaumont explains in an interview.[15] The "loyal customers" can then opt for Margherita, Prosciutto or another according to the color code.

The pizza is depicted by a retouched photograph ("the very heart of the design"). The overall design is exactly the same on each box of the series, except for the type of pizza depicted. The photo shows the baked pizza on a plate on a table covered with a white tablecloth, silver cutlery and a glass of red wine ("sophisticated and authentically Italian"). Only the pizza is in focus; the rest is blurred, bathed in soft light. A single slice is cut and lifted just a few millimeters above the rest of the pizza and seems to levitate, a levitation only noticed when looking twice. On the first look, your own hand appears to be holding the slice that is positioned at the lower right corner of the box. This use of heavily retouched photography to signify "the real thing" in combination with the trick of the hovering slice and the purposeful incompleteness of the image of the missing hand as an opening for a play or a narrative between the user and the designed object allow us to qualify this design as post-modern.

This play takes place between the real materiality of the cardboard box and the illusion of reality produced by the photograph. Burning into the illusory space, the laser etchings excavate the raw pulp of the cardboard to form another layer, not on top but below the print. Bennewith turned the pizza box into an object that makes our visual culture visible. He points to the fact that "all the reproduced materials represent the connection between telemetry, UI design/culture and daily life." The user interface of the Health app, a pictogram for dancing drawn on the grid designed by Otl Aicher for the graphic identity of the 1972 Olympic games in Munich, the word 'HOUSE,' an image of an ear and other strangely familiar visuals appear as ghost images.

They articulate a visual essay about repetition in daily life, catalyzed by industrially reproducible things, (self) surveillance and optimization.

David Bennewith, Ristorante Telematics (Funghi), Dancing, 2023

David Bennewith, Ristorante Telematics (Quattro Formaggi), Crystals, 2024

Materials: Collected Dr. Oetker 'Ristorante' line pizza box, .indd, PDF, Lasercutting Zing 16 @ LaserStraat, Wormerveer.

16
In a text about the Socialist object, art historian Christina Kiaer gives this reading of a fragment of Walter Benjamin's *Arcades Project*: "Benjamin imagined that the dreaming collective of bourgeois culture would awaken from the 'dream sleep' of the commodity phantasmagoria into a socialist culture, when the wish-images of what he called the 'ur-past' – the mythic, egalitarian society of material abundance – are made visible in the newest technological forms." Christina Kiaer, *"Into Production!": The Socialist Objects of Russian Constructivism,* https://transversal.at/transversal/0910/kiaer/en, last consulted on October 4th 2022. Re-published in Binna Choi, Maiko Tanaka (ed.), *Grand Domestic Revolution Handbook*, Amsterdam/Utrecht: Valiz, Casco, 2014.

In their respective manner, both David Bennewith's and Raisa Šmuriginaitė's works make a mythical abundance visible in the newest technological forms of their times.[16]

The one closer to us deals with the myths and technologies we have in 21st century Europe. Designed as the box for a product of Germany based on pharmaceutical and military inventions, it bears a photograph conjuring a "sophisticated and authentically Italian" atmosphere. There, through the melted cheese and the mushrooms slices, the interface of a device from a Silicon Valley company displays the amount of human energy burnt during one night (1150 KCAL).

The other made a mythical abundance visible in the newest technological forms of its time in order to give shape to a desirable socialist culture: modern, rational yet connected to the traditional. International yet idiosyncratic. Informational yet cool and colorful. But, ironically, as a part of the façade of a totalitarian regime, they became containers without contents.

Thankfully though, Tara's work has been conserved, archived and researched, allowing us to shift our attention beyond the clichés of socialist macaroni and capitalist pizza, away from "heroes", and onto these containers that do make such colorful complex and layered characters for stories about design to be told.

p is for public spaces:
advertising for hotels and restaurants

In the 1960s and 1970s, Lithuanian public spaces, interiors in particular, experienced a gust of modernist projects. These were partly caused by the financial regulation at the time, which obliged an allocation between 1 per cent and 3 per cent of budget for the creation of unique art and design objects.

New cafés, restaurants and hotels were built, inviting artists, architects and designers to create and implement new modernist projects for the public interiors. In the 1960s and 1970s, it was a special phenomenon of the Baltic countries, where cafés and restaurants became points of attraction shaping a distinctly Baltic urban atmosphere. However, some of them remained in the realm of "dreams", as they appeared in restricted public spaces that were often only accessible to the elite or oriented towards foreigners. The advertising booklets designed by the artists of the Tara bureau have gained a new value today, as most of these interiors have been destroyed (with the exception of the legendary café *Neringa* by architects Vytautas Nasvytis (1928–2016) and his twin brother Algimantas (1928–2018).

KAUNO

RESTORANAI IR KAVINĖS
RESTORANAI IR KAVINĖS
RESTORANAI IR KAVINĖS
RESTORANAI IR KAVINĖS
RESTORANAI IR KAVINĖS
RESTORANAI IR KAVINĖS
RESTORANAI IR KAVINĖS

INFORMACIJA
TELEFONAI

INFORMACIJA
TELEFONAI

45

VIEŠBUTIS
GINTARAS
HOTEL

[E]xport   [O]p-Art   [P]lay

The *Gintaras* Hotel (currently the renovated Panorama Hotel) was designed by the architect
Stasys Bareikis and opened in 1964 next to the Vilnius Railway Station.

p is for public spaces: advertising for hotels and restaurants

LŽL. sp. Užs. 4417. 69.20.000. LV

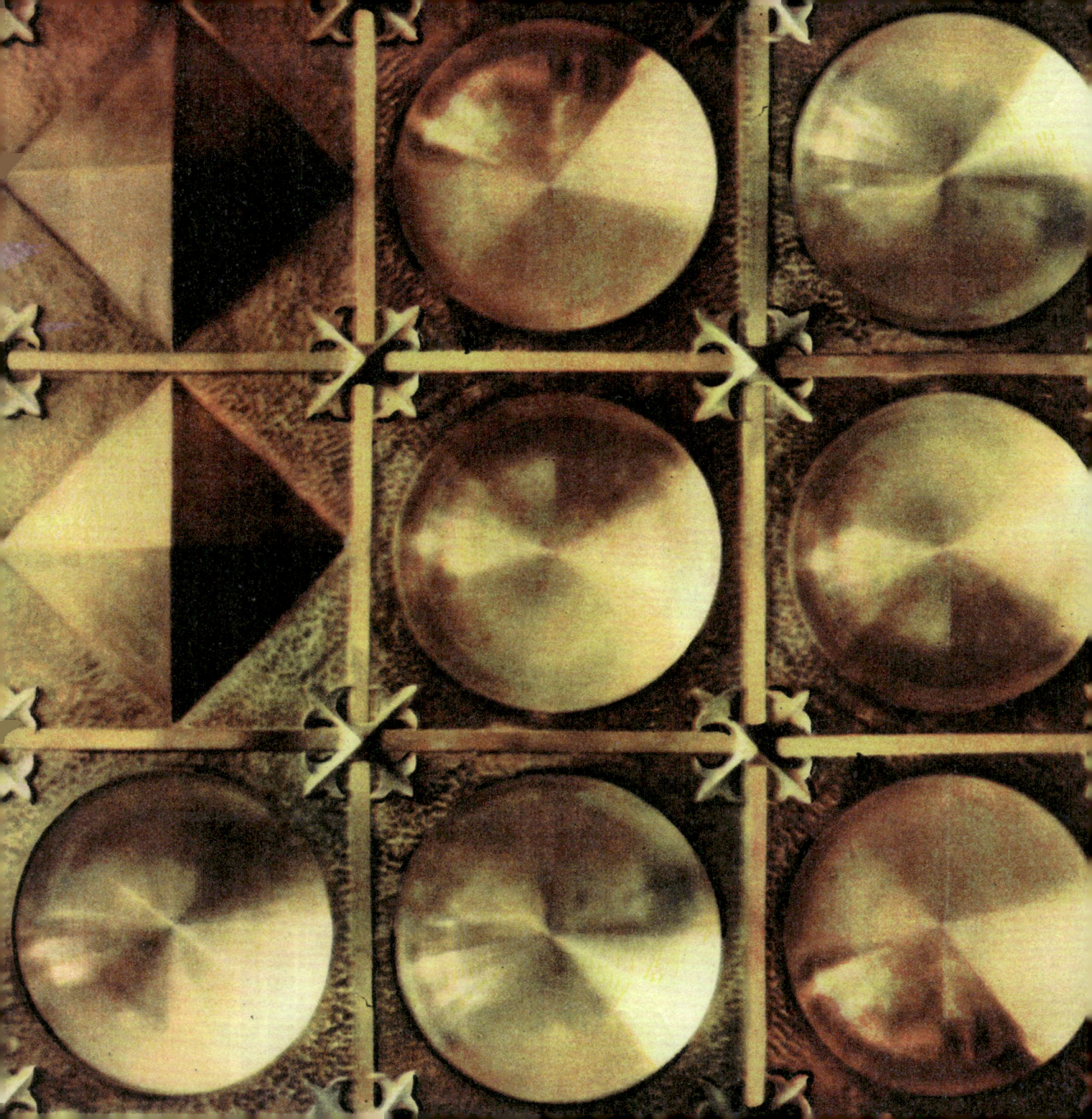

VILNIAUS MIESTO VALGYKLŲ TRESTAS

ВИЛЬНЮССКИЙ ТРЕСТ СТОЛОВЫХ
DINING-ROOM TRUST OF VILNIUS

ET|KB

Leid. Nr. 2296. V. Kapsuko sp. Užsak. Nr. 1309. LV 13000.

636238 1686

Gintaras

rage of amberlike colour, the „Gintaras".

Should you wish to celebrate a family anniversary, a jubilee or take part at a wedding party — be it your own or your friend's — we invite you to our Banquet Hall.

Customers are welcome from midday to 12 p.m.

Those who are fond of beer are welcome to the **beer bar** where they can have some cold foamy beer with dried Lithuanian cheese, toast of rye bread with garlic, or „fingers" with cheese and caraway seeds.

You are welcome in the Beer Bar from 11 a.m. 11 p.m.

Our address: Sodų str. 14, Vilnius, Lithuanian SSR.

[E]xport   [L]ithuanian   [O]p-Art   [P]lay

175

p is for public spaces: advertising for hotels and restaurants

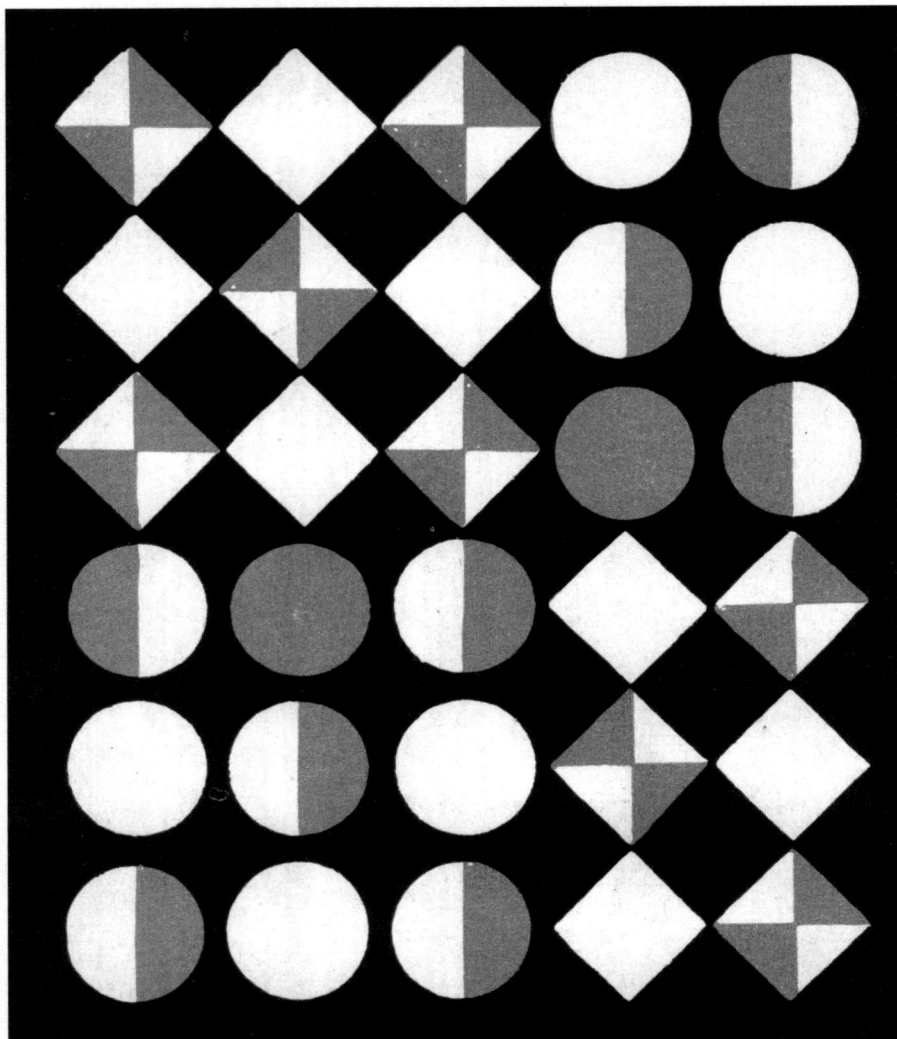

[E]xperimentation   [O]p-Art   [P]lay   [W]estern

The furniture for the hotel's restaurant was designed by Tadas Baginskas (b. 1936), who in turn invited Teodoras Kazimieras Valaitis (1934–1974) to create a metal decorative partition, which became the emblematic symbol of this place.

p is for public spaces: advertising for hotels and restaurants

HOTEL

VILNIUS г. ВИЛЬНЮС

Gintaras

VIEŠBUTIS

neRinGa VILNIUS

p is for public spaces: advertising for hotels and restaurants

VIEŠBUTIS
HOTEL
VILNIUS

INFORMACIJA
TELEFONAI

The advertising prospectus, designed by Juozas Gelguda in 1969, presents the two famous hotels in Vilnius in the 1960s and 1970s – *Neringa* and *Vilnius*. Hotel *Vilnius* was located on the central street of the city, now Gediminas Avenue.

p is for public spaces: advertising for hotels and restaurants

[F]ear [M]odernisation

The emblematic café *Neringa*, whose interior design made pioneering use of combining national motifs, Nordic modernity and Western trends was designed by architect brothers Nasvytis, and opened its doors in Vilnius in 1959. It was the tribute to their beloved Neringa, the sunny and sandy peninsular that separates the Curonian Lagoon from the Baltic Sea. The café became a showcase for modernism in Lithuanian architecture, as well as a renowned meeting place for artists and intellectuals, and a home to Lithuanian jazz.

One of the novelties implemented while realizing *Neringa* project was that it was created as an *ensemble* caring down to the smallest detail. The project included the whole team of professional artists and designers.

Lithuanian Baltic seaside-themed artistic and design variations are reflected in the forms, colours, ornaments and materials of the furniture, lighting, textile choices and ceramic objects. All of them designed, constructed and manufactured especially for this project. Regarding the stylistic evaluations the impact of Festival style could be mentioned, as well as echoes of interwar famous cafés in Kaunas, and the tradition of Nordic modernism. Despite the freedom declared by the young architects, from the very beginning the architectural plans for the café included a "broadcast room" – we now know that it was in fact a KBG listening booth under the stairway.

p is for public spaces: advertising for hotels and restaurants

627739

871

VILNIAUS MIESTO VALGYKLŲ TRESTAS
DINING-ROOM TRUST OF VILNIUS
ВИЛЬНЮССКИЙ ТРЕСТ СТОЛОВЫХ

NERINGA

ETIKB Leidinio Nr. 2291. V. Kapsuko sp. Užsak. Nr. 1305. LV 12999.

T. 6000   1969

[L]ithuanian   [N]ational

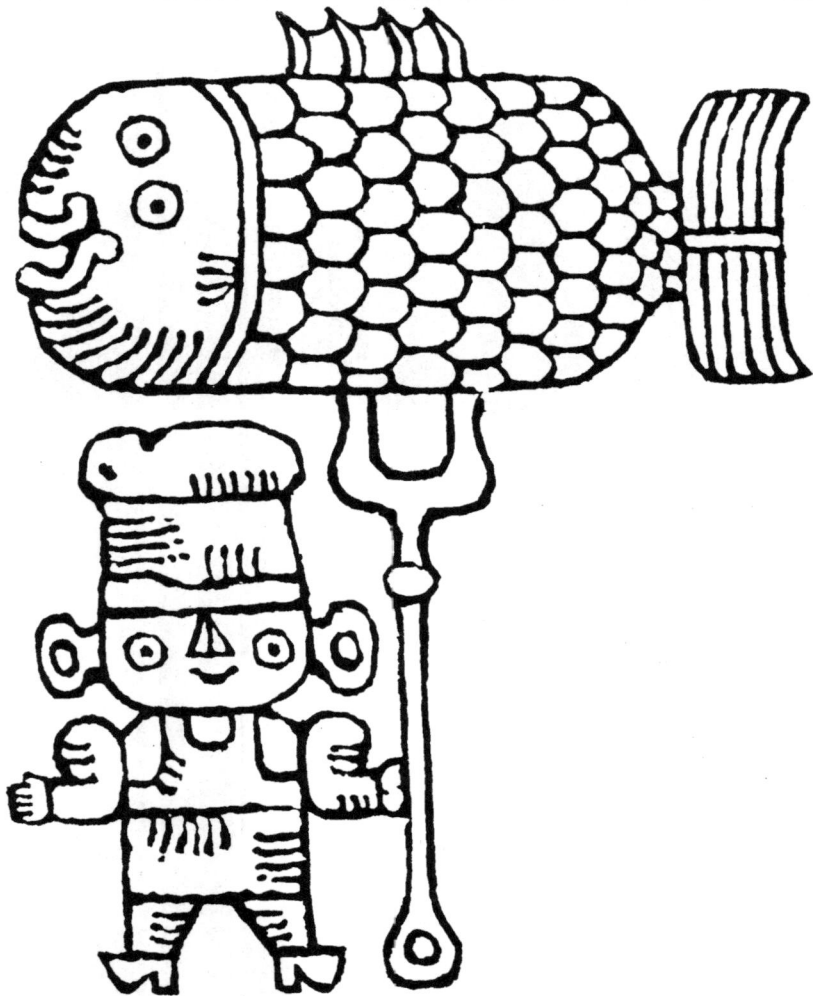

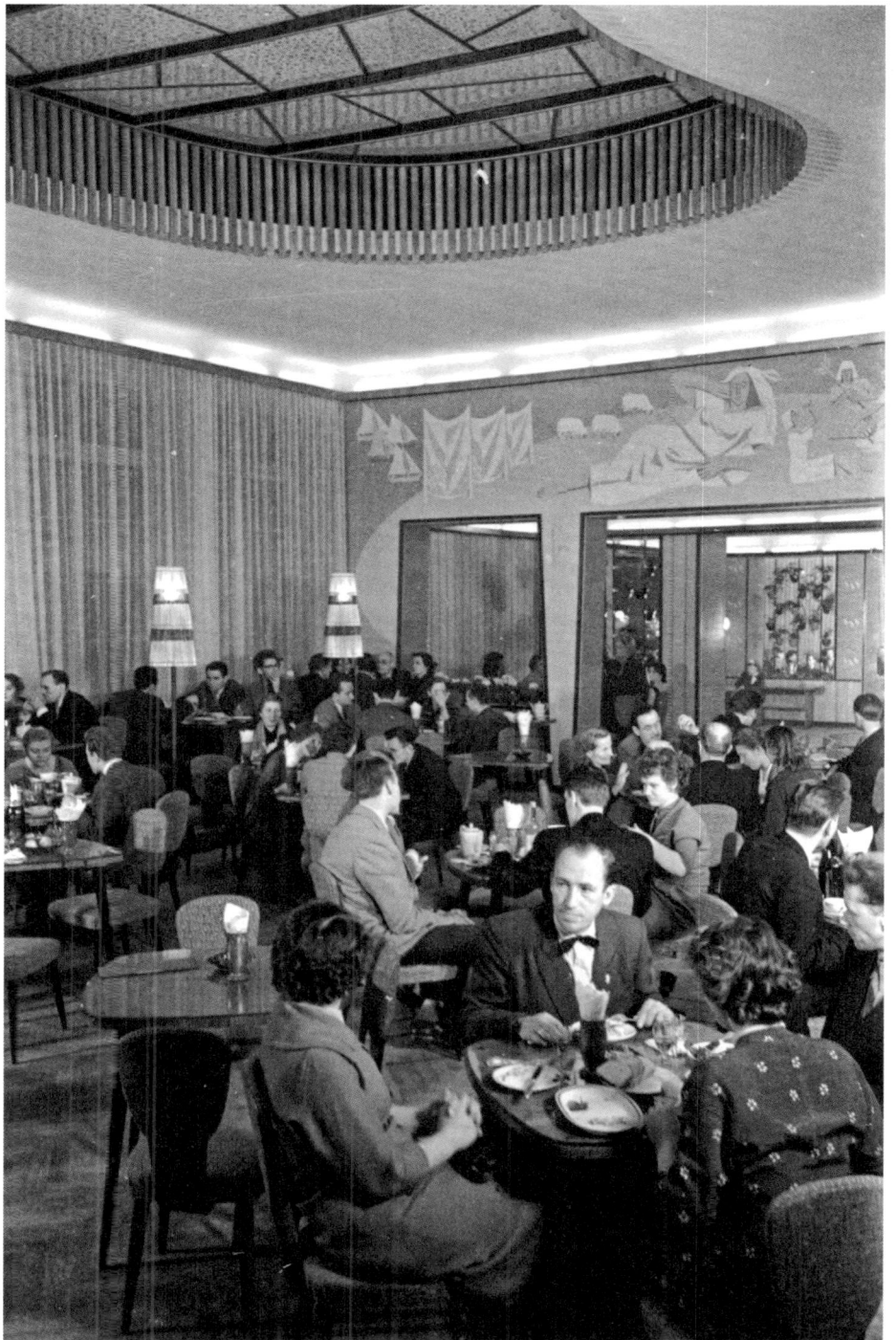

p is for public spaces: advertising for hotels and restaurants

Linkime maloniai praleisti laiką Vilniuje.

Желаем Вам приятного пребывания в Вильнюсе.

Wir wünschen Ihnen einen angenehmen Aufenthalt in Vilnius.

Welcome to Vilnius!

KAPSUKO G-VE

LENINO PR.

L. GIROS G-VE

„Vilniaus" viešbutis
Lenino pr., 20/1
Tel. 2-36-65
„Neringos" viešbutis
Lenino pr., 23
Tel. 2-05-16

Hotel "Vilnius"
Lenin Ave., 20/1
Tel. 2-36-65
Hotel "Neringa"
Lenin Ave., 23
Tel. 2-05-16

Гостиница «ВИЛЬНЮС»
просп. Ленина, 20 1
телефон 2-36-65
Гостиница «НЕРИНГА»
просп. Ленина, 23
телефон 2-05-16

Hotel „Vilnius"
Leninprospekt, 20/1
Tel. 2-36-65
Hotel „Neringa"
Leninprospekt, 23
Tel. 2-05-16

Užs. Nr. 4416

HOTEL   VIESBUTIS   HOTEL   VIESBUTIS

VILNIUS

„Vilniaus" viešbutis ir jo filialas „Nerin-ga" yra Vilniaus miesto centre.

●

Гостиница «ВИЛЬНЮС» с филиалом «Неринга» расположена в центре столицы Советской Литвы гор. Вильнюс.

●

Das Hotel „Vilnius" mit der Filiale „Neringa" liegt im Zentrum der Hauptstadt

●

The hotels "Vilnius" and "Neringa" are situated in the centre of Vilnius, the capital of Soviet Lithuania.

[E]xport   [L]ithuanian   [P]ropaganda

Hotel *Vilnius* also owned the *Dainava* restaurant, which was famous for its modern interior, designed by Eugenijus Cukermanas (who himself worked at the Tara bureau for some time). The first Soviet-era nightclub in Vilnius had been operating in *Dainava* since 1967. It was difficult to get in and among the customers quite often you could meet some foreign tourists

p is for public spaces: advertising for hotels and restaurants

[B]altic   [F]açade   [M]odernisation   [N]ational

Dainava is also remembered for the iconic decorative accent – the Sun (1963), designed by Teodoras Kazimieras Valaitis. This symbolic metal sculpture, where one could discern a man, a woman and the sun all in one, was often chosen by the architects, who curated and designed the travelling export exhibitions in the 1960s.

p is for public spaces: advertising for hotels and restaurants

Aptarnavimo biuras teikia bet kokią informaciją jus dominančiais klausimais. Čia jūs galite užsisakyti bilietus į teatrą, koncertą, taip pat į lėktuvus, traukinius, autobusus. Aptarnavimo biuras padės jums sutvarkyti visus buitinius reikalus. Čia keičiama užsienio valiuta.

Бюро обслуживания гостиницы даст Вам информацию по интересующим Вас вопросам. Здесь можно заказать билеты в театр, на концерт, а также на самолеты, поезда, автобусы. Через бюро производятся все бытовые услуги, обмен иностранной валюты.

NERINGA

[E]xport   [F]açade   [L]ithuanian   [M]odernization   [S]oviet

s is for soviet exhibition in London: export products and their promotional materials

In August 1968, the Soviet Industry and Trade exhibition opened in London's Earls Court Exhibition Centre. It was the most important exhibition the Soviet Union held abroad in 1968. Next to the main space-themed section with the undertones of the Cold War rivalry, special attention was devoted to the presentation of the occupied 'soviet Baltic republics'. The Lithuanian pavilion was designed by architect Tadas Baginskas (b. 1936), who developed a pavilion that combined Lithuanian ethnic symbolism with minimalist pro-Western design solutions. Selected and approved samples of the best products of Lithuanian enterprises were sent to London. The lists of names of the products sent to the exhibition reveal that those were mostly exclusive, often one-off or export-only goods and luxury models.

A special promotional publication was printed for each group of products. This series of the 1968 London promotional materials is unique in the history of Lithuanian graphic design and reflects the style of export-oriented promotional publications of the time. The publications were designed by different artists of the Tara bureau: their format, style, conceptual and plastic solutions depended on the quality of the material received from the factories and different ministries, as well as the submitted photographs and texts, on which editors and translators worked intensely. The uniform design of this series is revealed by the *Rūta* logo designed by Vaidilutė Gruševskaitė especially for this exhibition. This memorable, laconic, even somewhat Op-Art-like sign became a symbol of Lithuania's presentation in London. The key motif of this modern plastic form is the traditional Lithuanian garden plant – the rūta (Latin *ruta graveolens*), mentioned in Lithuanian folk songs, tales and legends, and used as an important element in customs and rituals.

[E]xport   [F]açade   [F]ear   [L]ithuanian   [S]oviet   [W]estern

s is for soviet exhibition in London: export products and their promotional materials

LIETUVIŠKI SUVENYRAI

LITHUANIAN SOUVENIRS

One of the most provocative catalogues was the one dedicated to the *Lithuanian Souvenirs,* in which textile patterns, amber necklaces, images of the Baltic sea, the Nida dunes and photographs of the first nude portraits by Rimantas Dichavičius were inserted in addition to the wooden sculptures. This seemingly random, yet bold gesture shows that the Lithuanian pavilion in London was a political commission by Moscow, made in order to "shape the myth of the Soviet West and the export image of the USSR abroad". However, to use a quote by Czesław Miłosz, its creators were subjected to a *Hetman*-like strategy that aimed at showcasing non-existent freedoms, pseudo-modernity and phoney progress in the occupied Baltic countries.

s is for soviet exhibition in London: export products and their promotional materials

16

28

s is for soviet exhibition in London: export products and their promotional materials

He who but once has gazed on a
Lithuanian river
seemingly sunk in reverie
or heard the cool forest rustling
on its high banks,

has glimpsed Lithuania's lakes and fells
and watched the sun set
over the Baltic will never forget
her captivating beauty.
Coming to know more intimately
the people of Lithuania
and their cultural life,
enriched today by features born
of a socialist society,
the visitor will be filled
with warmth towards this small
country and her people.

TARYBŲ LIETUVOS ŽUVIES PRAMONĖ

[E]xperimentation   [E]xport   [J]okes   [K]itsch

s is for soviet exhibition in London: export products and their promotional materials

RIEBI SALTO RŪKYMO ATLANTO SILKĖ turi didelę paklausą vartotojų tarpe. Ji švelnaus skonio, sultinga. Rūkymui imamos tik rinktinės sūdytos silkės. Rūkymas suteikia šiam gaminiui aukštą gastronominę vertę.

ЖИРНАЯ АТЛАНТИЧЕСКАЯ СЕЛЬДЬ холодного копчения пользуется большим спросом у покупателей. Она отличается нежным вкусом, сочной консистенцией. Для ее приготовления используется отборная соленая сельдь, а последующая обработка копчением придает этому продукту высокую гастрономическую ценность.

SMOKE-DRY FAT ATLANTIC HERRING is one of the most popular representatives of smoked fish, distinguished for its delicate flavour and rich consistency. For its preparation choice salted herring is used, while the subsequent smoking of this fish makes it highly valuable as a food product.

UOTAS. Salto rūkymo uotas turi labai malonų rūkymo arcmatą ir baltą sultingą mėsą.

ПАЛТУС. По вкусовым качествам и внешнему виду палтус холодного копчения отличается приятным запахом копчености, белым сочным мясом.

TURBOT. As to its palatability and appearance the smoke-dry turbot is distinguished for its peculiar flavour of smokiness and white rich meat.

ŠALDYTA ŽUVIS
МОРОЖЕНАЯ РЫБА
FROZEN FISH

РЫБНОЕ ФИЛЕ МОРОЖЕНОЕ

VIDAUS VANDENŲ ŽUVININKYSTĖ

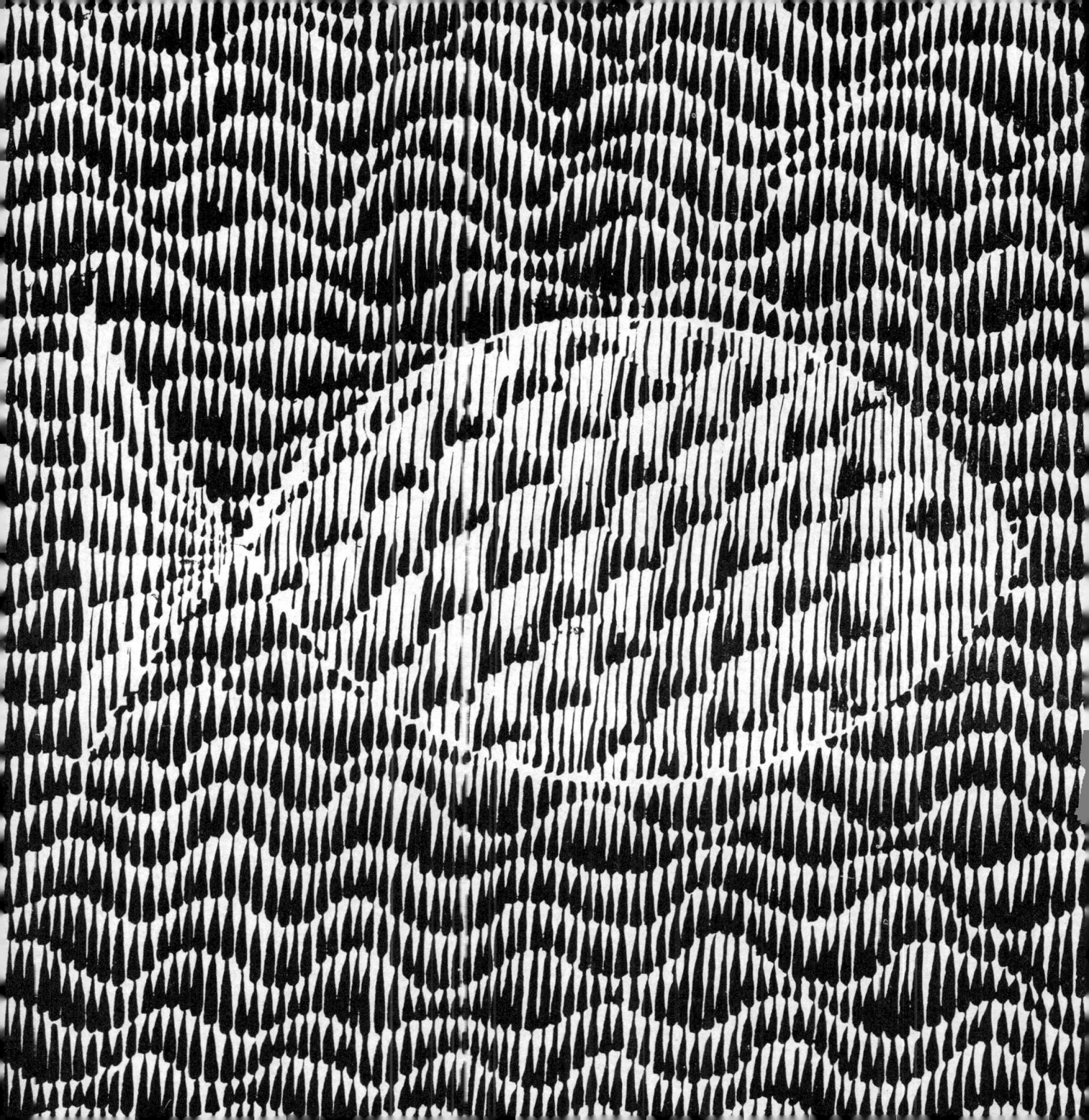

TARYBŲ LIETUVOS LENGVOJI PRAMONĖ
SOVIET LITHUANIAN LIGHT INDUSTRY

s is for soviet exhibition in London: export products and their promotional materials

LIETUVIŠKI AUDINIAI
IR TRIKOTAŽAS

LITHUANIAN WOVEN AND
KNITTED FABRICS

[E]xport   [F]açade   [K]itsch   [S]oviet   [Y]outh   [W]estern

s is for soviet exhibition in London: export products and their promotional materials

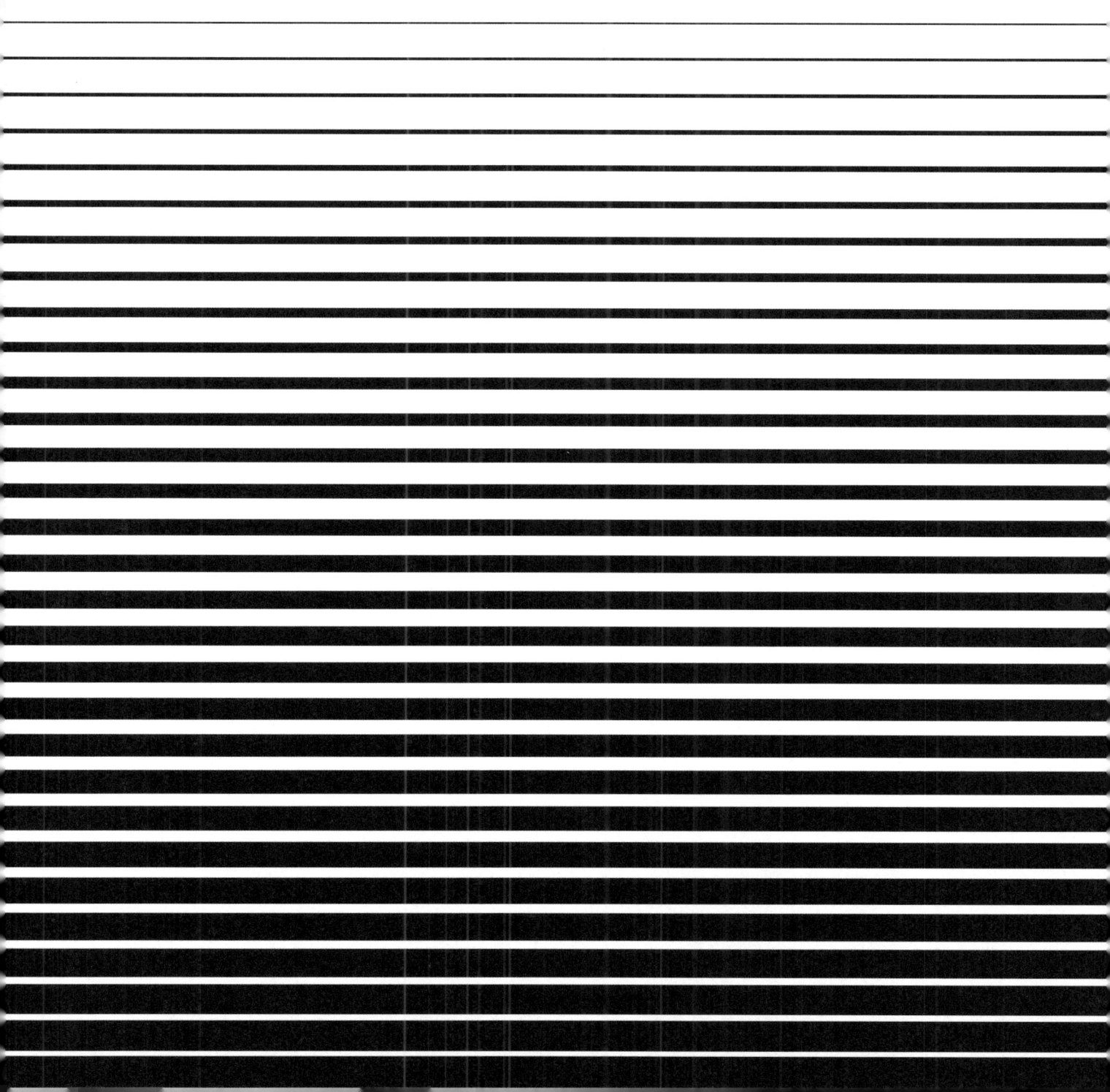

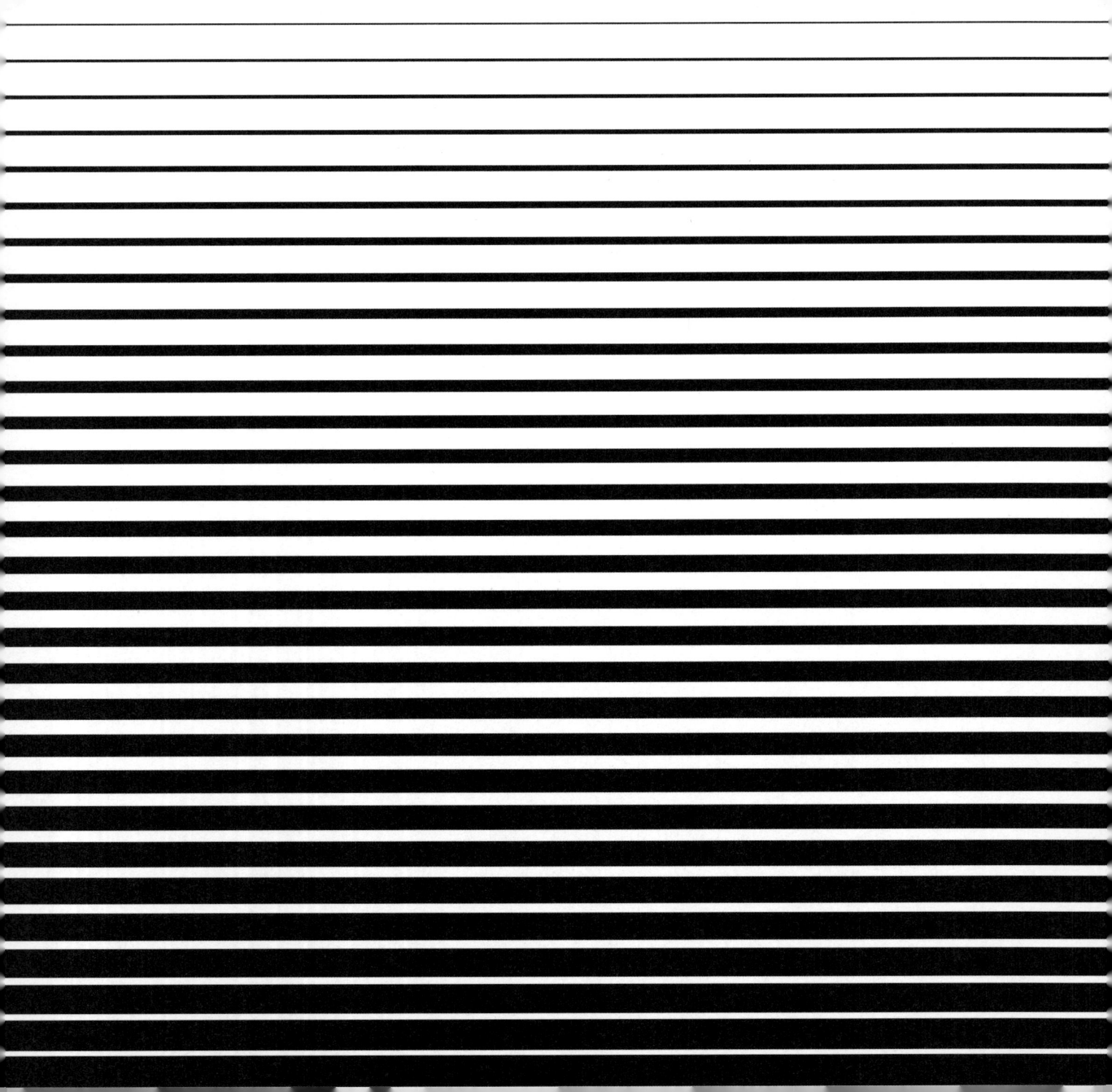

t is for technical aesthetics:
the staged images
and propagandistic catalogues

Technical aesthetics is a combination of words used during the soviet years to identify a wide range of design-related activities. Since 1966 the Vilnius branch of VNIITE, the internationally recognized acronym for the All-Union Scientific Research Institute for Technical Aesthetics, operated in Vilnius. The Lithuanian branch was advanced in many areas: industrial environment, city environment, urban furniture, precision mechanical products, and electronics. The technical aesthetic also refers to the soviet factories, where many people worked. Designers also worked there, often in collaboration with engineers and technologists. Some of them were even assigned to secret factories where equipment for the Soviet military industry was made.

In the course of 10 years of operation, the Tara bureau produced almost 1890 publications with a circulation of 1500 to 4000, and during preparations for foreign exhibitions it could go up to 10,000 copies. The artists of the Tara bureau put a lot of ingenuity and playfulness into the design, styling and layout of these factory catalogues. Collaboration with the photographers was very important here, as all catalogues were richly illustrated with both colour and black-and-white photographs. In these catalogues we see the reputed "staged images", which illustrated propagandistic reportages along with an entire system of ideological "brainwashing", the staging of unattainable fulfilment and a false promise "that we too have such things", to quote the famous phrase from the "Kitchen debates". Now we know that in reality people lacked the simplest household items, and in most cases, had to live among ugly things, standing in queues sometimes even waiting years to buy more aesthetically designed objects, the so-called *deficit* goods. Ironically, the designers and engineers who created those things couldn't see or experience them.

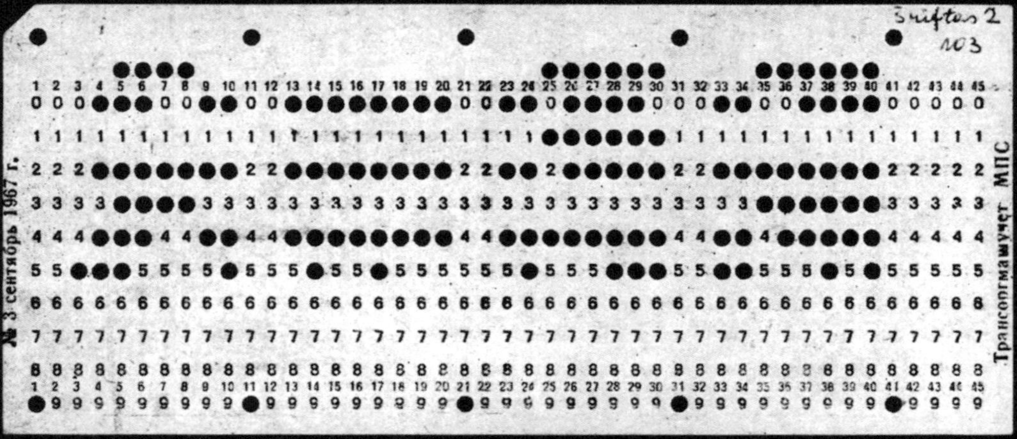
Šriftas 2
103
№ 3 сентябрь 1967 г.
Трансоргмашучет МПС

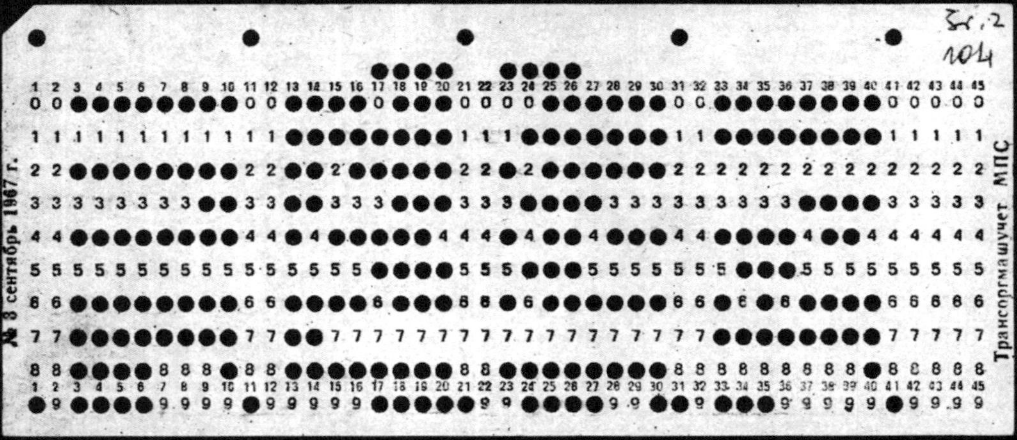
Šr. 2
104
№ 3 сентябрь 1967 г.
Трансоргмашучет МПС

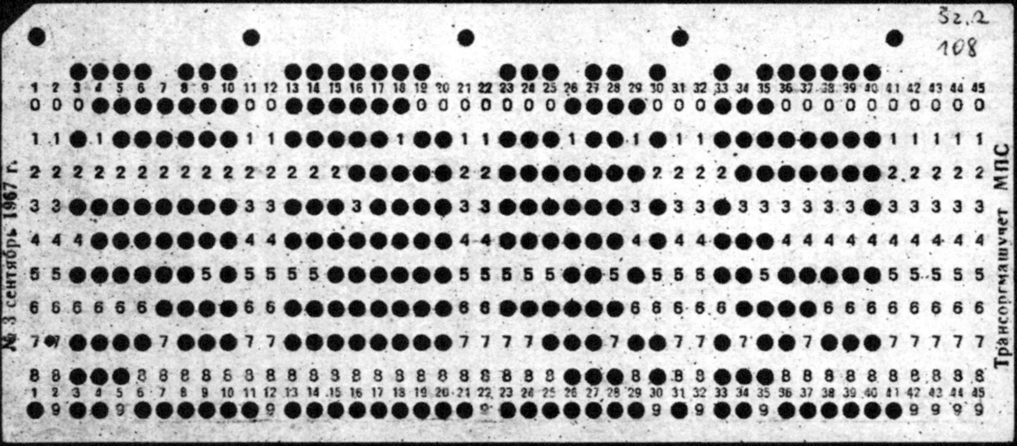
Šr. 2
108
№ 3 сентябрь 1967 г.
Трансоргмашучет МПС

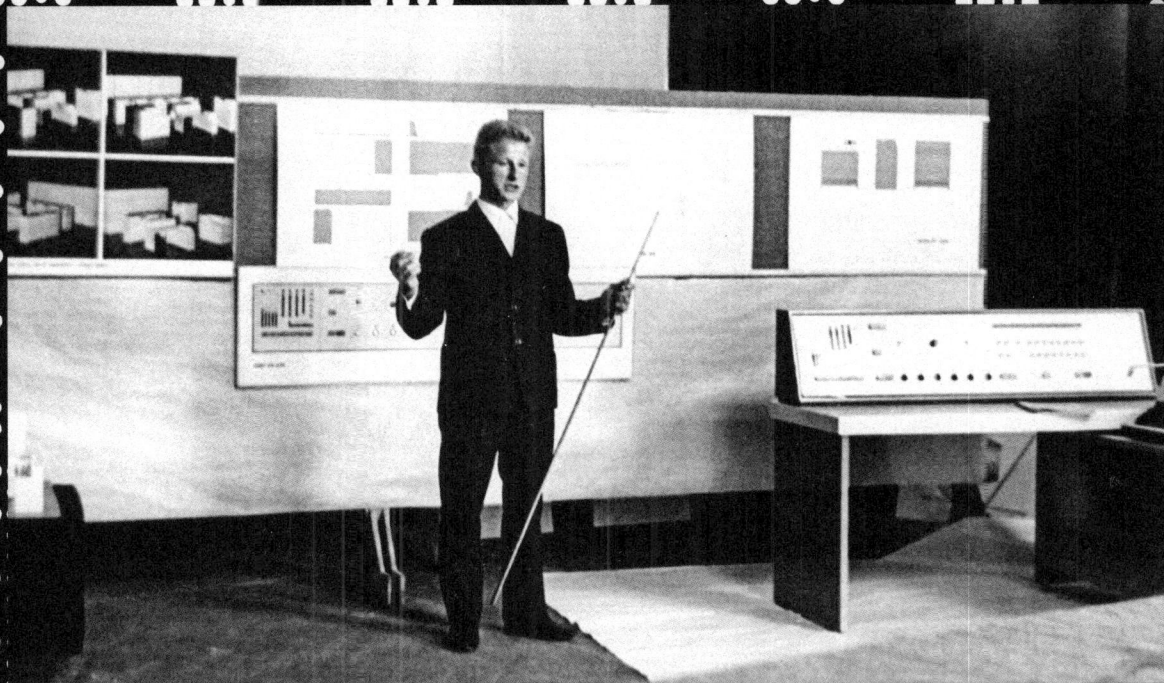

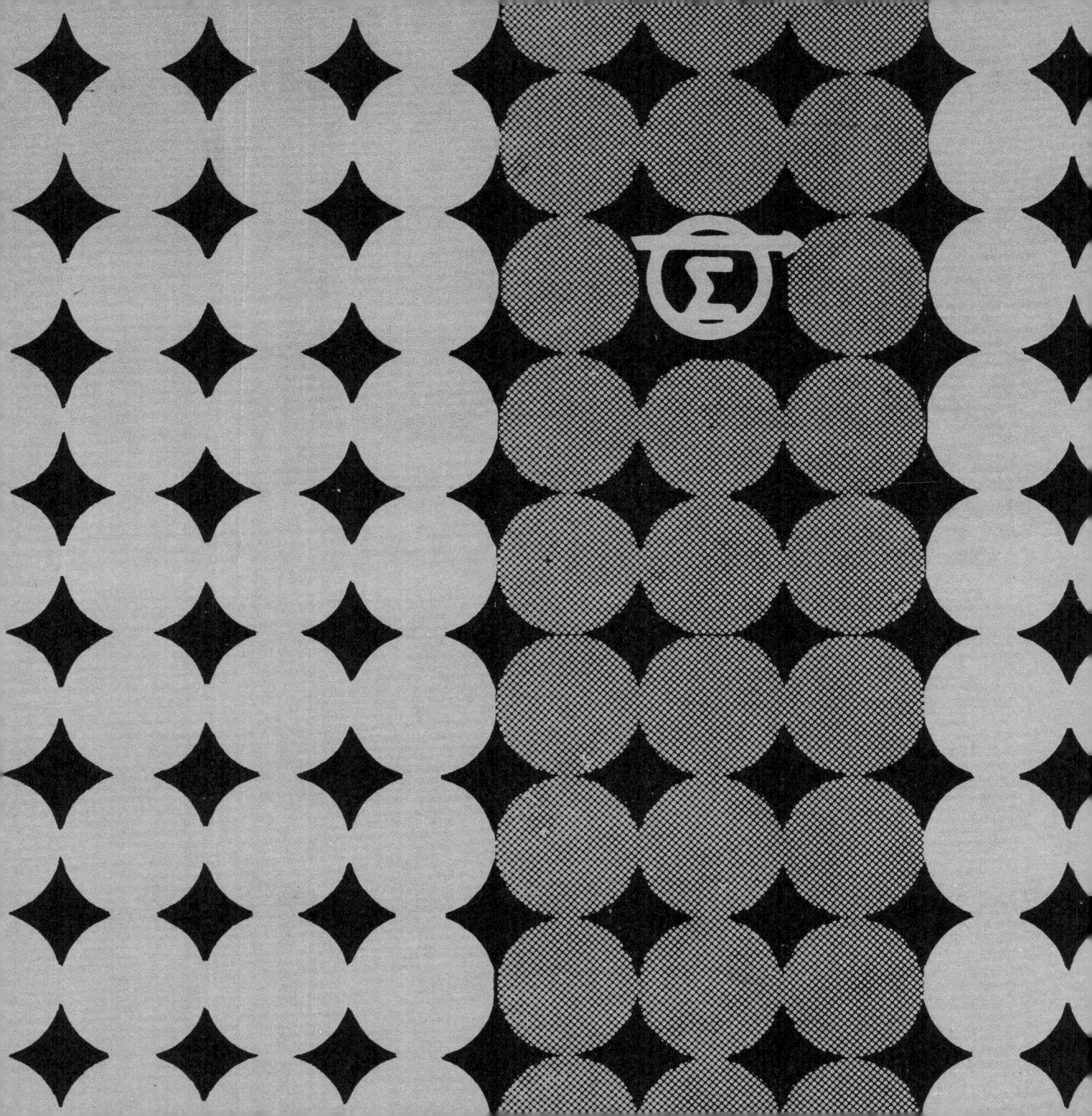

Vilniaus
skaičiavimo mašinų gamykla

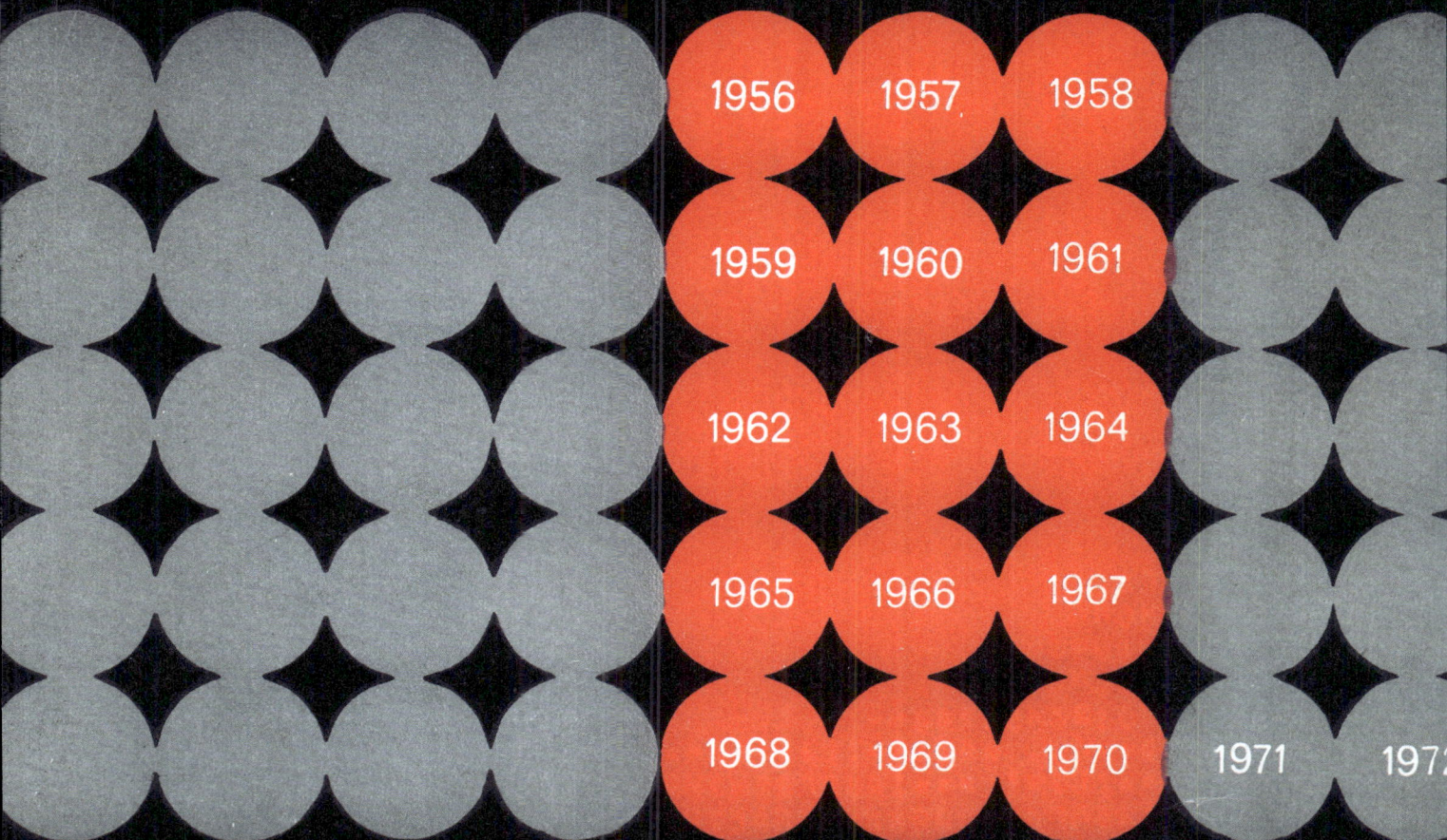

1956	1957	1958
1959	1960	1961
1962	1963	1964
1965	1966	1967
1968	1969	1970	1971	1972

RŪTA 110

P 50I

The *Rūta* was also the name of the first Lithuanian computer. The second-generation computing machine, registered in 1962, had a small memory, but could process large amounts of data kept on punched cards. It was designed at the Special Constructing Bureau, which operated next to Sigma, the computing machine factory in Vilnius. The idea to construct a unique computing machine was developed by a team of young mathematicians, engineers and constructors, who had been given the task of modernising a copy of the American IBM computing machine. Due to the defects of the Russian version, a decision was made to create a brand-new ferri-transistor, elements-based machine.

The first *Rūta* was quite a compact machine; it was the basis for the bigger computing machine *Rūta 110*, which was the diploma project of Algirdas Šarka (b. 1937), one of the first three design graduates from the Department of Industrial Design in 1965. *Rūta 110* consisted of multiple devices which needed much space to fit into. In order to produce one single system, 410 kilometres of wires and 16,000 transistors and diodes had to be used. Its creators now admit that it had not been a successful project; only 37 of them were produced.

t is for technical aesthetics: the staged images and propagandistic catalogues

Elektros technikai

Radijo technikai

Metalistai

PANEVĖŽIO
TIKSLIOSIOS MECHANIKOS GAMYKLA
ПАНЕВЕЖСКИЙ ЗАВОД ТОЧНОЙ МЕХАНИКИ

SKAIČIAVIMO TECHNIKOS GAMYBINIS-TECHNINIS SUSIVIENIJIMAS „SIGMA"

ПРОИЗВОДСТВЕННО-ТЕХНИЧЕСКОЕ ОБЪЕДИНЕНИЕ ВЫЧИСЛИТЕЛЬНОЙ ТЕХНИКИ „СИГМА"

PANEVĖŽIO TIKSLIOSIOS MECHANIKOS GAMYKLA

ПАНЕВЕЖСКИЙ ЗАВОД ТОЧНОЙ МЕХАНИКИ

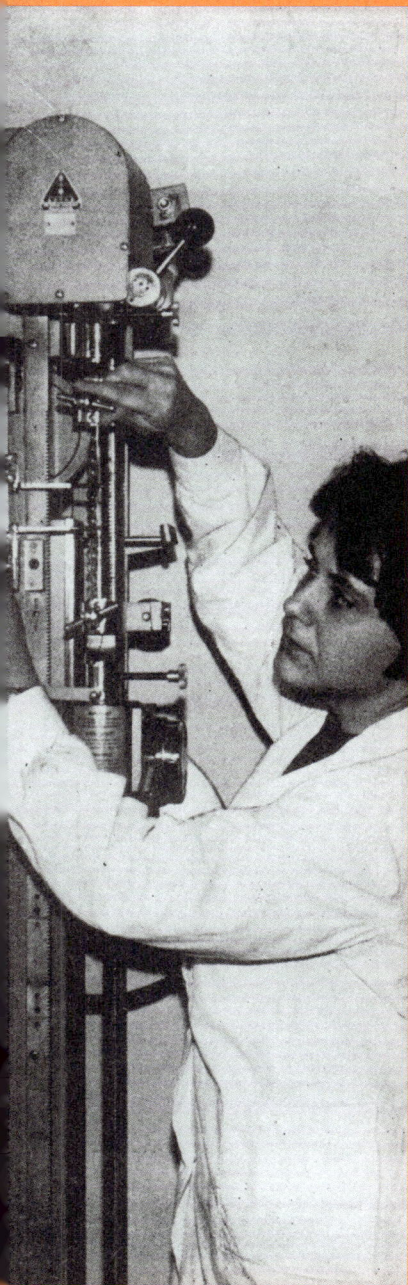

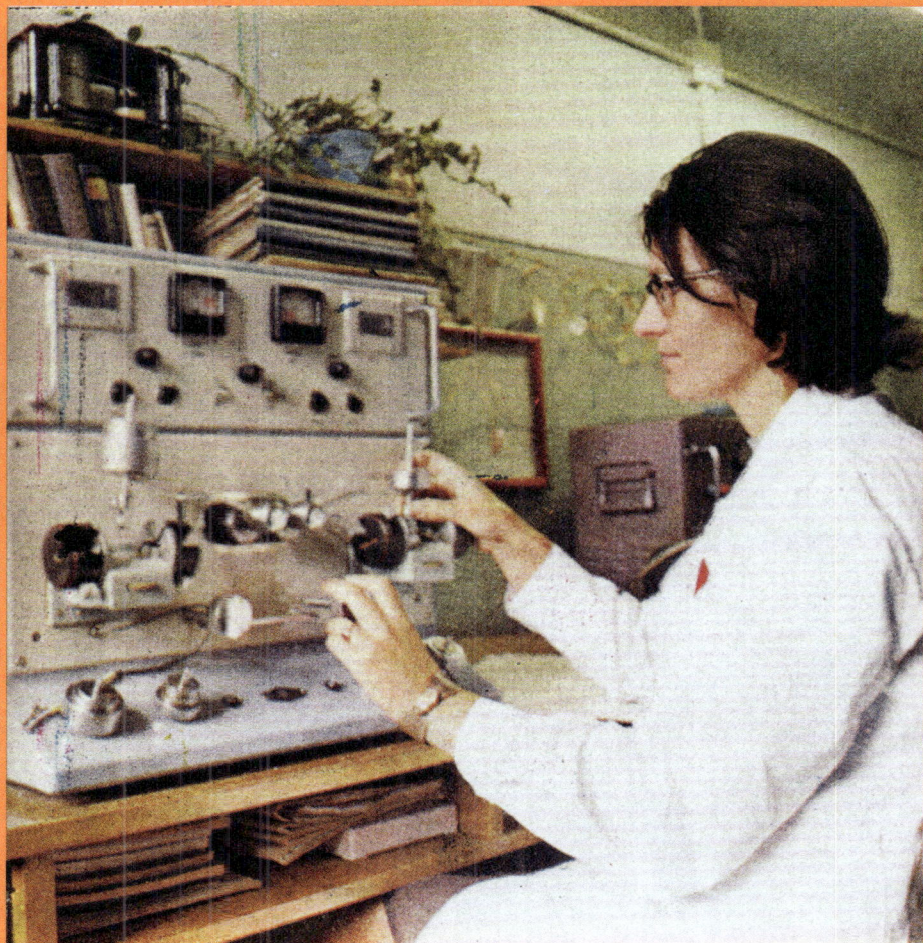

t is for technical aesthetics: the staged images and propagandistic catalogues

t is for technical aesthetics: the staged images and propagandistic catalogues

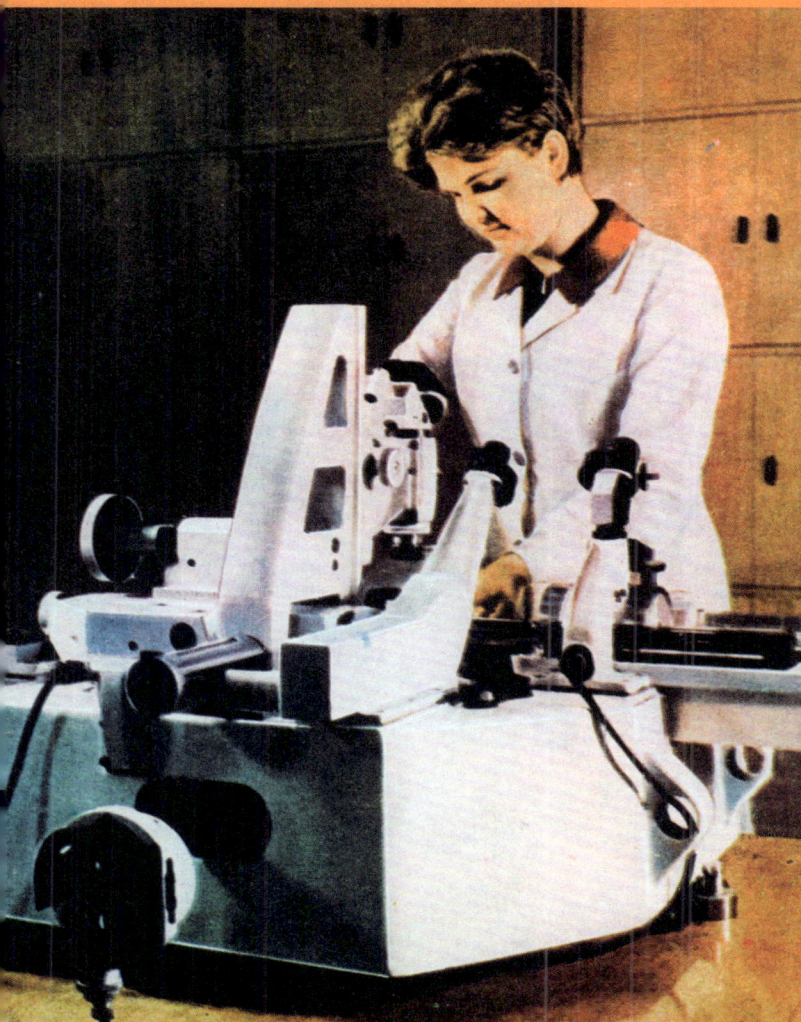

[F]açade   [M]achinery   [P]ropaganda   [S]oviet   [Y]outh

233   t is for technical aesthetics: the staged images and propagandistic catalogues

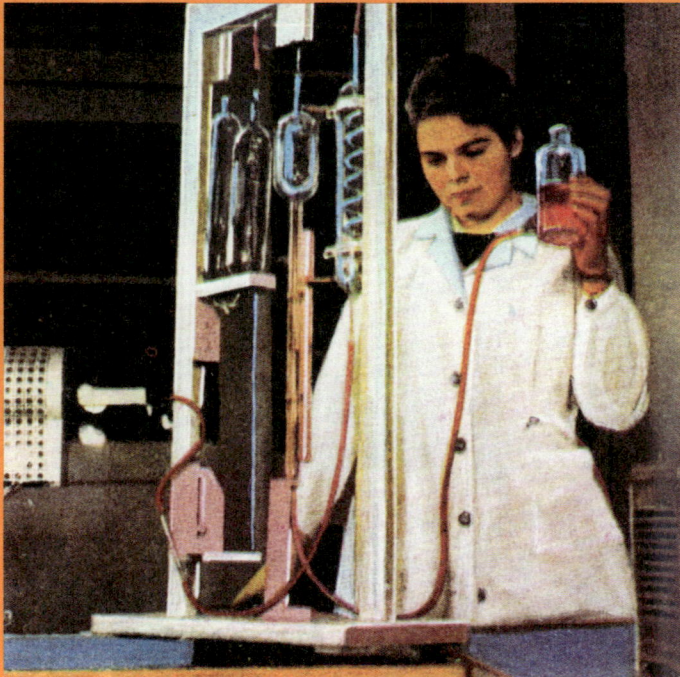
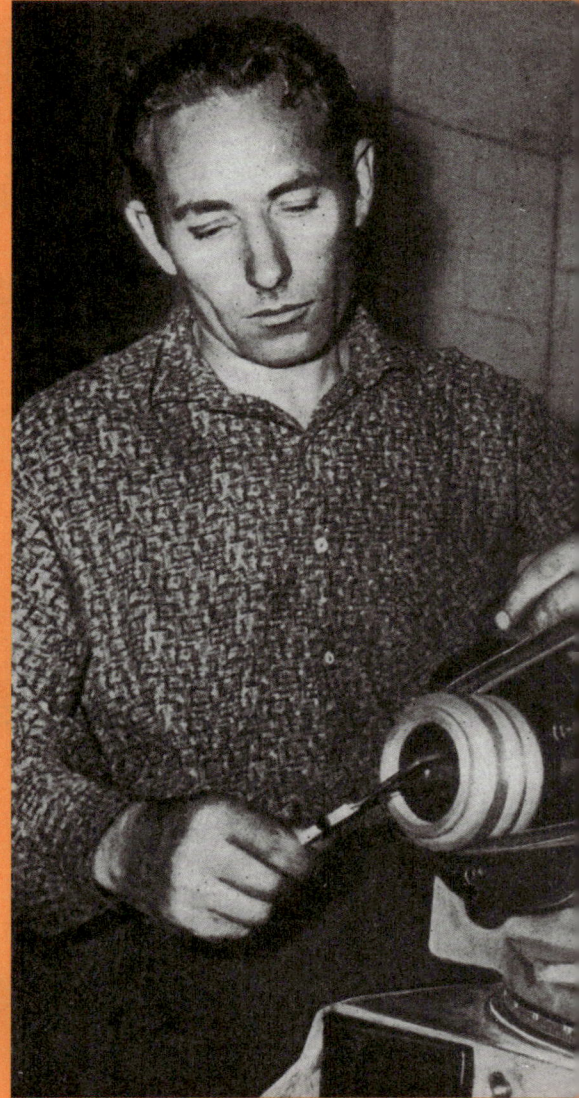

t is for technical aesthetics: the staged images and propagandistic catalogues

[M]achinery   [P]ropaganda   [S]oviet   [Y]outh

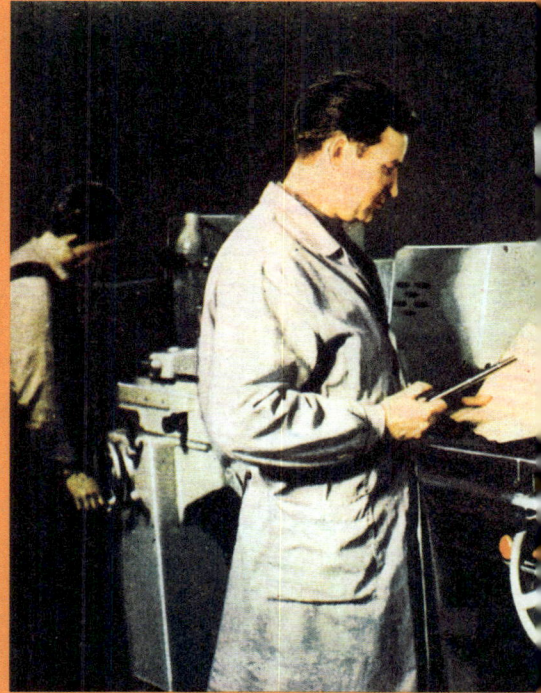

t is for technical aesthetics: the staged images and propagandistic catalogues

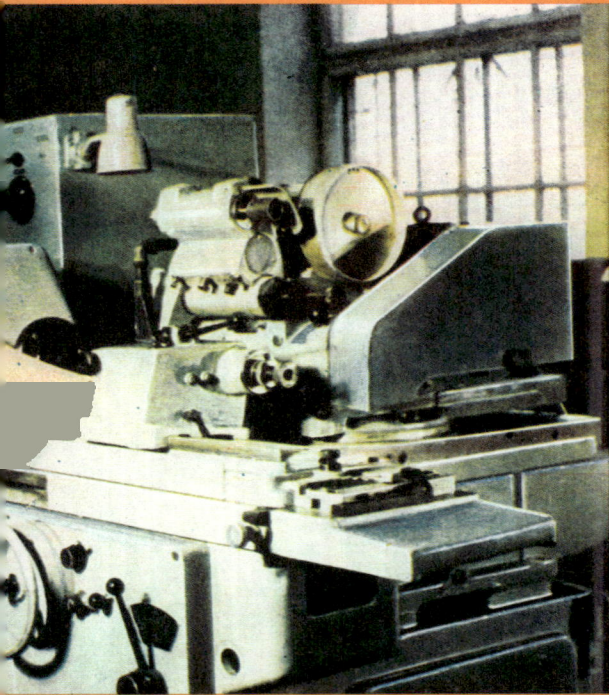

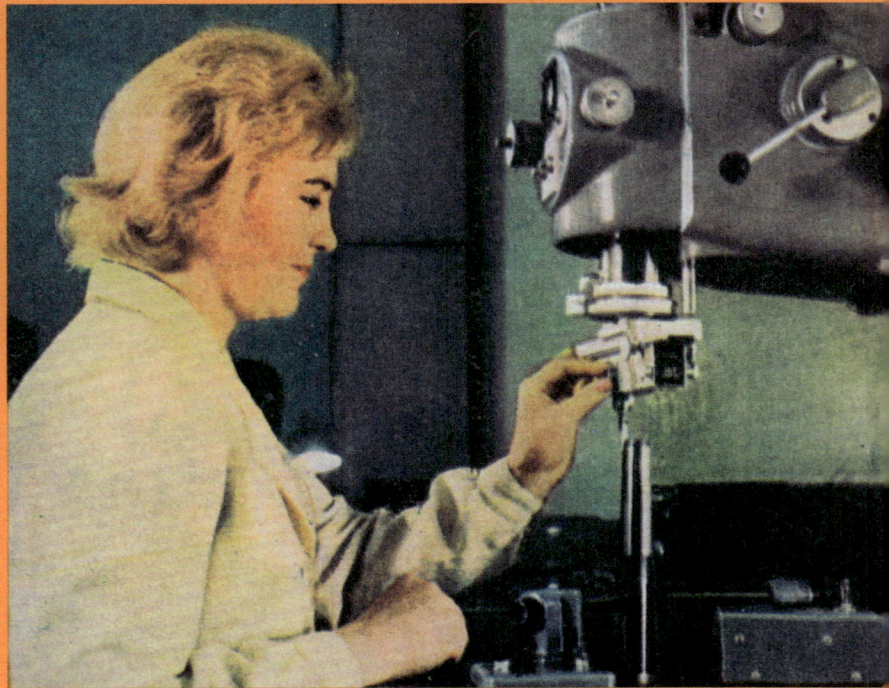

t is for technical aesthetics: the staged images and propagandistic catalogues

t is for technical aesthetics: the staged images and propagandistic catalogues

[I]deology   [M]achinery   [S]oviet   [Y]outh

    t is for technical aesthetics: the staged images and propagandistic catalogues

TAURAGĖS KERAMIKOS GAMYKLA

t is for technical aesthetics: the staged images and propagandistic catalogues

elektrinis dulkių siurblys

Министерство
электротехнической промышленности СССР

ГАТURNAS

VILNIAUS
ELEKTRINIO
SUVIRINIMO
ĮRENGIMŲ
GAMYKLA

VESIG

ВИЛЬНЮССКИЙ
ЗАВОД
ЭЛЕКТРОСВАРОЧНОГО
ОБОРУДОВАНИЯ

ĮTAMPA
НАПРЯЖЕНИЕ

IŠLEIDIMO DATA
ДАТА ВЫПУСКА

Nr.
№

Kaina 40 rub.
Цена 40 руб.

ГОСТ 10230-62

электропылесос

[C]osmic   [D]esign   [J]okes   [M]odernisation   [O]p-Art   [P]lay

The *Saturnes* vacuum cleaners had been produced by the Vilnius Electric Welding Equipment Factory since 1962. The ball-shaped, bright-coloured, portable electric vacuum cleaner was an accurate reflection of the space-age aesthetics of the era. Credit for the design should go to Vytautas Didžiulis, although the development process involved several others. According to the engineers, they were unaware of the American-made *Hoover Constellation* at the time. However, they do admit to industrial espionage.

t is for technical aesthetics: the staged images and propagandistic catalogues

[F]açade   [O]p-Art   [R]eklama

t is for technical aesthetics: the staged images and propagandistic catalogues

mūsų šviestuvai

ūsų buičiai.Madingi,patogūs,gražūs. Panevėžio eksperimentinė elektrotechnikos gamykla

t is for technical aesthetics: the staged images and propagandistic catalogues

ПОДВЕС ТИПА 167

Подвес (ГОСТ 8607-63) предназначен для освещения жилых и общественных помещений.

Колпак и потолочная розетка деревянные.

Абажур из молочно-белого стекла, декорированный, подвешен на проводе марки ШППВ 2×0,75

ЛЮСТРА ТИПА 171

Люстра (ГОСТ 8607-63) предназначена для освещения жилых помещений.

Потолочная розетка, крышка и стеклодержатели пластмассовые черного цвета.

Видимые металлические детали никелированные.

Абажуры пластмассовые.

ПОДВЕС ТИПА 168

Подвес (ГОСТ 8607-63) предназначен для освещения жилых помещений.

Колпаки и потолочная розетка деревянные.

Абажуры из молочно-белого стекла, декорированные, подвешены на проводе марки ШППВ 2×0,75

ТЕХНИЧЕСКИЕ ДАННЫЕ

Высота, мм	— 680±10
Номинальное напряжение, в	— 220
Число ламп накаливания, шт.	— 1
Максимальная мощность лампы, вт	— 60

Лампы накаливания в комплект поставки не входят.

ТЕХНИЧЕСКАЯ ХАРАКТЕРИСТИКА

Высота люстры, мм	— 570±10
Диаметр абажура, мм	— 120
Номинальное напряжение, в	— 220
Число ламп накаливания, шт.	— 3
Максимальная мощность лампы, вт	— 60

Лампы накаливания в комплект поставки не входят.

ТЕХНИЧЕСКИЕ ДАННЫЕ

Высота, мм	— 620±10
Номинальное напряжение, в	— 220
Число ламп накаливания, шт.	— 2
Максимальная мощность лампы, вт	— 60

Лампы накаливания в комплект поставки не входят.

[A]bstract advertising   [H]andmade   [O]p-Art   [R]eklama   [S]low   [S]oviet

t is for technical aesthetics: the staged images and propagandistic catalogues

·ekranas·  PGE

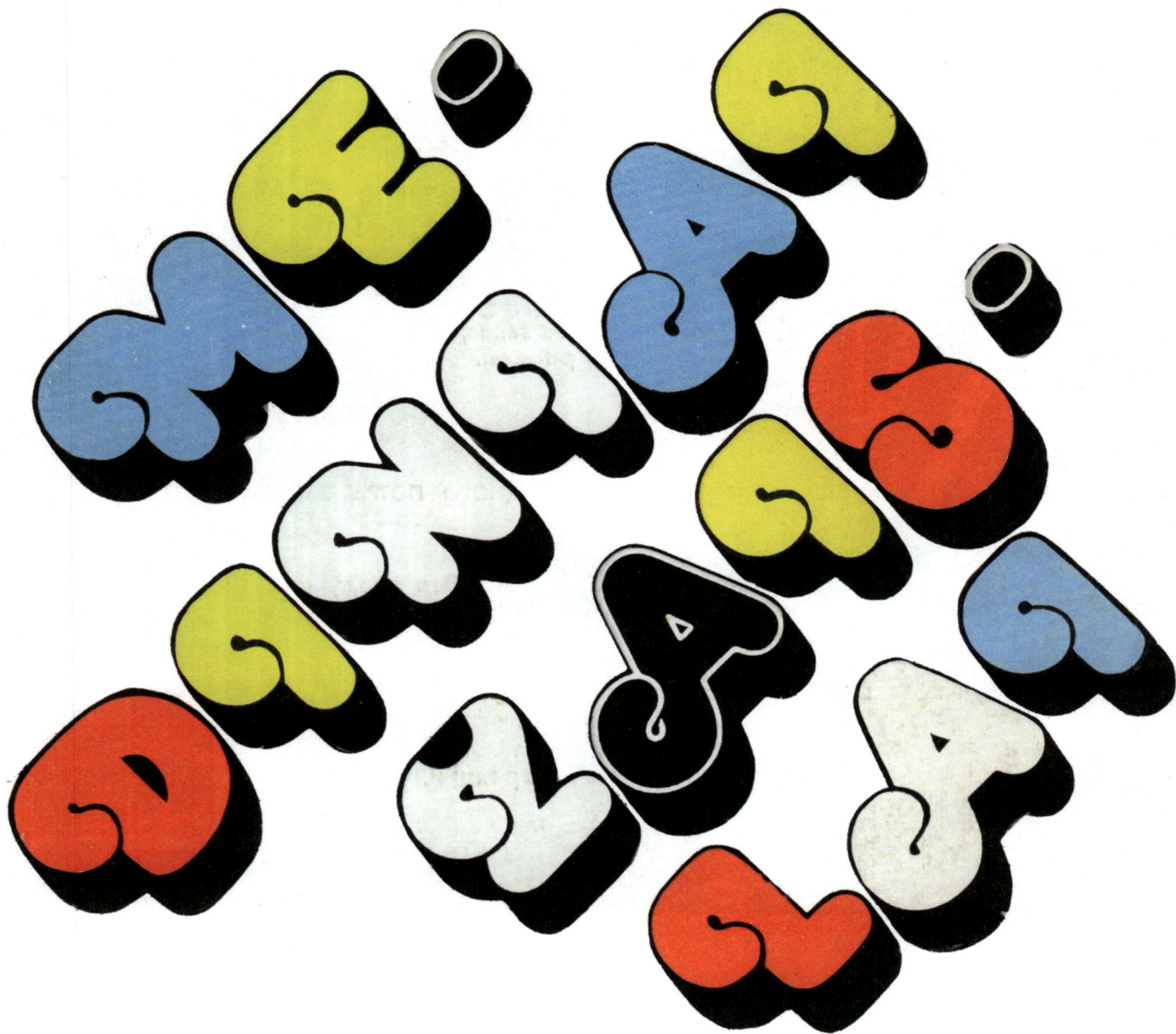

[E]xperimentation   [P]lay   [T]ypography

t is for technical aesthetics: the staged images and propagandistic catalogues

ŽAISLŲ KATALOGAS

LIETUVOS TSR VIETINĖS PRAMONĖS MINISTERI
МИНИСТЕРСТВО МЕСТНОЙ ПРОМЫШЛЕННОСТИ ЛИТ. С

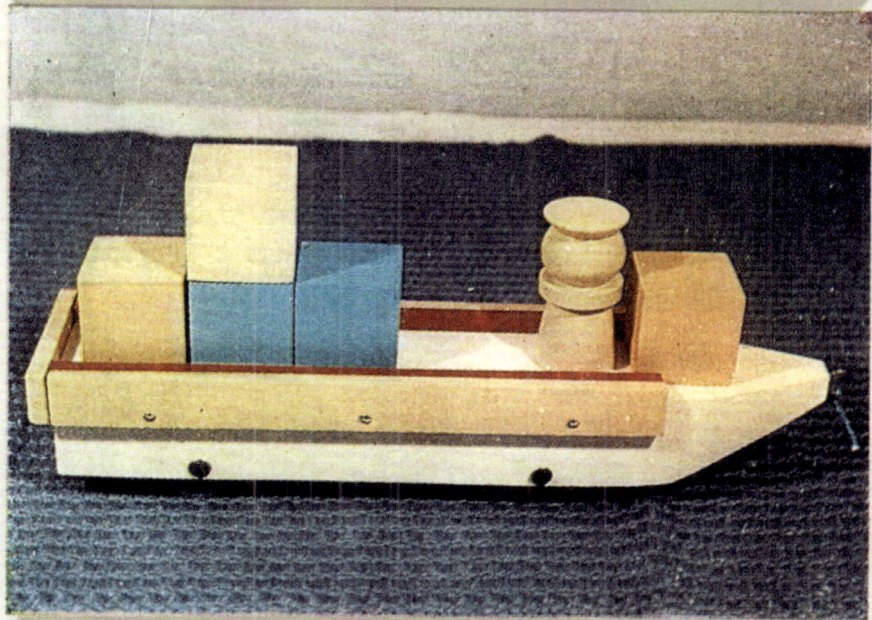

z is for zooming in:
researching and rediscovering
Tara's archives and practices

Conversation between Karolina Jakaitė and Deimantė Jasiulevičiūtė

How did it all begin? How did we both (from different starting points) come across the same idea of a book about the history of Lithuanian graphic design?

1
Karolina Jakaitė, *Lithuanian graphic design in the 1950s–1970s: between National and International* (supervised by Assoc. Prof. Dr. Lolita Jablonskienė), [manuscript], Vilnius Academy of Arts, 2012.

DJ After graduating in graphic design from the Gerrit Rietveld Academie in Amsterdam, I became interested in exploring the history of Lithuanian graphic design. Having left Lithuania at a young age, I saw this as an opportunity to reconnect with my cultural roots. At that time, finding information online about these topics was quite challenging. However, through extensive research, I discovered your doctoral thesis[1] on the Tara bureau. After corresponding, we met for the first time in Vilnius in November 2019. This meeting marked the beginning of a nearly five-year journey of research, exploration, and collaboration. The study and the resulting book focus on themes of identity, the preservation of design history, and its relevance to contemporary contexts.

KJ The beginning of my research on the Tara bureau was related to the preparation of my dissertation (2012–2016) and the research of the 1960s–1980s which I started during my PhD studies at the Vilnius Academy of Arts. Initially, I faced a challenging situation: the archives of Soviet-era bureaus had been largely destroyed, creating a sense that "nothing had survived" and that there was hardly any material to be found. Library inquiries often yielded negative responses, with slips of paper marked *NURAŠYTA* ("written off").
In 2008, a pivotal moment occurred when I first met Kęstutis Gvalda, a long-time artist-constructor of the Tara bureau and one of the key figures in this book. Right until his passing in 2011 we communicated very intensely. Gvalda had preserved a significant amount of

authentic material from the bureau's archives. His apartment in Vilnius was filled to the brim with artifacts, specialized books, catalogues, poster prints, and original drafts, all stored in a variety of boxes and envelopes. I had the opportunity to visit this treasure trove several times. Gvalda had an unyielding passion for storytelling, sharing his knowledge, and preserving the bureau's legacy for future generations. His creative motto, "create the way the world did," reflected his vision. After his death, accessing some of these artifacts became more difficult, and navigating the material he left behind proved challenging. Nevertheless, I remain profoundly grateful for the chance to have met him, learned from him, and preserved part of his archive.

Research processes and dialogues, what were the stages and methods of our research?

DJ   I was interested in the material from the beginning, but I didn't anticipate how intricate and involved the process would become. This was not a straightforward investigation of a classified archive; it required a methodical approach, uncovering information piece by piece by studying each newly discovered logo, catalogue, or brochure, and analyzing their endpapers.

Advertising brochures and leaflets from the Tara bureau archive

Now, after years of research, I appreciate the necessity of this extensive process, including the numerous trips to Lithuania, meetings, photoshoots, scans, and revisions. It was a thorough journey of

z is for zooming in: researching and rediscovering Tara's archives and practices

discovery, delving into the complex history and memory of the Soviet era, uncovering various layers, and confronting both difficult and often uncomfortable aspects.

I was particularly captivated by the experiences of the artists themselves. For them, the bureau was not just a workplace but a significant part of their lives. Despite the staged nature of some photographs and simulations, their commitment to each project was evident. I was especially moved by the video recording of the joint interview with Vladas Lisaitis, his personal recollections, the story of *Tariukas*, and their vision of it traveling around the world and through space. I see the story of *Tariukas* as a metaphorical vehicle for this book – one that journeys, explores, and reveals untold stories.

Sketch by Vladas Lisaitis, "Tariukas on the Moon, Tariukas traveling around the world", drawn by Lisaitis during his interview, 2021

KJ   From my very first meeting with Gvalda, I realized how crucial it was to connect with and interview living witnesses. Gvalda introduced me to around 20 other Tara artists and witnesses to the bureau's processes. During the quarantine, we managed to bring back from Klaipėda the archive of Tara's logos preserved by Vincentas Sakas. This search for witnesses and surviving artifacts has been an ongoing journey, and in fact, it continues to this day. From the start, I understood

z is for zooming in: researching and rediscovering Tara's archives and practices

the existential importance of these personal collections. Without timely discovery and documentation, the unique materials they held would be irretrievably lost – something I've already experienced on several occasions when I arrived too late.

It wasn't just about uncovering a new, never-before-seen artifact or finally finding something that had long been sought after but never found. It was equally important to hear and preserve their authentic stories, to glimpse the behind-the-scenes lives of designers from that era, and to learn as much as possible about the various circumstances that shaped their work. These insights allowed for new interpretations and unexpected connections with the broader history of design and the present day.

I found great meaning in naming those unknown graphic designers and recording their names into the fragmented history of Lithuanian design. Many of these artists were completely unknown in the art and design fields of their time, while others had been undeservedly forgotten, their often tragic biographies difficult to trace. Yet, these individuals were bright, modest, unpretentious people who radiated wisdom and optimism. This has been an empathic process – deeply sensitive, emotional, and profoundly enriching, both professionally and in terms of our shared humanity. For me, these connections and personalized stories have been the greatest gift.

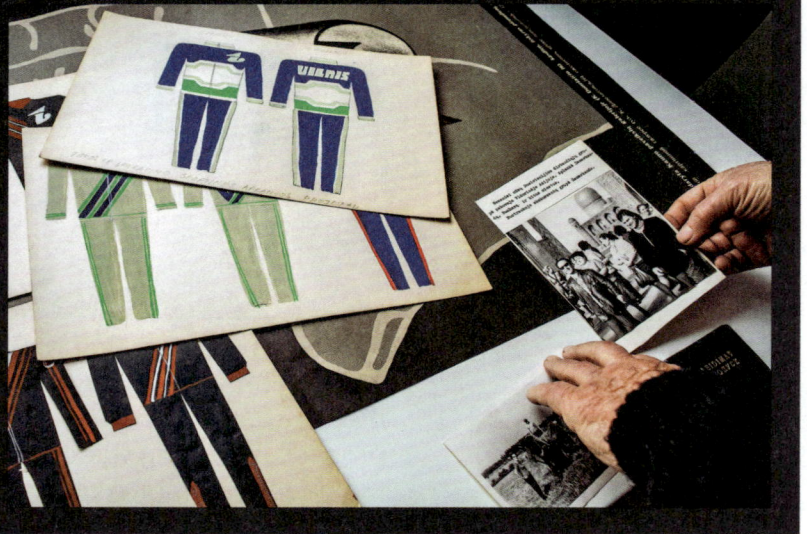

Vladas Lisaitis holding his sketches of the branded sports clothing for the team of the Tara bureau designed in the 1970s and photos from his personal archive during his interview at the Design Foundation's Exhibition space at SODAS 2123 in Vilnius, 2021, photo by Goda Šuminaitė

The 'zooming in' method and artistic experiments, what elements influenced and determined our selection process?

KJ   I felt it was essential to showcase the rarest and most unique samples that held true aesthetic and artistic value. Your involvement in the research process was instrumental, as it led us to create high-quality scans and detailed photo documentation, allowing us to zoom in on specific details. With a sense of wonder, care, and empathy, we fully immersed ourselves in the artistic research, analyzing individual case studies. This approach enabled me to see certain artifacts in a new light – pieces I had initially "written off" due to their perceived strangeness, banality, or even kitschiness. Your often unexpected questions challenged me to reconsider my own perspectives.

Karolina Jakaitė at the exhibition "Gvalda's Room: designed by the Tara bureau" in front of the posters by Kęstutis Gvalda at the Design Foundation's Exhibition space at SODAS 2123 in Vilnius, 2020, photo by Edvardas Blažys / LRT

2
Visitors' impressions of the first Exhibition of Applied Graphics, 1967, Lithuanian Central State Archives, Fund R-396, List 4, File 24, Sheets 1–20.

This process of rediscovery was deeply immersive. Revisiting examples of graphic design I had encountered before or analyzing sources after a significant period made me notice new aspects. For instance, while flipping through the visitors' book of the first 1967 exhibition in the archives,[2] I came across an entry that read, "It is a pity you believed the promises of propaganda", which reminded me, with regret, that the entire Tara bureau was initially conceived to serve the Soviet propaganda machine.

Revisiting these exhibitions and unfulfilled projects – often the most interesting and experimental – made me realize that by presenting them, we were revealing fragments of a "failed or unfinished design history". It was as if we were showcasing something that never fully came to be, yet at the same time, uncovering the visionary world that the Tara artists had created. The result was both subjective and fragmented, achieved through the careful highlighting, juxtaposing, and interpretation of individual details.

DJ   From the start, my aim was to present the material through a contemporary lens while carefully choosing elements from the archive that highlighted both the personal stories of the artists and their artistic qualities. The packaging designs, in particular, featured intricate and highly decorative elements. I was especially drawn to works that showcased optical patterns from Lithuanian folk art – such as circles, suns, and motifs symbolizing the circle of life – as well as organic, psychedelic forms. Monika Jonaitienė's designs, preserved and documented by her son Kęstutis Jonaitis, were particularly influential. I also noted the incorporation of archaic elements, folklore references, and playful depictions of Lithuanian nature.

Sketches by Monika Jonaitienė, preserved and documented by her son Kęstutis Jonaitis, photo by Kęstutis Jonaitis

By searching for various assonances and unexpected connections, I found that even simple items like boxes and candy wrappers – often considered "discarded graphic design" – could conceptually merge to reveal new insights into Lithuanian identity. This approach allowed me to uncover how elements of the archive, through their intricate

z is for zooming in: researching and rediscovering Tara's archives and practices

details and unconventional choices, could challenge or expand our understanding of design.

"Unfinished processes" and a playful approach: how was the idea of the Glossary conceived and developed?

DJ   Together with Zuzana, who is also the graphic designer of this book, we initially conceived the idea while brainstorming design solutions and repeatedly noticing the many variations of Tara logos. It started with our focus on logos that felt more alive, each having its own voice and identity – like an *A* resembling a flame or a growing flower, and a *Z* resembling a snake, a symbol often seen in Lithuanian mythology. This process led me to search for additional letter variations, eventually discovering the entire alphabet, which is how the idea of creating the Glossary was born. At the same time, we explored how to present these logos in a less conventional way, seeking solutions that would give them deeper meaning rather than just displaying them in a straightforward manner.

KJ   I was immediately inspired by the idea of the Tara alphabet, even though t emerged almost in the final stages of the book, when it seemed that all that remained was to write the introductory text. However, I had already been interested in various alphabetically constructed stories and books.[3] I had also dreamt of engaging in the immersive writing of design history using this collage-alphabet method.[4] As I saw more of Deimantė's, Zuzana's and Oriol's graphic experiments, I realized that it wouldn't be feasible to insert textual commentary everywhere, and that some contextual waymarks for the graphic images would be highly beneficial.

So, we began this process from the perspective of graphic design, and after much deliberation and discussion, we filled it with meaningful keywords that would help to better understand the era of Tara, the contexts of the bureau, and the narratives encoded within them, as well as the often complex layers of Soviet reality. This is how the threads of collage stories and incomplete narratives were woven together. The resulting Glossary, though somewhat fragmented due to certain limitations (such as finding only a single equivalent for some of the letters), is specifically designed to help readers delve deeper into the Tara archive and uncover its stories.

3
Some of my inspirations: Deyan Sudjic, *B is for Bauhaus, Y is for YouTube: Designing the Modern World from A to Z*, New York: Rizzoli Ex Libris, 2015; *Marija Teresė Rožanskaitė: vaizdai ir tekstai* [albumas-žodynas], sud. Laima Kreivytė, Vilnius: Tarptautinės dailės kritikų asociacijos Lietuvos skyrius, 2011; *Marija Teresė Rožanskaitė. X-Rays of Art and Life*, eds. Laima Kreivytė, Mykolas Piekuras, Vilnius: MTR Art Foundation, 2024.

4
In 2020, together with a fellow Estonian design researcher Triin Jerlei we had started creating a Baltic design alphabet and even wrote paragraphs of several letters. We were inspired by the beautiful coincidence that A and B could correspond to the collaboration between two design personalities, Estonian Vello Asi and Lithuanian Tadas Baginskas, in organizing joint design exhibitions of the Baltics.

z is for zooming in: researching and rediscovering Tara's archives and practices

5
Therefore, the numerous books,
scientific studies, exhibition catalogues indicated in the Bibliography
list were very valuable in rethinking
the meanings of the stories of the Tara
bureau. I am also extremely grateful
to my colleagues (especially to Lolita
Jablonskienė and Giedrė Jankevičiūtė
for the very valuable remarks during
the reviewing process) who listened,
advised and supported me during
this long process of research, doubts,
disappointments and discoveries.

6
Lithuanian Central State Archives,
„Nauja taros ir įpakavimo įmonė",
1965, N°. 1677-16.

7
The Design Foundation's studio
"Gvalda's Room", which was exhibited
in the creative complex SODAS2123
in Vilnius between 2020–2022, offered
an opportunity of residence while
studying the Tara bureau's archive.

The concept of translation plays a significant role in this alphabet, as it required not just the simple translation of my texts from Lithuanian to English, but also the exploration of possible meaningful variants of design translations from that time and place (from *Then* to *Now*, from *Here* to *There*) to convey these ideas to someone unfamiliar with the Soviet era, with all its discrepancies, misunderstandings, and nuances. I also faced the challenge of translating from conventional scientific language[5] into a more narrative form, imagining it as the curator's commentary to visitors of an exhibition about the Tara bureau.

Additionally, during the research process, I discovered an archival film[6] with valuable images from the bureau's early years, though the sound had been lost. This presented another layer of translation – interpreting silent images into words. For this, I often relied on testimonies from interviews to provide the missing context, which I was trying to explain in the Glossary descriptions.

Because newly discovered archive photographs can give a false and sometimes even misleading picture. Therefore, we tried to introduce a certain contextual balance with these sporadic and somewhat fragmented Glossary annotations. Eventually, some conceptually meaningful Glossary terms that we had devoted a lot of time to, such as *blat*, *boredom*, *fictitious*, *misunderstandings*, *uniform* or *shortages*, remained in the drafts because we simply ran out of visual letters.

Failures and unfulfilled ideas: reflecting on the most difficult challenges we faced both collectively and individually.

KJ   The research was significantly affected by the pandemic, making it difficult to conduct interviews and meet with respondents.[7] Later, Russia's war against Ukraine had a deeply painful impact on the project. Throughout the research, one of the most challenging aspects was grappling with the Soviet nature of the graphic design artifacts and the processes related to them. This idea of "Soviet-ness" emerged as a third concept or approach, alongside the national and international perspectives I had been exploring – something that Alfonsas Andriuškevičius had suggested I consider back in 2013. I was inspired by his texts and particularly one poem which prompted to introduce the more poetic concept of "gray" in the Glossary:

The sky's turned a little more pink.
A little more blue is the earth.
Only me, as I was, I am still:
Cement-like
And gray (of the shade of non-love)[8]

8
I was very glad to receive a commentary of my already defended thesis by Alfonsas Andriuškevičius, a very important professor to me personally and my BA art history thesis supervisor. See Alfonsas Andriuškevičius, *Aisopika/ Aesopica,* ed. Rūta Junevičiūtė, Vilnius: Ariel Ink, 2023, 2–3.

I would examine the brightly decorated candy and chocolate wrappers and colorful boxes, only to realize that these were also signs of the Soviet occupation. The system needed this kind of glamorous façade to mask the tastelessness, greyness, ugliness, deprivation, and other painful experiences that prevailed in many areas. The hypocrisy and uncertainty encoded in these "simply dangerously beautiful" graphic design artifacts were deeply oppressive and often triggered a rejection reaction. It's easy to admire the playful design of those booklets, but the overall impression is heavy and unsettling.

On the other hand, delving into the artists' intentions, the sincere support from their relatives, their belief in what they were doing, and their often traumatic personal stories made the process easier. Among the designers of the bureau there were people who had suffered exile, interrogation, and persecution at the hands of the KGB. Their determination to continue creating, even with the knowledge that their work might never see the light of day or not the way they imagined, was inspiring. This experience was like a constant balancing act between love and *non-love.*

In the final stages of writing the book, we faced funding problems. It was difficult not to give up, but we persevered, seeking private sponsors and other opportunities to complete the work we had started.

DJ   One of the biggest challenges was the risk of presenting the designs from the Tara bureau in an overly idealized manner, which could distort their true context. To address this, we employed a "glossary" approach and provided contextual explanations that complement the visual narrative. This method helps to give meaning to the intricate details that stand out against the grey backdrop of the era. There's a universal understanding that beauty can emerge even in the most challenging times – a night of hardship often gives way to a new dawn.

Additionally, the failure to recognize and the marginalization of the Tara artists, along with the various limitations they faced – whether in print or expression – ironically provided a creative advantage. These constraints pushed their creativity in ways that might seem excessive today. Despite these challenges, their drive to express their artistic ambitions allowed them to continue creating and surviving under restrictive conditions.

Deimantė Jasiulevičiūtė in her studio in Amsterdam, photo by Angela Blumen

On supportive signs and fateful coincidences, or the question: what are the most important insights and discoveries?

DJ   I was inspired the most by works that radiated this authenticity, that seemed created from the depths of one's heart and roots. Then there are those modern connections in terms of sustainability or slowness that we now long so much for and that they seemed to have. Even the whole process of creating the book seemed to be based on Tara's slow design principle – lots of work on the selection process and the concept, and then, after scanning began, new angles and works emerged, as well as new connections. In the end, a lot of scans and shots – about 500 – remained unused. However, this whole process was very enriching.

Even though we were exploring the period of occupation, I wanted to include a certain sense of freedom so that the readers could make their own associations. It would create a kind of discussion that would leave space and help to avoid that *staged* moment. Because the whole archive is in the process. It seems alive, because there still are undiscovered moments. It is like a living history and at the same time an unfinished subject, but in a good way, because there is life in it.

KJ   It is a very enriching process. The most supportive thing was that connection with the artists or their relatives. Also, those unexpected coincidences seem like signs of support, showing that we are moving in the right direction. For example, while working on the alphabet idea, I took a fresh look at a sweets box full of random letters from the personal archive of Vaidilutė Gruseckaitė, while Petrutė Masiulionytė found an envelope with a large number of cut-out alphabets from the times of Tara and several alphabet games created by the artists of the bureau. Also, while we were recording fragments of this conversation, Vidas Poškus found and hung a term project poster by Kęstutis Šveikauskas, one of the most mysterious heroes of Tara, in the *Titanikas* exhibition hall of the Vilnius Academy of Arts. Another seemingly random, but in fact more programmed was the coincidence of years, which became apparent in the very final stages of the book because of the longer-than-planned delay in the research and the printing of the book being moved to 2024–2025. This will be the anniversary year – six decades from the founding of the bureau in 1964, while 2025 will be the 100th anniversary of Gvalda's birth. All this in a way confirms the dedication of our book to the creators of the Tara bureau. It is an expression of our respect and gratitude.

Die Schutzmarke by Kurt Siegfried Kraft, published in Berlin by Verlag Die Wirtschaft, 1970, original copy with autograph (by the Author?), reader's card and designers' names from the library of the Tara bureau

z is for zooming in: researching and rediscovering Tara's archives and practices

Also, a really good sign for us was the relationship we made with Spector Books, because one German book "Die Schutzmarke" was of particular importance to the designers of Tara bureau and it was exactly in Leipzig in 1966, probably for the first time *Then*, that the Tara bureau logo was introduced. True, *Then* it was hung backwards, but *Now*, as if to correct that accidental but also fateful mistake (which can also be seen as a kind of promise) – after almost 60 years it will be published "the way the artists designed it".

The rest house *Gelmė* ("Deep Water") of the Tara bureau in Preila, 1978, photo from the Archive of *Grafobal Vilnius*

And finally, an almost mystical coincidence – when I was already working on the layout of the book, I had an unexpected opportunity to stay at the rest house *Gelmė* ("Deep Water") in Preila, which in 1978 had been built on the shore of the lagoon for the employees of the Tara bureau and for nearly several decades had been a space where the Tara bureau's artists were able to rest and search for inspiration near the Baltic Sea. It was a kind of identification with Tara's spaces and the merging of our chosen point of view of *Then* and *Now*, and in a metaphorical sense, a reflection of our expectations and efforts, where throughout the whole process, while feeling not only the ephemeral nature of the artifacts that we were researching, but also the fragility and transience of the surrounding world, we were also trying to unravel the depths of design and the stories that surrounded it. We invite you to dive into them too!

z is for zooming in: researching and rediscovering Tara's archives and practices

TEXT AND IMAGE CREDITS

We have endeavored to trace the copyright holders of all images and texts reproduced in this publication. We thank all those who have granted reproduction rights. We apologize for any errors or omissions.

a is for archive

12   Antanas Kazakauskas, Layout from the catalogue *Lithuania London'68,* published in English, 1968
13   Text by V. Jurevičius about the Tara bureau exhibition *Ženklai ir plakatai* (Signs and Posters), published in the evening newspaper *Vakarinės naujienos* (Evening News), 1984, June 27. The photograph shows "Sigma" trademark modifications designed by Pranas Markevičius
15   Kostas Katkus, Cover of the Tara bureau catalogue, 1970, personal archive of Karolina Jakaitė
16   Kęstutis Gvalda in Stalin's gulag in Krasnoyarsk Krai, Siberia, ca. 1950s, personal archive of Regina Pranskevičienė
18   Vladas Lisaitis, Sketches for the Poster *Respublikinė taikomosios grafikos paroda* (The Republican Exhibition of Applied Graphics), 1984, personal archive of Vladas Lisaitis
19   Vladas Lisaitis holding printed sheets of design proposals next to one of the factories, ca. 1980s, personal archive of Vladas Lisaitis
20   Logo of the Tara bureau (upside-down) and next to it – a display of food production of the Soviet Lithuania Republic at the 1966 Leipzig Spring Fair, 1966. Architect Albinas Purys, photograph from Lithuanian Central State Archives
21   The Tara bureau's logos and packaging at the Baltic Food Exhibition, ca. 1960s, photograph by Vytautas Zaranka, Lithuanian Archives of Literature and Art
22   East German visitors are viewing the display of Soviet Lithuanian souvenirs and packagings by the Tara bureau in Erfurt at the 'Litauen 70', 1970, architect Albinas Purys, photograph from Lithuanian Central State Archives, Fund R-396, List 4, File 36

b is for bureau

24   Various titles and logos of the Tara bureau
26   Page from the catalogue of the 1967 Tara bureau exhibition, personal archive of Karolina Jakaitė
27   The Artist-constructors employed at the Experimental Package Design Bureau, 1970s, photographs from the personal archive of Vladas Lisaitis
28   Envelope of the Tara bureau, personal archive of Karolina Jakaitė
29   Kęstutis Ramonas defending his dissertation at the Department of Artistic Constructing of Industrial Products, then LSSR State Art Institute, now Vilnius Academy of Arts, 1965, personal archive of Kęstutis Ramonas
30–32   Kęstutis Ramonas, Packagings and containers for household chemicals, 1965, personal archive of Kęstutis Ramonas
33   Kęstutis Ramonas, Containers for machine oil, 1965, personal archive of Kęstutis Ramonas
34   Romualdas Svaškevičius, Cover of the magazine *Tara. Reklama* (Packaging. Advertising), 1966

35   Romualdas Svaškevičius, Cover of the magazine *Tara. Reklama* (Packaging. Advertising), 1967
36–39   Stills from the archival film about the Tara bureau *Nauja taros ir įpakavimo įmonė* (The New Packaging Company), 1965, cameraman Rimantas Juodvalkis, Lithuanian Central State Archives, No. 1677–16
40   Kęstutis Gvalda, Trademark registration card Žuvininkystės ūkis *„Pajūris"* (Fishing farm Seaside), 1968, personal archive of Karolina Jakaitė
41   The Tara bureau's artists at the methodological office (left to right: unidentified artist, Teresė Ivanauskaitė, Faisa Šmuriginaitė, Pranas Markevičius, unidentified artist), photograph from Advertising catalogue about the Tara bureau, ca. 1970s
42   The Tara bureau's methodological office, 1966, photograph by Antanas Dilys, Lithuanian Central State Archives
43–47   Labels and calendars on the back side of posters, personal archive of Karolina Jakaitė
48   The Tara bureau's packaging factory worker B. Stankevičius is preparing packaging for canning industry, 1974, photograph by Eugenijus Šiško (Spyglinis), Lithuanian Central State Archives
49   Photomechanical bar and its manager Pranas Jonaitis (1937–2014), ca. 1970s, personal archive of Kęstutis Jonaitis
50–53   Monika Jonaitienė, Packaging designs for *Cotton*, 1960s, Archives of Lithuanian Artists' Association
54–55   Monika Jonaitienė, Candy wrappers *Pilotas* (Pilot) and *Rudens sodas* (Autumn Garden) for confectionery factory *Pergalė* (Victory), 1960s, Archives of Lithuanian Artists' Association
56–57   Monika Jonaitienė, Candy wrappers *Kregždutė* (Swallow) and *Taika* (Peace), 1960s, personal archive of Kęstutis Jonaitis
58   Candy wrappers by the Tara bureau from the catalogue of the 1967 Tara bureau's exhibition
59   Confectionery packagings, examined by production manager S. Steponavičienė and confectionery workshop technologist O. Bagdonienė at confectionery factory *Pergalė* (Victory), 1976, Lithuanian Central State Archives
60–61   Monika Jonaitienė, Chocolate wrappers for confectionery factory *Pergalė* (Victory), 1960s, personal archive of Kęstutis Jonaitis
62–63   Gediminas Karosas, Advertising brochure for confectionery factory *Gegužės Pirmoji* (May Day), published in Lithuanian, Russian, English and German, 1976
64   New designs of chocolate boxes demonstrated by S. Grigaitė at the confectionery factory *Pergalė* (Victory), 1976, photograph by Algis Palionis, Lithuanian Central State Archives
     Representatives of the confectionery companies' association of the German Democratic Republic are visiting the confectionery factory *Pergalė* (Victory), 1976, Lithuanian Central State Archives
65   New chocolate boxes at the confectionery factory *Pergalė* (Victory), 1974, photograph by Tadas Žebrauskas, Lithuanian Central State Archives
66   Monika Jonaitienė, Chocolate box *Palydovai* (Satellites), 1960s, personal archive of Kęstutis Jonaitis
67   Teresė Ivanauskaitė, Chocolate box *Nida* (Nidden), 1960s, personal archive of Kęstutis Jonaitis
     Monika Jonaitienė, Chocolate box *Paukščių pienas* (Bird's Milk), 1960s, personal archive of Kęstutis Jonaitis

m is for macaroni and pizza

p is for public spaces

s is for soviet exhibition in London

190 Photograph from the Soviet Lithuanian Pavilion at the Earls Court exhibition Centre in London, 1968, personal archive of Tadas Baginskas
191 Author unknown, Cover of the catalogue *Lietuviški suvenyrai* (Lithuanian Souvenirs), published in Lithuanian and English, 1968
192–195 Author unknown, Layouts and excerpts from the catalogue *Lietuviški suvenyrai* (Lithuanian Souvenirs), published in Lithuanian and English, 1968
196 Nude photograph by Rimantas Dichavičius from the catalogue *Lietuviški suvenyrai* (Lithuanian Souvenirs), published in Lithuanian and English, 1968
197–198 Author unknown, Excerpts from the catalogue *Lietuviški suvenyrai* (Lithuanian Souvenirs), published in Lithuanian and English, 1968
199 Photograph by Rimantas Dichavičius from the catalogue *Lietuviški suvenyrai* (Lithuanian Souvenirs), published in Lithuanian and English, 1968
200–201 Antanas Kazakauskas, Layout from the catalogue *Lithuania London'68,* published in English, 1968
202–203 Author unknown, Cover and layouts from the catalogue *Tarybų Lietuvos žuvies pramonė* (Soviet Lithuanian Fish Industry), published in Lithuanian, Russian, and English, 1968
204–207 Photographs and Illustrations from the catalogue *Vidaus vandenų žuvininkystė* (Inland fisheries), designed by Monika Urmanavičiūtė-Jonaitienė, published in Lithuanian, Russian, and German, ca. 1960s
208–209 Author unknown, Cover and layouts from the catalogue *Tarybų Lietuvos lengvoji pramonė* (Soviet Lithuanian Light Industry) showcasing the newest fashion designs by Vilnius House of Clothing Design, published in Lithuanian and English, 1968
210–212 Author unknown, Photographs from the catalogue *Tarybų Lietuvos lengvoji pramonė* (Soviet Lithuanian Light Industry) showcasing the newest fashion designs by Vilnius House of Clothing Design, published in Lithuanian and English, 1968

t is for technical aesthetics

216 Pranas Markevičius, Illustrations from the catalogue *Vilniaus skaičiavimo mašinų gamykla* (Vilnius computing machine factory), in Lithuanian, Russian, and German, 1970
217 Algirdas Šarka, one of the first three design graduates from the Department of Industrial Design at then LSSR State Art Institute, 1965, photograph from Archive of Design Department of Vilnius Academy of Arts
218–219 Pranas Markevičius, Illustrations from the catalogue *Vilniaus skaičiavimo mašinų gamykla* (Vilnius computing machine factory), in Lithuanian, Russian, and German, 1970
220–221 Kostas Katkus, Covers of the catalogues *Rūta 110* and *Rūta 701*, published in Russian, ca. 1970
222–223 Kostas Katkus, Illustrations from the catalogue *Rūta 110* and *Rūta 701*, published in Russian, ca. 1970

224 The constructors Povilas Jašinskas and Romualdas Žlabys in front of *Rūta 701*, 1968, photograph by V. Vilaniškis and B. Akstinas, Lithuanian Central State Archives
225–227 Authors unknown, Excerpts from the advertising brochure *Elektros technikai* (Electrical technicians), *Radijo technikai* (Radio technicians), *Metalistai* (Metal workers), published in Lithuanian, ca. 1960s
228 Vladas Lisaitis, Cover of the catalogue *Panevėžio tiksliosios mechanikos gamykla* (Panevėžys Precision Mechanics Plant), published in Lithuanian and Russian, 1974
229 Vladas Lisaitis, Endpaper of the catalogue *Panevėžio tiksliosios mechanikos gamykla* (Panevėžys Precision Mechanics Plant) with the stamps and signatures by the members of Artistic Committee with permission for printing, published in Lithuanian and Russian, 1974
230 Vladas Lisaitis, Endpaper of the catalogue *Tauragės keramikos gamykla* (Tauragė ceramics factory), published in Lithuanian and Russian, 1976
231–238 Photographs of the workers, engineers and constructors from the catalogues *Tauragės keramikos gamykla* (Tauragė ceramics factory), *Panevėžio tiksliosios mechanikos gamykla* (Panevėžys precision mechanics plant), *Panevėžio gamykla "Ekranas"* (Panevėžys factory "Ekranas"), photographs by Algirdas Staišys, Ramūnas Krupauskas and others, ca. 1970s
239 Vladas Lisaitis, Illustration from the cover of the catalogue *Tauragės keramikos gamykla* (Tauragė ceramics factory), published in Lithuanian and Russian, 1976
240 The factory packer M. Kuznecova from the Vilnius Electric Welding Equipment Factory prepares the *Saturnas* (Saturn) vacuum cleaners for shipment, 1966, photograph by Marius Baranauskas, Lithuanian Central State Archives
241 Kęstutis Ramonas, Label for electric vacuum cleaner *Saturnas* (Saturn), published in Lithuanian and Russian, ca. 1960s, personal archive of Kęstutis Ramonas
242 At the exhibition in Panevėžys, visitors examine newly planned lighting objects produced by the Panevėžys Electromechanical Factory, 1972, photograph by Leonas Grubinskas, Lithuanian Central State Archives
243 Author unknown, Excerpts from the advertising brochure of the Panevėžys Electromechanical Factory *Svetilniki* (Lamps), published in Russian, ca. 1960s
244 Kęstutis Gvalda, Original of the poster *Mūsų šviestuvai* (Our Lamps), 1976, personal archive of Karolina Jakaitė
244 Author unknown, Layout from the advertising brochure of the Panevėžys Electromechanical Factory *Svetilniki* (Lamps), published in Russian, ca. 1960s
246–247 Feliksas Ivanauskas, Endpaper and dust jacket of the catalogue *Panevėžio gamykla "Ekranas"* (Panevėžys factory "Ekranas"), published in Lithuanian, Russian, and English, ca. 1970
248 Author unknown, Illustration from the cover of the advertising catalogue *Mediniai žaislai* (Wooden Toys), published in Lithuanian, Russian, English, Germain, 1977
249 Author unknown, Cover of the advertising catalogue *Žaislų katalogas* (Toy Catalogue), published in Lithuanian and Russian, ca. 1970s

BIBLIOGRAPHY

Archival sources

Lithuanian Central State Archives (LCSA)

Archival film about the Tara bureau *Nauja taros ir įpakavimo įmonė* (The New Packaging Company), 1965, cameraman Rimantas Juodvalkis, LCSA, No. 1677–16.

Archival film about the Tara bureau *Kad prekės atrodytų gražiau* (The New Packaging Company), 1965, cameraman Juozas Gustaitis, LCSA, No. 1699–16.

Photos from the Baltic Food Exhibition in Tallinn, 1966, LCSA, Fund R-396, List 5, File 7.

Photos from the Baltic Food Exhibition in Riga, 1966, LCSA, Fund R-396, List 5, File 8.

Photos from the Lithuanian Exposition at the Spring Leipzig Fair, 1966, LCSA, Fund R-396, List 5, File 4.

Photos from the Exhibition of Industrial Aesthetics in Vilnius, 1968, LCSA, Fund R-396, List 5, File 22.

Photos from the Exhibition *Tara un Iepakojums* (Container and Packaging) in Riga, 1975, LCSA, Fund R-396, List 5, File 62.

Photos from the Exhibition in Erfurt *Litauen-70* (Lithuania-70), 1970, LCSA, Fund R-396, List 4, File 36.

Proposals for the Establishment of the Pilot Bureau for Container and Packaging Construction at the National Economy Council, LCSA, Fund R-239, List 4, File 140.

Visitors' Impressions of the First Industrial Graphic Art Exhibition of 1967, Lithuanian Central State Archives, Fund R-396, List 4, File 24.

List of Exhibits for Erfurt exhibition *Litauen-70* (Lithuania-70), LCSA, Fund R-396, List 1, File 78.

Archives of Lithuanian Artists' Association

Personal file of Juozas Gelguda.
Personal file of Monika Urmanavičiūtė-Jonaitienė.
Personal file of Kostas Katkus.

Interviews

Interview with Antanas Morkevičius, recorded by K. Jakaitė, Vilnius, January 19, 2010.

Interview with Juozas Gelguda, recorded by K. Jakaitė, Vilnius, June 22, 2023.

Interview with Lidija Glinskienė, recorded by K. Jakaitė, Vilnius, October 15, 2010.

Interviews with Petrutė Masiulionytė, recorded by K. Jakaitė, Vilnius, October 20, 2011 and January 15, 2024.

Interview with Kęstutis Jonaitis, recorded by K. Jakaitė, Vilnius, February 1, 2024.

Interview with Teresė Ivanauskaitė, recorded by K. Jakaitė, Vilnius, October 28, 2010.

Interview with Juozas Galkus, recorded by K. Jakaitė, Vilnius, August 10, 2021.

Interview with Kęstutis Ramonas, recorded by Karolina Jakaitė and Šarūnas Šlektavičius, Design Foundation, Vilnius, March 18, 2016.

Interviews with Vaidilutė Gruseckaitė, recorded by K. Jakaitė, Vilnius, March 8, 2018 and October 15, 2019.

Interviews with Antanas Kazakauskas, recorded by K. Jakaitė, Vilnius, September 4, 2013, October 9, 2015 and April 13, 2018.

Interviews with Kęstutis Gvalda, recorded by K. Jakaitė, Vilnius, March 6, 2008, June 5, 2008, October 2, 2008, December 9 and 16, 2009, January 13, 2010, July 9, 2010, February 6, 2011.

Interview with Laimutė Puodžiūnaitė-Ramonienė, recorded by K. Jakaitė, Vilnius, September 27, 2021.

Interviews with Raisa Šmuriginaitė, recorded by K. Jakaitė, February 10 and October 6, 2010.

Interview with Vladas Lisaitis, by Karolina Jakaitė and Deimantė Jasiulevičiūtė, recorded by Design Foundation, Vilnius, November 11, 2021.

Reviews, articles in periodicals about the Tara bureau, published in the 1960s–1980s

„Problema Nr. 1: diskusija apie plataus vartojimo prekių kokybę" (Problem No. 1: Discussion about the Quality of Consumer Goods), in: *Mokslas ir technika*, 1965 No. 1, p. 4–7.

„Respublikos įmonių prekiniai ženklai" (Trademarks of Companies of the Republic), in: *Tara. Reklama*, Vilnius: EMKB, 1966, p. 16.

„Taikomoji pramoninė grafika – vakar, šiandien, rytoj" (Applied Industrial Graphics – Yesterday, Today, Tomorrow), in: *Kultūros barai*, 1986, No. 4, p. 18.

Aleksynaitė, Daina, „Ar taikomoji grafika – Pelenė?.." (Is Applied Graphics – a Cinderella?..), in: *Kauno tiesa*, 1984 07 01.

Bielskis, Algimantas, „Gaminys ir vartotojas" (Product and User), in: *Mokslas ir technika*, 1965, No. 12, p. 7–9.

Daukantas, Feliksas, „Kodėl žmogus susipyksta su daiktais" (Why do People get Angry with Things?), in: Švyturys, 1968, No. 17, p. 21–23.

Gedminas, Antanas, „Plakatas – tai vaizdinė agitacija" (A Poster is Visual Propaganda), in: *Literatūra ir menas*, 1968 01 06, p. 4.

Gedžius, Arūnas, „Ar konservų dėžutė – meno kūrinys?" (Is a Tin Box can be a Work of Art?), in: *Literatūra ir menas*, 1972 03 11, p. 4.

Gedžius, Arūnas, „Reikia mums reklamos?" (Do We Need Advertising?), in: *Mokslas ir technika*, 1971, No. 1, p. 12–13.

Katkus, Kostas, „Nauja stiklinė tara" (New Glass Container), in: *Tara. Reklama*, 1968, Vilnius: ETĮKB, p. 15–18.

Kulvietis, Povilas, „Gaminiai bus puikūs" (The Products will be Great), in: *Mokslas ir technika*, 1965, No. 2, p. 2–3.

Kulvietis, Povilas, „Mūsų gaminiai turi būti geriausi pasaulyje" (Our Products Must be the Best in the World), in: *Mokslas ir technika*, 1965, No. 5, p. 2–3.

Matijošaitytė, Birutė, „Unifikuota vaisių-uogų ir daržovių konservų etikečių sistema" (Unified Labeling System for Canned Fruits, Berries and Vegetables), in: *Tara. Reklama*, 1968, Vilnius: ETĮKB, p. 15.

Ramonas, Kęstutis, „Kai grožis ateina į namus" (When Beauty Comes Home), in: *Literatūra ir menas*, 1974 11 16, p. 12.

Ramonas, Kęstutis, „Ženklai – simboliai" (Signs – Symbols), in: *Dailė*, 1970, p. 42–43.

Rimeika, Henrikas, „Prekinis ženklas ir mes" (The Logo and Us), in: *Mokslas ir technika*, 1969, No. 9, p. 24–26.

Rimkus, Vytenis, „Taikomoji grafika" (Applied Graphics), in: *Kultūros barai*, 1985 No. 4, p. 33–37.

Urbonas, Jonas, „Į kiekvienus namus ateinantis grožis" (Beauty Coming to Every Home), in: *Literatūra ir menas*, 1968 02 17, p. 2.

Urbonas, Jonas, „Nauja meno tarybų darbo metodika" (New Methodology for the Work of Artistic Committees), in: *Tara. Reklama*, Vilnius: Eksperimentinis taros ir įpakavimo konstravimo biuras, 1967, p. 39.

Valantinaitė B., „Prekės išvaizda turi būti graži" (The Appearance of the Product Must be Beautiful), in: *Literatūra ir menas*, 1958 04 05.

Valdonis G., „Prekei reikia gražaus rūbo" (The Product Needs a Nice Cloth), in: *Gimtasis kraštas*, 1974 10 31, p. 6–7.

Ryumina, Itta, "Litovskaya promgrafika" (Lithuanian Industrial Graphics), in: *Dekorativnoye iskusstvo SSSR* (Decorative Art of the USSR), 1972, No. 10, p. 18–22.

Sil'vestrova, S. A., "Opyt proyektirovaniya upakovki v Vil'nyusskom EKHKB" (Experience of Packaging Design at the Vilnius EKMKB), in: *Tekhnicheskaya estetika* (Technical aesthetics), 1979, No. 6, p. 8–11.

Urbonas, Jonas, "Tovar litsom" (The Product's Face), in: *Dekorativnoye iskusstvo SSSR* (Decorative Art of the USSR), 1969, No. 136, p. 48–49.

VARIA

Aynsley, Jeremy, *A Century of Graphic Design*, London: Octopus Publishing Group, 2001.

Aisopika/ Aesopica, ed. Rūta Junevičiūtė, Vilnius: Ariel Ink, 2023.

Cold War Modern: Design 1945–1970, eds. by David Crowley, Jane Pavitt, London: V&A Publishing, 2008.

Crowley, David, „Pop Effects in Eastern Europe under Communist Rule", https://faktografia.com/2014/01/26/pop-effects-in-eastern-europe-under-communist-rule/.

Crowley, David, „Writing about heroes", https://faktografia.com/2012/06/09/writing-about-heroes/.

Cubbin, Tom, „Open Form and the Polish Influence on Soviet Design in the 1960s", in: *Herito*, Special Issue: *Patterning Design in Central Europe*, 2016, No. 24, p. 82–93.

Drėmaitė, Marija, *Baltic Modernism. Architecture and Housing in Soviet Lithuania,* Berlin: DOM Publishers, 2017.

Drėmaitė, Marija, „Vakarietiškumo kaukė: sovietų Lietuvos manifestacijos" (The Mask of Westernization: Manifestations of Soviet Lithuania), in: *Pasakojimas tęsiasi: modernizacijos traukinyje. Lietuvos šimtmetis: 1918–2018*, sud. Giedrė Jankevičiūtė, Verijus Šepetys, Vilnius: VDA leidykla, 2018, p. 50–60.

Eijnde, Jeroen N. M. van den, *Exploring the Space for Design. Research Between I-We-Do-Think*, Arnhem: ArtEZ Press, 2016.

Ernst, van Alphen, *Staging the Archive: Art and Photography in the Age of New Media*, London: Reaktion Books: 2015.

Forty, Adrian, *Words and buildings: a Vocabulary of Modern Architecture*, London: Thames & Hudson, 2004.

Galkus, Juozas, *Lietuvos plakato istorija* (Lithuanian Poster History), Vilnius: Vilniaus dailės akademijos leidykla, 2015.

Gedminas, Antanas, Galkus Juozas, *Lietuvos plakatas* (Lithuanian Poster), Vilnius: Mintis, 1971.

Girst, Thomas, *The Duchamp Dictionary*, London: Thames and Hudson, 2014.

Grigoravičienė, Erika, „Modernizacija, (post)modernizmai, naujasis modernizmas: Lietuvos dailės nuo XX a. 6 dešimtmečio pabaigos istorijos sąvokos" (Modernisation, (Post)modernities, and New Modernism: The Concepts of Lithuanian Art History Starting from the Late 1950s), in: *Acta Academiae Artium Vilnensis 95,* Vilnius: Vilniaus dailės akademijos leidykla, 2019, p 53–85.

Hardziej, Patryk, *Karol Śliwka*, Gdansk: Gdynia City Museum, 2018.

Heller, Steven, Veronique Vienne, *100 Ideas that changed Graphic Design,* London: Lawrence King Publishing, 2012.

Jablonskienė, Lolita, „Lietuvos dizaino istorijos kuravimas" (Curating the History of Lithuanian Design), in: *Acta Academiae Artium Vilnensis*, Vilnius, 2022, Vol. 107, *How to Tell About Art? Art History, Criticism, Texts and Narratives in Lithuania*, p. 57–80.

Jablonskienė, Lolita, „Trumpa judėjimo „Meną į buitį" istorija / A Brief History of the "Art into Everyday Life" Movement, in: *David Mabb: Menas kasdienybei* (David Mabb: Art for Everyday Life), ed. Simon Rees, Vilnius: Šiuolaikinio meno centras, 2006, p. 12–18.

Jakaitė, Karolina, „Lietuvos grafinis dizainas XX a. 6–8 deš.: tarp nacionalumo ir internacionalumo" (Lithuanian Graphic Design in the 1950s–1970s: between National and International) supervised by Assoc. Prof. Dr. Lolita Jablonskienė, (manuscript of PhD thesis), Vilnius Academy of Arts, 2012.

Jakaitė, Karolina, „The Lithuanian Pavilion at the 1968 London Exhibition", translated by Jurij Dobriakov, *Art in Translation*, Volume 7, 2015, Issue 4, p. 520–551.

Jakaitė, Karolina, *Antanas Kazakauskas. Viskas užprogramuota / Everything is Programmed*, Vilnius: Vilnius Graphic Art Centre, Vilnius Academy of Arts, 2022.

Jakaitė, Karolina, Šaltojo karo kapsulė: lietuvių dizainas Londone 1968 (Cold War Capsule: Lithuanian Design in London in 1968), Vilnius: Lapas, 2019.

Jankevičiūtė, Giedrė, „*Swinging sixties* sovietų Lietuvos vaikų knygų iliustracijose" (Swinging sixties in Soviet Lithuanian Children's Book Illustrations), in: *Acta Academiae Artium Vilnensis 83*, Vilnius: Vilniaus dailės akademijos leidykla, 2016, p. 109–133.

Jankevičiūtė, Giedrė, *Lietuvos grafika 1918–1940* (Lithuanian Graphic Arts 1918–1940), Vilnius: E. Karpavičiaus leidykla, 2008.

Janulevičiūtė, Rasa, *Tadas Baginskas. Dizaino liudininkas* (Tadas Baginskas. Design Witness), Vilnius: Vilniaus dailės akademijos leidykla, 2020.

Janulevičiūtė, Rasa, *Vilniaus dailės akademijos dizairo katedra: 1961–1990: profesionalaus Lietuvos dizaino pagrindas* (Vilnius Academy of Arts, Department of Design: 1961–1990: The Foundation of Professional Lithuanian Design), Vilnius: Vilniaus dailės akademijos leidykla, 2011.

Jaškūnienė, Eglė, *Fotografija Lietuvos grafiniame dizaine 1953–1988: technologijos, komunikacija, propaganda, estetika* (Photography in Lithuanian Graphic Design 1953–1988: Technologies, Communication, Propaganda, Aesthetics), Vilnius: Vilnius Gedimino technikos universitetas, 2021.

Jerlei, Triin, „And We Had to Do Better Than Abroad: the Local Vilnius Branch of VNIITE, All-Union Research Institute of Industrial Design, in Soviet Lithuania", in: *Acta Academiae Artium Vilnensis 103*, Vilnius: Vilniaus dailės akademijos leidykla, 2021, p. 149–188.

Jerlei, Triin, „Baltiški suvenyrai kaip bandymas sukurti "sovietinę Europą" (Baltic Souvenirs as an Attempt to Create a "Soviet Europe"), in: *Vilkas, bokštas ir bažnyčia. Vilniaus suvenyrai*, ed. Rūta Miškinytė, Vilnius: Lapas, 2023, p. 128–139.

Jerlei, Triin, „My Address is the Soviet Union – or is t? Baltic Identity in Souvenir Production within the Soviet Discourse", in: *Journal of material culture*, 27 (2), 2022, p. 147–165.

Klimaitė, Indrė, *On Continuous and Systematic Nutrition Improvement*, Maastricht: Jan Van Eyck Academie, 2013.

Klimas, Audrius, *Lietuvos prekių ženklai. Istorija, funkcija, klasifikacija* (Lithuanian Trademarks. History, Function, Classification), Vilnius: Vilniaus dailės akademijos leidykla, 2009.

Lietuvos grafinio dizaino kūrėjai 1964–1984 (Lithuanian Graphic Design Creators 1964–1984), (reconstructed exhibition catalogue), ed. Karolina Jakaitė, Vilnius: Vilniaus dailės akademijos leidykla, 2022.

Maciuika, John V., Drėmaitė, Marija, eds, *Lithuanian Architects Assess the Soviet Era: The 1992 Oral History Tapes*, Vilnius: Lapas, 2020.

Marija Teresė Rožanskaitė: vaizdai ir tekstai (albumas-žodynas) (Marija Teresė Rožanskaitė: Images and Texts (album-dictionary), sud. Laima Kreivytė, Vilnius: Tarptautinės dailės kritikų asociacijos Lietuvos skyrius, 2011.

Marija Teresė Rožanskaitė. X-Rays of Art and Life, eds. Laima Kreivytė, Mykolas Piekuras, Vilnius: MTR Art Foundation, 2024.

Miłosz, Czesław, *The Captive Mind*, New York: Vintage Books, 1955.

Modernizacija. XX a. 7–8 deš. Baltijos šalių menas, dizainas ir architektūra / Modernization. Art, Design and Architecture of the Baltic States in the 1960s and 1970s: catalogue, ed. Lolita Jablonskienė, Vilnius: Lietuvos dailės muziejus, 2011.

Mood ja külm sõda / Fashion and the Cold War, ed. by Eha Komissarov, Berit Teeäär, Tallinn: Art Museum of Estonia – Kumu Art Museum, 2012.

Narušytė, Agnė, *The Aesthetics of Boredom: Lithuanian Photography 1980–1990*, Vilnius: Vilniaus dailės akademijos leidykla, 2010.

Pleasures in Socialism: Leisure and Luxury in the Eastern Bloc, ed. by David Crowley, Susan E. Reid, Evanston: Northwestern University Press, 2010.

Ogólnopolskie Wystawy Znaków Graficznych, eds. Patryk Hardziej, Rene Wawrzkiewicz, Karakter, 2016.

Pavitt, Jane, *Fear and Fashion in the Cold War*, London: V&A Publishing, 2008.

Péteri, György, „Nylon Curtain – Transnational and Transsystemic Tendencies in the Cultural Life of State-Socialist Russia and East-Central Europe", in: *Slavonica*, Vol. 10, No. 2, 2004, p. 113–123.

Piotrowski, Piotr, „Why Were There No Great Pop Art Curatorial Projects in Eastern Europe in the 1960s?", in: *Art in Transfer in the Era of Pop*, ed. Annika Öhrner, Stockholm: Södertörn University, 2017, p. 21–35.

Piotrowski, Piotr, *In the Shadow of Yalta. Art and the Avant-Garde in Eastern Europe 1945–1989*, London: Reaktion Books, Ltd., 2009.

Pleasures in Socialism: Leisure and Luxury in the Eastern Bloc, ed. by David Crowley, Susan E. Reid, Evanston: Northwestern University Press, 2010.

Postmodernism: Style and Subversion, 1970–1990, ed. by Glenn Adamson, Jane Pavitt, London: V&A Publishing, 2011.

Ramonas, Kęstutis, „Taros" biuras sovietmečiu: profesionalaus grafinio dizaino Lietuvoje pradžia" (The Tara bureau in Soviet era: the beginning of professional graphic design in Lithuania), in: *SKŪL001*, ed. by Jogaila Jurgelis, BA Final project, Vilnius College of Design, 2016, p. 17–27.

Reid, Susan E., „Khrushchev Modern. Agency and modernization in the Soviet home", in: *Cahiers du monde russe*, 2006/1, Vol. 47, p. 227–268.

Retrotopia. Design for Socialist Spaces, ed. By Claudia Banz, Berlin: Verlag Kettler, Kunstgewerbemuseum, 2023.

Stories of Things. Lithuanian Design 1918–2018, eds. Karolina Jakaitė, Giedrė Jankevičiūtė, Ernestas Parulskis, Gintautė Žemaitytė, Vilnius: Lietuvos dailės muziejus, 2018.

Symbol to Logo: Polish Graphic Marks 1945–1969, 2000–2015, Patryk Hardziej, Rene Wawrzkiewicz, Gdansk: Gdynia City Museum, 2017.

Streikus, Arūnas, *Minties kolektyvizacija: cenzūra sovietų Lietuvoje* (Collectivization of Thought: Censorship in Soviet Lithuania), Vilnius: Naujasis Židinys-Aidai, 2018.

Sudjic, Deyan, *B is for Bauhaus, Y is for YouTube: Designing the Modern World from A to Z*, New York: Rizzoli Ex Libris, 2015.

Sutkaitis, Rokas, *Soviet Logos: Lost Marks of the Utopia*, Kaunas, 2019.

Šatavičiūtė-Natalevičienė, Lijana, „Suderinti (ne)suderinamą: tapatumo paieškos ankstyvajame sovietiniame tekstilės dizaine („Kauno audinių» atvejis)" (To Match the (Un)matchable: The Search for Identity in Early Soviet Textile Design (The Case of Kauno Audiniai)), in: *Acta Academiae Artium Vilnensis* 103, Vilnius: Vilniaus dailės akademijos leidykla, 2021, p. 17–56.

Šepetys, Nerijus, „About an Intellectual Creator, (un)Favorable Time, Penetrating Contexts, (un)Surmountable Boundaries", Teodoras Kazimieras Valaitis 1934–1974: supplement of the catalogue, ed. Giedrė Jankevičiūtė, Vilnius: Lietuvos dailės muziejus, Vilniaus dailės akademijos leidykla, 2014, p. 9–20.

Taul, Gregor, *Monumentality Trouble. Monumental-Decorative Art in Late Soviet Estonia, Latvia and Lithuania / Sekeldused monumentaalsusega: monumentaal-dekoratiivkunst hilisnõukogude Eestis, Lätis ja Leedus* (PhD research and thesis) (supervised by Dr. Anu Allas), Tallinn: EKA, 2024.

Tutlytė, Jūratė, „Dizainas socialistiniame (Lietuvos) ūkyje, arba žmogus ir daiktinė aplinka visuotinio nepritekliaus sąlygomis" (Design in a Socialist (Lithuanian) Economy, or Man and the Material Environment in Conditions of Shortages), in: *Darbai ir dienos*, 2007, No. 47, p. 139–160.

Uz lielās dzīves trases / On the Track of Great Life: Graphic language on the 1960s in Latvia, Riga: Raktuve, 2016.

Vukić, Fedja, *The Other Design History*, Zagreb: Upi2M Books, 2015.

Žuklytė-Gasperaitienė, Deima, „Lietuvos grafinis dizainas XX a. 7–8 dešimtmečiais: psichodelinio meno įtakos" (Lithuanian Graphic Design in the 1960s and 1970s: Influences of Psychedelic Art), in: *Acta Academiae Artium Vilnensis* 103, Vilnius: Vilniaus dailės akademijos leidykla, 2021, p. 57–90.

Žuklytė-Gasperaitienė, Deima, *Hei, poparte! Lietuvos grafikų kūryba XX a. 7–8 dešimtmečiais* (Hey, Pop Art! The Work of Lithuanian Graphic Artists in the 1960s and 1970s), Vilnius: Vilniaus grafikos meno centras, 2020.

Teodoras Kazimieras Valaitis 1934–1974, ed. Giedrė Jankevičiūtė, Vilnius: Lietuvos dailės muziejus, Vilniaus dailės akademijos leidykla, 2014.

ACKNOWLEDGEMENTS

We would like to extend our gratitude to the Tara bureau artists, their families, private individuals, public collections and archives. We cordially thank our partners, colleagues, friends for their support, cooperation and trust.

Agnė & Monika Jakaitė
Aistė Kisarauskaitė
Aleksandras Kavaliauskas
Alfonsas Andriuškevičius
Alfreda Pilitauskaitė
Algė Gudaitytė
Andrius Kaušinis
Angela Blumen
Anne König
Antanas Šnaras
Audra Baranauskaitė
Clint Soren
Daina Kamarauskienė
Dalia Klajumienė
Dalius Tauraitis
David Bennewith
David Crowley
Deima Žuklytė-Gasperaitienė
Diāna Mikāne
Edgar Walthert
Edvardas Kavarskas
Egidijus Razmus
Eglė Pernarė
Elina Birkehag
Ernestas Parulskis
Eva Körber
Gailė Pranckūnaitė
Giedrė Jankevičiūtė
Gintautė Žemaitytė
Goda Šuminaitė
Grafobal Vilnius
Gregor Taul
HLabs (T/A HanSpringett Ltd)
Ieva Pleikienė (1971–2024)
Iliana Veinberga
Jolana Sýkorová
Jolita Liškevičienė
Jonė Juchnevičiūtė
Julijus Balčikonis
Juozas Galkus
Juozas Gelguda
Jurgis Lietunovas
Jurgita Juodytė
Justas Jurkuvėnas
Justina Zubaitė-Bundzė
Jūratė Tutlytė
Kai Lobjakas
Kęstutis Jonaitis
Kristina Dambrauskienė

Laslo Strong
Laura Petrauskaitė
letterspace.amsterdam
Lithuanian Artists' Association
Lithuanian Central State Archives
Lolita Jablonskienė
Mayra Rodríguez Castro
Margarita Čepukienė
Mari Laanemets
Mariana Bruni
Marija Repšytė
Marius Iršėnas
Marius Žalneravičius
Márk Redele
Meilė Šveikauskienė
Neringa Černiauskaitė
Nida Art Colony
Patryk Hardziej
Paulius Vitkaukas
Petrutė Masiulionytė
Pieter Verbeke
Raimonda Meyer
Rasa Janulevičiūtė
Regina Pranskevičienė
Rene Wawrzkiewicz
Rimantas Dichavičius
Rokas Sutkaitis
Rolandas Rastauskas (1954–2024)
Rolandas Skarbauskas
Rūta Eglinskienė
Sigutė Chlebinskaitė
Shadi Ekman
Šarūnas Nakas
Šarūnas Šlektavičius (1977–2023)
Tadas Baginskas
Tim Ochser
Triin Jerlei
Ugnė El Bouhali
Ugnius Gelguda
Ūla Ambrasaitė
Valdas Vilutis
Vida Valeckaitė
Vilnius Academy of Arts
Violeta Kasevičienė
Virginija Januškevičiūtė
Vladas Lisaitis
Vytautas Kumža
Wooseok Jang
Yana Ustymenko

ABOUT AUTHORS

Deimantė Jasiulevičiūtė is a Lithuanian-born, Amsterdam-based graphic designer. Since graduating from the Gerrit Rietveld Academie in 2018, her focus is on research-based projects with a strong emphasis on collaborative practices within the fields of art and design. In addition to her independent work, Deimantė has collaborated with studios, brands, and publications such as Studio Veronica Ditting, Frame Magazine, Mados Infekcija, HLabs, and others. Her work includes editorial design, visual identities, digital and print matter, as well as various publishing activities in fashion, culture, and technology.

Karolina Jakaitė is a design historian and researcher at the Vilnius Academy of Arts Institute of Art Research. She holds a PhD in Art History, teaches design history courses at Vilnius Academy of Arts and is co-founder of the Design Foundation. Jakaitė is the author of *The Cold War Capsule: Lithuanian Design in London in 1968* and *Antanas Kazakauskas: All is Programmed*. She has curated design exhibitions, and co-curated *Stories of Things. Lithuanian Design 1918–2018, Retrotopia: Design for Socialist Spaces*. Since 2023 she has been working on a research project *Baltic Way: Design Histories from Lithuania, Latvia, and Estonia in the Late 1980s–1990s* (with Triin Jerlei) under the initiative of New European Bauhaus at Vilnius Academy of Arts.

Paul Gangloff is a graphic designer and teacher based in Amsterdam. He works upon commissions as well as through self-initiated research, writings and exhibitions. He has published on subjects such as punkzines (*Punk: Periodical Collection*, Jan Van Eyck Academie, 2012), the typeface Hollandse Mediaeva (*Type & Characters*, self-published, 2012), the Lettrist concept of hypergraphy (*Rules of Hypergraphy*, Extrapool, 2014) and the magazines written, typeset and printed by children on the letterpresses of the Freinet schools (*Freinet Techniques*, Rollo press, 2024). He teaches at the Gerrit Rietveld Academie.

Oriol Cabarrocas is a graphic designer from Barcelona, currently based in Amsterdam. He understands his work as a constant exploration of the social life of images and their symbolic meanings. In 2021, he moved to the Netherlands to pursue a master's degree at Werkplaats Typografie, where he deepened his engagement with the arts and culture sector. He has collaborated with institutions such as the Stedelijk Museum, MACBA, Public Art Abu Dhabi Biennial, and the Miró Foundation, among others. He enjoys working on transversal projects that involve different formalizations and materialities, ranging from printed matter to spatial design.

Zuzana Kostelanská has run her practice for graphic design and typography in Amsterdam since 2018. She holds a BA from the Gerrit Rietveld Academie and a MA from the Werkplaats Typografie. She has worked with artists, art institutions, curators, researchers, and designers, focusing mainly on identities, printed matter, archives, and digital works. She works with and for de Appel, Warehouse, Woonhuis de Ateliers, Manifesta Biennial, Public Art Abu Dhabi Biennial, Valiz, Sternberg Press, Casco Art Institute, and Onomatopee Projects, among others. She is currently a tutor at the MA Critical Fashion Practices at ArtEZ Arnhem.

COLOPHON

Tara: Then and Now, Here and There
Archives and Practices of the Experimental
Design Bureau in Vilnius 1960s–1980s

Editors:
Karolina Jakaitė, Deimantė Jasiulevičiūtė

Texts:
Karolina Jakaitė

Reviewed by:
Prof. dr. Lolita Jablonskienė
(Vilnius Academy of Arts)
Prof. dr. (hp) Giedrė Jankevičiūtė
(Lithuanian Institute for Culture Research)

Additional essay:
Paul Gangloff

English language editing:
Tania Theodorou

Translations from Lithuanian:
Laima Bezginaitė

Graphic design:
Zuzana Kostelanská with Oriol Cabarrocas

Editorial design:
Deimantė Jasiulevičiūtė

Proofreading:
Laima Bezginaitė, Anne König

Image correction:
ScanColor Reprostudio GmbH Leipzig

Printing and binding:
Druckhaus Sportflieger Berlin

Typefaces:
Univers, FX Matrix

Paper:
Kraftkarton, Munken Print White 1.8,
Maxi Gloss

Front cover:
Fragment from the chocolate box *Kaip gi
gražus gražus rūtelių darželis* (What a lovely,
lovely rue garden) by Monika Jonaitienė,
1970s, personal archive of Kęstutis Jonaitis

Distribution:

Germany, Austria: GVA, Gemeinsame
    Verlagsauslieferung Göttingen
    GmbH&Co. KG,
    www.gva-verlage.de
Switzerland: AVA Verlagsauslieferung AG,
    www.ava.ch
France, Belgium: Interart Paris, www.interart.fr
UK: Central Books Ltd,
    ww.centralbooks.com
USA, Canada, Central and South America,
    Africa: ARTBOOK/ D.A.P.,
    www.artbook.com
Japan: twelvebooks,
    www.twelve-books.com
South Korea: The Book Society,
    www.thebooksociety.org
Australia, New Zealand:
    Perimeter Distribution,
    www.perimeterdistribution.com
Baltic distribution:
    Lithuanian publisher LAPAS,
    www.leidyklalapas.lt

Financed by:
Stimuleringsfonds Creatieve Industrie
Lithuanian Council for Culture
"Grafobal Vilnius" Lithuanian and Slovak Public LLC

Translation financed by:
Lithuanian Culture Institute

Institutional partners:
Design Foundation (www.dizainofondas.lt)
Vilnius Academy of Arts
LAPAS Publishing House
SODAS 2123

Published by:
Spector Books
Harkortstraße 10
04107 Leipzig
www.spectorbooks.com

© 2025, authors, editors and Spector Books, Leipzig

First edition: 2025

Printed in the EU

ISBN 978-3-95905-860-5

creative
industries
fund NL

LITHUANIAN
COUNCIL FOR
CULTURE

grafobal
VILNIUS

LCI Lithuanian
Culture
Institute

Vilnius
Academy
of Arts

DESIGN
FOUNDATION

LAPAS

Glossary

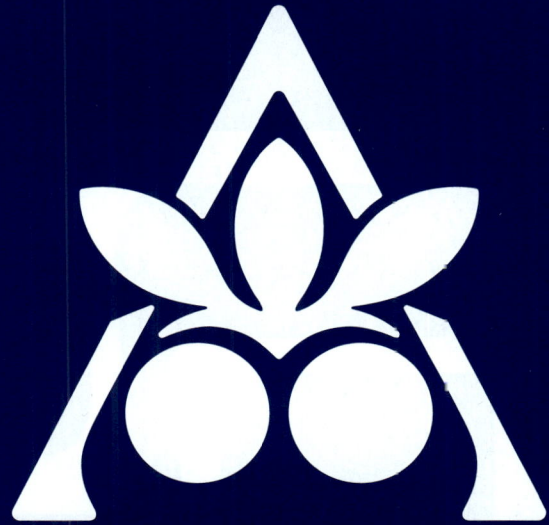

[A] is for abstract advertising

The artists who worked in the Tara bureau often advertised products they never had the opportunity to see. Even when these products were produced – often in small quantities – they did not necessarily make it to shops. Each time, the artists had to create new and aesthetically stylish packaging for products that, in most cases, remained one-off examples exhibited at specialised or foreign exhibitions. Even if these products did reach shops, they were not easily available to ordinary customers and could not be chosen based on aesthetics or flavour preferences. The artists would design striking, artistic logos for companies that, unfortunately, operated under the constraints of the Soviet system and rarely made real use of those logos. The abstraction of this kind of advertising was also evident in the fact that, in many instances, the advertisement was not for a specific product or brand of a particular manufacturer, but simply for an object or foodstuffs. Additionally, multiple visual identities were sometimes created for the same product. Design artists worked in a hermetic bubble, disconnected from most of the aspects that ordinary design requires. They did not need to reflect on the product, consult with the client, think about sales, the needs of consumers, or profitability. On the other hand, this sometimes afforded them more freedom of expression, and the outcome they desired was of high artistic quality, aesthetic taste, and importantly for them, was characterised by a distinctive author's style.

[A] is for artist-constructors

Most of the artists held degrees in fields such as graphic art, scenography, fresco-mosaic, ceramics, painting, textiles, and industrial art. The latter specialisation was introduced in 1961 at the then LSSR State Art Institute (now Vilnius Academy of Arts) and had since evolved into design studies, though the names of the specialisations did not include this English word. The job title "artist-constructor" was used for designers across various fields. The second keyword in this phrase – constructor – is important because the artists working at the Tara bureau also had to develop constructing solutions for new packaging projects, such as creating different shapes of boxes, and packaging for various branded products. Another specific term from the Soviet era worth mentioning is "formgiver" or "decorator" (in Lithuanian *apipavidalintojas*) which placed more emphasis on form rather than function, and on exterior decor rather than problem-solving. The several dozen artists working at the Tara bureau particularly appreciated the "free schedule." Although each had their own desk there, they would typically come in only a few times a month to pick up commissions and attend Art Council, Artistic Committee meetings. After becoming employees of the Tara bureau, artists essentially learned "on the job," studying foreign examples from magazines and specialised books. However, they were not involved in the subsequent processes of bringing the project to production or market release. Usually, these artists chose one area of graphic design as their main, preferred field, and then aimed to excel in it. Not everyone loved this work – some saw it as *khaltura* (a meaningless side job to earn money), while for others, it became a place for lifelong dedication and professional fulfilment.

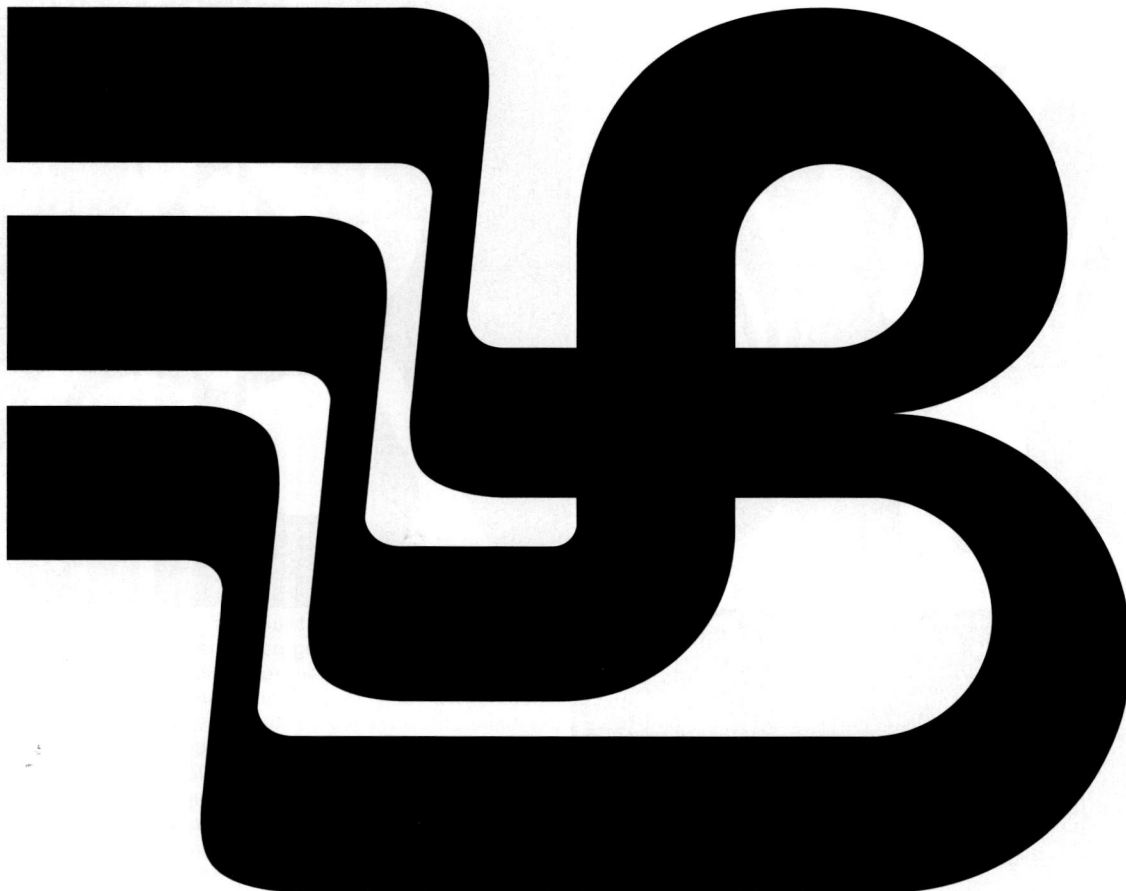

[C] is for cosmic

Tara's packaging and some of their advertisements reflect on one of the leading themes of the 1960s – space, which was inspired by real space flights and the Cold War race. This theme was supported and promoted by the Soviet propaganda, but space also became the object of more abstract dreams and visions, as an escape from the constrained reality of the Soviet era. The artists of the Tara bureau also dreamt of space while drawing the characters and their journeys in the visionary cartoon "Tariukas on the Moon".

54 66 240–241 257

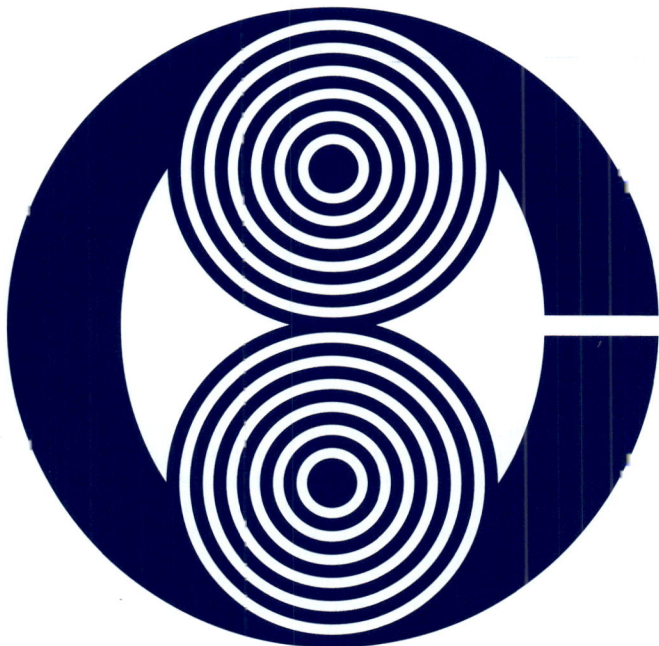

[C] is for censorship

During the Soviet era, all press and publishing processes were strictly controlled. Before printing, every Tara brochure or promotional catalogue had to be approved by *Glavlit* (Main Administration for Literary and Publishing Affairs) or *Gorlit*. In the world of images and signs, special care was taken to avoid any allusion to the symbolism of Christianity or inter-war statehood. Knowing the principles of censorship, the artists had mastered not only the so-called Aesopian language, but also the mechanisms of self-censorship. For instance, members of the Tara bureau knew from experience that it was dangerous to use the motif of an apple, because for any depiction of it a variation of three colours – yellow, green or red – would have to be used, which would be associated with the flag of independent Lithuania. Sometimes problems occurred with a photograph of church steeples, used for decorating a chocolate box, or even a motif of arms open wide in which the censors would discern the shape of a cross. Export publications offered much more freedom, allowing the use of not only nude photographs, which would have been censored in the local context, but also of bolder artistic language.

64 81 191 196 229

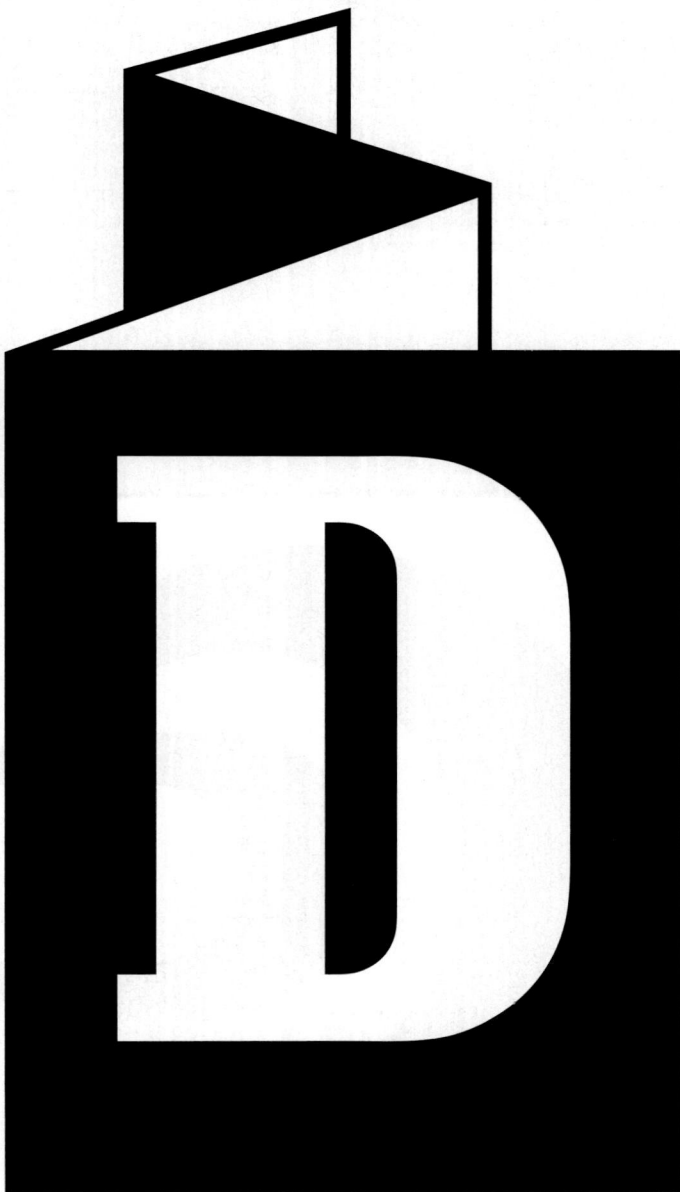

[D] is for design

In the Tara bureau's environment, the now common word "design" was replaced by several other words: industrial graphics, artistic constructing or technical aesthetics. This way the Soviets aimed to avoid using the English word "design" in order not to be identified with the capitalist system that had given birth to this phenomenon. However, both the accounts of the authors who had worked during that period and the surviving sources, show that the terms "design" and "designer" were certainly known to professionals. Some of Tara's artists were graduates of the newly emerging design specialisations of industrial art or industrial graphics, who worked while drawing inspiration from foreign magazines, found design solutions intuitively or through practice, and in time had acquired a certain professional mastery. However, the existence of these activities between technology and aesthetics, between industry and art shaped certain clefts which in turn influenced numerous discrepancies and paradoxes. At the time, the Tara bureau belonged to the Ministry of Local Industry of the LSSR, so the bureau's artistic activities and exhibition processes were somewhat detached from the field of art and architecture, which pushed the design creators into a certain periphery. The launch of their projects into production and later into commerce depended on completely different, highly bureaucratic links of the system, which under the conditions of planned economy did not act according to the principles of design and depended heavily on the proactivity, and more often than not, inactivity, of many institutions, their policies, and their leaders. From the consumer's point of view, the word *deficit* would have been more appropriate than *design* for reflecting the processes of the time, because everything was scarce, consumers could not choose based on aesthetic qualities, they had to wait in long queues, they had to have a *blat* (use of informal contacts and personal networks to obtain goods and services) and, eventually, to settle for low-quality products.

29–33   98–103   223   240–241

This was one of the key words in the first title of the Tara bureau – Experimental Package Design Bureau – and it had remained in the longest-used title – Experimental Artistic Constructing Bureau. In the Soviet context, this word implied that an establishment with such a title would have more possibilities and greater financial capacity. In terms of creative processes, the creators of the Tara bureau were constantly experimenting: they took on commissions without knowing the exact task and used intuition, improvisation, and a variety of creative methodologies, while constantly being subject to variable conditions. Sometimes they would submit a dozen or even several dozen sketches for a single project. To sum up, in the context of the Soviet era graphic design and the bureau itself were like an experiment, and some of its goals and especially the artists' visionary projects remained unfulfilled.

29–33 36–37 60 82 101 106 116–117 170–171 174–177 248–249

[E] is for export

From the very beginning, the objectives for the establishment of the Tara bureau were programmed for export. The Soviet Union invested heavily for propaganda purposes in the presentation of Soviet pavilions at world exhibitions as well as in the presentation of various industrial achievements at industrial trade fairs. One of the first presentations by the Tara bureau took place at the 1966 Leipzig fair, and the bureau played a particularly important role in shaping the overall image and layout of the promotional publications for the Soviet exhibition in London in 1968. Among other export exhibitions, mention should be made of the Zagreb trade fair, the presentation of Soviet Lithuania at the Litauer-70 in Erfurt, and the trade fairs held in Copenhagen in 1974 or Paris in 1977. Packaging designs and promotional publications intended for export were printed in the highest possible quality using improved quality inks, gold plating, and screen-printing techniques. Sometimes they were even printed in foreign printing houses. Export publications were printed in several languages: in Russian Cyrillic and in the language of the foreign country where the exhibition was to be held. Again, this was a paradox: the world was divided by the Iron Curtain, but the projects created by the artists of the Tara bureau traveled, albeit along somewhat closed roads. The artists would not get the chance to attend those export exhibitions, but in their personal catalogues of their works, they would mention the names of the exhibitions and the countries where their projects were presented.

12 20 22 142 174–175 178–181 184 186 190–212

[F] is for façade

Much of the Tara bureau's production contained a lot of façade culture and the corresponding fakeness, coercion, lies and uncertainty, especially in those export examples. Everything was done just for the sake of the "show", displaying "the best and highest quality products" that were not really available to common people. This fake demonstrative façade is very clearly revealed in the entries of the Visitors' Books. This façade also existed in the bureau's environment: it is well reflected in the photograph of the bureau, where the artists had to pose in identical white jackets that they in fact never wore. And in everyday life, behind this façade, they had to face absurdity and hopelessness, as is well illustrated by the photograph preserved in the archive of Vladas Lisaitis, where he is frustrated, flouncing next to a factory with sheets of design proposals that need to be coordinated.

19   36–37   41   42   59   64   100–101   105   186   190   209   242

[F] is for fear

Fear is the feeling that pierces the entire Cold War period, from arms races and military conflicts to the atomic bomb threat. The atmosphere of fear and mistrust was also familiar to the creators of the Tara bureau, who had experienced the terrible fear of exile, threats of being reported to the KGB; fear not only for themselves, but also for their loved ones. Finally, there were fears and uncertainties that accompanied the creative processes: the fear of saying too much, the fear of being misunderstood, or simply of being criticized and ridiculed at the Artistic Committee meetings.

41   180   190   250–251

[G] is for graphics

The Tara bureau was staffed mainly by artists who had graduated from the graphics speciality, some of them – from the industrial graphics speciality that was introduced in the 1960s. The majority, however, were simply graphic artists who had worked not only at the Tara bureau, but also in the fields of book illustration and print making. As professional graphic artists, for some of the graphic design projects they sometimes used fragments of their original sheets created using etching or woodcutting techniques. Looking at some of the abstract examples of the Tara bureau's packaging, it seems that the chocolate box covers or abstract compositions used in factory brochures could easily be framed and exhibited as graphic prints on their own right.

[G] is for gray

It is a poetic keyword that comes from a quote by Kestutis Gvalda: "If not for the Tara bureau, everything would have remained gray". The reality of the Soviet era was full of grayness, boredom, and lack of love. This grayness can also be understood directly: most of the surviving photographs of the Tara bureau are black and white, and the illustrations of the primary sources are only in shades of gray. This is also related to the printing processes, where artists were simply afraid to see the printed works because of colour changes, grayness, darkening and poor paper quality. However, looking at the newly reproduced brightly coloured Tara boxes now, we can try to imagine the meaning of Gvalda's words, which together with the intentions of other artists, had a programmed aspiration to brighten up that gray everyday life. This is evidenced by the Tara bureau's chocolate boxes and other prettier packaging which to this day have been preserved by ordinary people for storing letters, threads, buttons, and stationery.

[H] is for handmade
All of Tara bureau's creative processes included a lot of manual work – cutting and then gluing in letters, signs, digits, or illustrations.
In their stories, the artists of the Tara bureau emphasized the difficult conditions of the manufacturing processes, which took a lot of time, as even small corrections required infinite patience. The glue that was used for creating collage advertising compositions was of extremely poor quality, because better ones were not available.

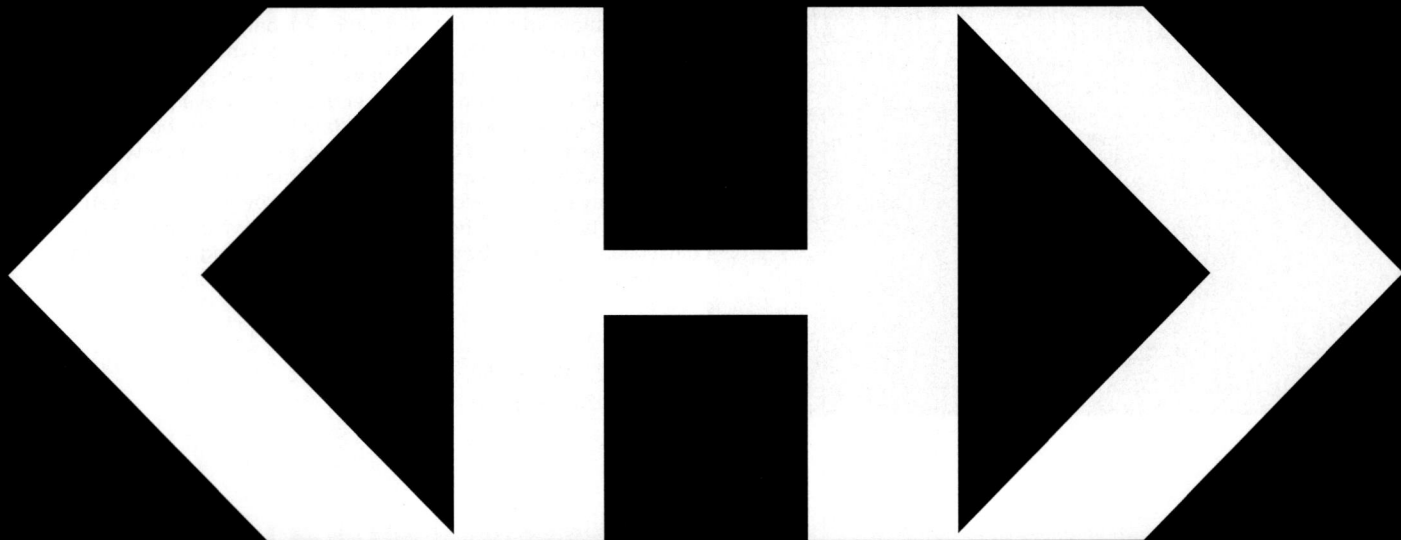

[I] is for ideology

During the Soviet era, when everything was controlled by the ideologized regime under compulsory orders from Moscow, various ministries and councils, the artists working at the Tara bureau also had to carry out ideological commissions. In general, there was definitely less ideological content in advertising, however even the titles or symbolism used on some of the seemingly innocent covers of chocolate boxes betray the ideologized, sometimes abstracted themes – *Peace*, *Friendship*, *Unity*, *Jubilee*. On the other hand, the capitalist principles of graphic design were essentially incompatible with the socialist communist ideology, according to which everyone should be equal, there should be no competition, and everything should be freely available to everyone. As we know, in reality this did not work, and there were even reversed examples of this distorted reality, where the most exclusive products were only available to party leaders and their family members or were obtained through a *blat* (use of informal contacts and personal networks to obtain goods and services).

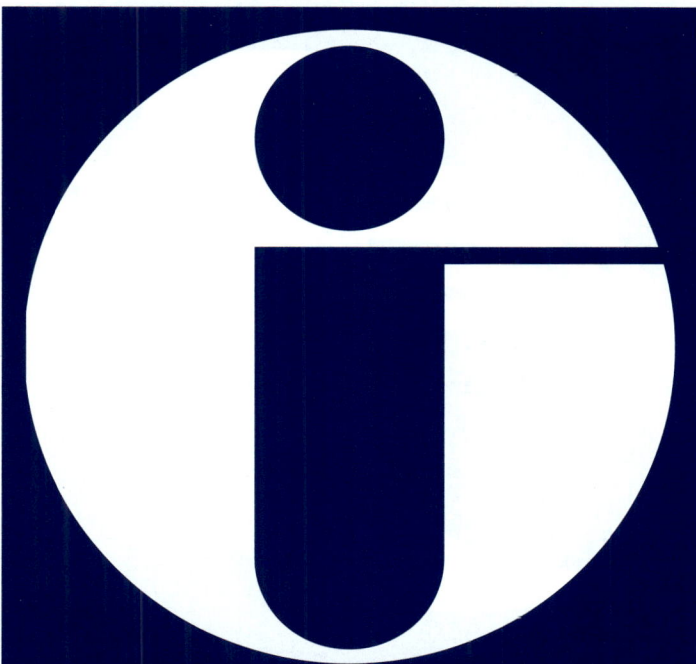

[I] is for imaginary design

The Tara bureau's creators lived and worked in a slightly closed, more imaginary world. They worked for these implied clients without seeing the products they were advertising while flipping through foreign magazines. They had to use a lot of imagination in the whole process. And now, as those singular, unrealised examples are discovered, an unfulfilled, but rather imaginary design history is being (re)created or reconstructed.

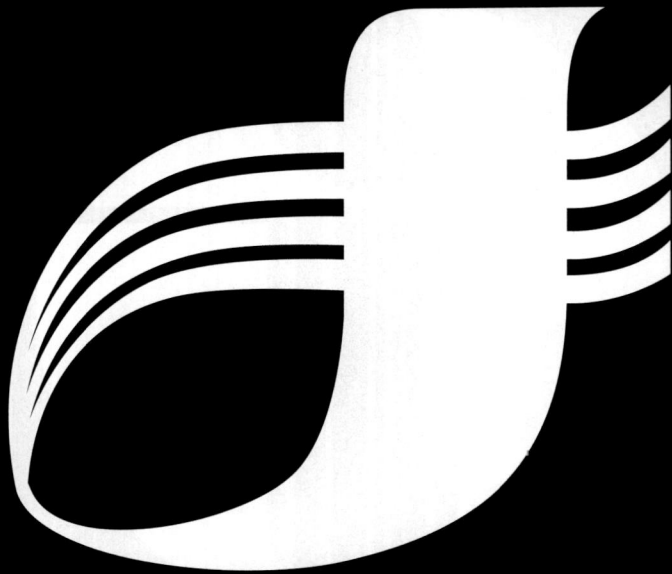

[J] is for jokes

Catalogues and brochures produced by Tara's artists reveal many humorous pictures and funny characters, as if from a comic book. According to the artists' own testimonies, they were so affected by the absurdity of the Soviet reality and the constant demands to insert all kinds of cliché details, slogans and staged images, that all they could do was look at it ironically, with a smile and humour, or "just try to laugh and cheer up others". On the other hand, those funny drawings also reveal certain naivety, professional fatigue, disbelief, or even helplessness.

[J] is for jury

Every project created in the bureau had to be considered by the Artistic Committee before it could be published, produced and circulated. The Artistic Committee's objective was to judge packaging, label, brochure, poster, catalogue and other projects on the basis of 5 key criteria, among them – the appropriateness of the layout and the use of materials, the functionality of the form, graphic composition, advertising impact, the appropriateness of the font, and the correspondence of the form and the graphic design to the product. However, this proposal, like many others, was mostly employed at a more theoretical level. The members of the Artistic Committee, among which there were representatives of various ministries, industry, trade and art fields, tended to judge the designs created by the artists based on their level of expertise, artistic inclinations, and taste. At different times, well-known Lithuanian artists have "worked" at the bureau's Artistic Committee, but in the field of art, graphic design commissions remained more of a "marginal" area, which hardly gained any recognition as an art phenomenon.

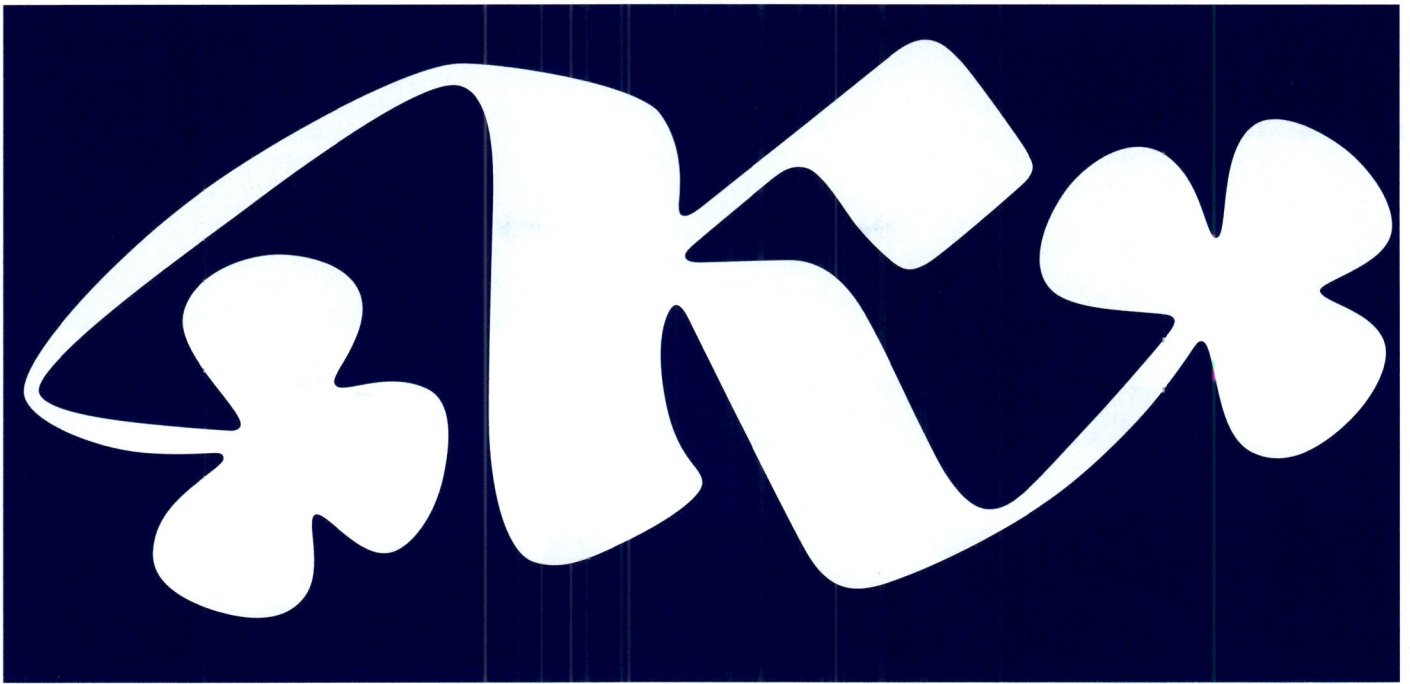

[K] is for kitsch

The Soviet environment was full of awkwardness, ugliness and tastelessness. During the Khrushchev Thaw period, efforts were made to oppose this and to aesthetically affect the surrounding environment. The Tara bureau was one of such examples. The bureau's artists used minimalist solutions for mitigating the tastelessness of the Stalinist period, as if to purge themselves of cluttered compositions and overcrowded fonts. However, some of the examples by the Tara bureau also contain a certain eclecticism: staged photographs, strange colour solutions, incoherent compositions. This was related to numerous corrections that took place during the creative process, when it was necessary to include certain obligatory segments to satisfy the often strange requirements of the Artistic Committee, and to correct the same project many times. In such cases, works sometimes came dangerously close to becoming kitsch. Kitsch can also be a form of protest, but it is less characteristic to the examples by the Tara bureau.

Given the context of the Soviet era and the threat of Russification, the Lithuanian language and its use in posters, labels, or packaging was very important to the Tara bureau's artists. They also made considerable personal efforts to prevent the disappearance of inscriptions in Lithuanian, which had to be accompanied by obligatory Russian translations. This is evident in one of the quotes by Kęstutis Gvalda: "*If there is no Lithuanian language, I am refusing the order*". When designing labels and embedding the names of new products, the artists paid a lot of attention to the inscriptions of Lithuanian place names and authentic historical names, which sometimes contain references to the inter-war period and the glorious history of the past. These Lithuanian names and titles were the expression of their love for Lithuania, its nature and history and the signs of modern Lithuanian identity.

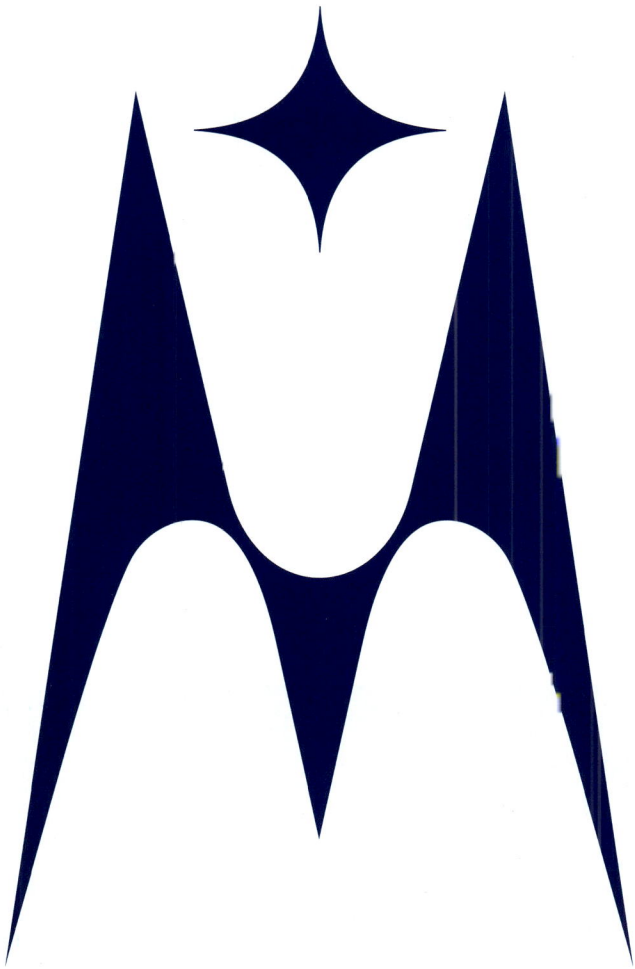

[M] is for modernisation

This is one of the key words of the Soviet era, inseparable from the Khrushchev Thaw and the modernisation processes related to industrialisation, scientific and technical progress. It also marks the processes of modernisation in art, architecture, and design. The artists of the Tara bureau sought to modernise labels, brand marks and packaging in order to move away from the prevailing naturalistic drawing compositions, intricate fonts, and overcrowded logos. This led to minimalist solutions, stylised drawing elements, the introduction of photographs, functional colour codes, simplified fonts and decorative elements.

[M] is for machinery

Sovietisation also took place at the industrial level – there were the Five-Year Plans and the socialist race. It is estimated that around one million people of Soviet Lithuania worked in factories. The Vilnius branch of the Institute of Technical Aesthetics, which had been in operation since 1966, and its designers also specialised in the machine industry, particularly in the design of machine tools. Therefore, the promotional brochures published by the Tara bureau contain a lot of industrial images, depictions of people working, photographs of machinery, and graphic design that was influenced by all of this.

[N] is for national

A famous slogan of the era was "Socialist in content, national in form", which suggested that national form was suitable for conveying socialist ideals. Souvenirs were usually made of local materials and employed traditional national ornaments. Nationalism was imposed from above and was meant to mask and soften the imperial ambitions of the totalitarian state, however, it should be noted that in some cases it encouraged the search for the roots of Lithuanianness. The Tara bureau's artists were genuinely inspired by authentic examples of Lithuanian folk art – fairy tales, songs, folk writings – and in their graphic design projects they looked for a pastiche of folklore and modern interpretations of it.

61 70-71 80-81 82 88-89 181-183 185 192-193

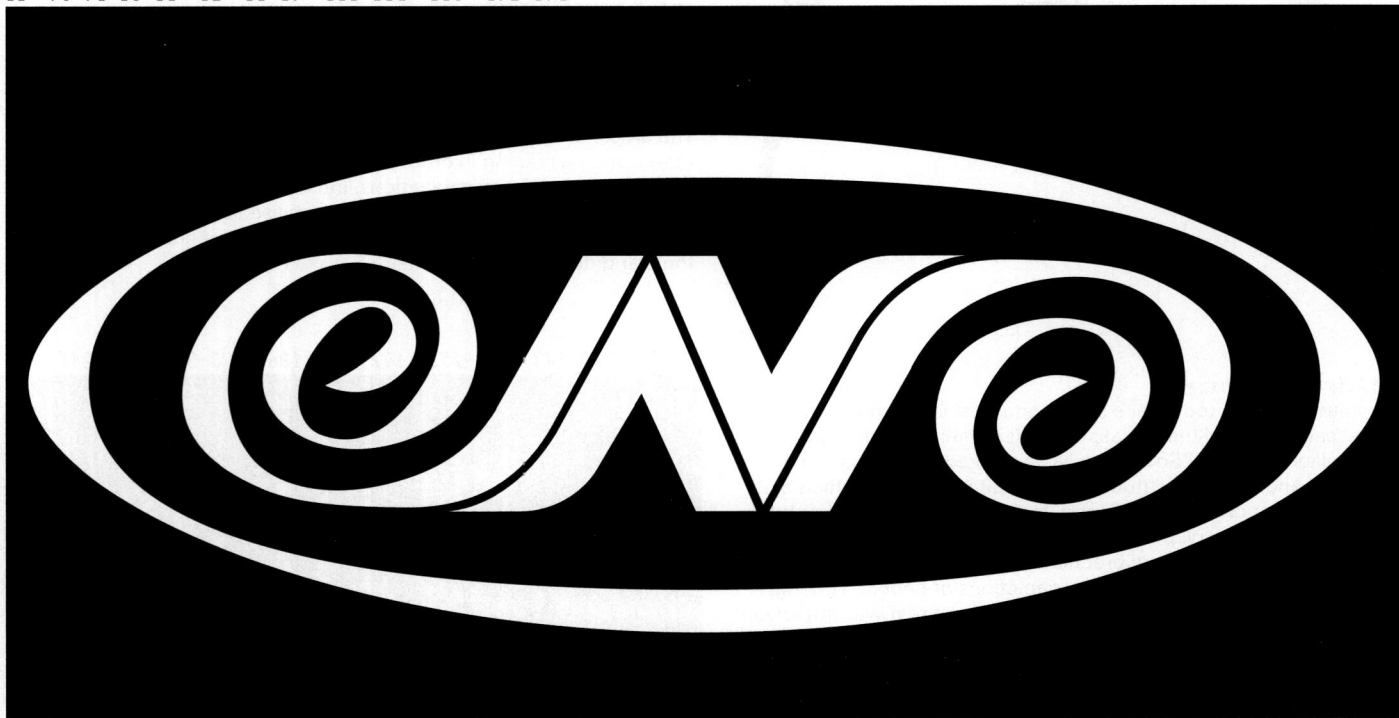

[O] is for Op-Art

In the late 1960s, the creators of the Tara bureau, just like other artists of the time, were overwhelmed by the optical art fashion, which circulated mainly through foreign magazines and their citations in the local press. Artists were fascinated by the play of sharp, regular geometric shapes, sometimes irritating to the eye, yet attractive in its unexpected movement. According to the testimonies of the Tara bureau's artists, some of them simply immersed themselves in drawing Op-Art patterns. For some, it offered a certain detachment from the depressing reality, a form of creative meditation, and sometimes an opportunity to distance themselves from the dictate of ideological themes. It was also related to practical considerations – the choice of repetitive motifs ensured less worrying about compositional inaccuracies during the printing process.

[P] is for play

Playfulness was one of the most important creative strategies of the Tara bureau's artists. Playfulness is illustrated by their artistic ambitions in providing so many different proposals for the same product or object. Playfulness was necessary for survival, because the surrounding environment was full of standardisation, various instructions, rules and displays of power, so one had to think of ways to play around these prohibitions and limitations or interpret them creatively. The Tara bureau was also directly related to toys and games: its artists designed very characterful packaging for toys and many catalogues promoting them. Some of the children's sweets packaging was designed to have a second function: once the sweets were eaten, the packaging could be used as a toy. A creative solution for a society of scarcity or, in today's terms, an example of sustainability. Later on, the scope of activities of the Tara bureau expanded and the artists themselves started designing, constructing and drawing various games, mostly lotto and board games.

[P] is for propaganda

The Tara bureau was one of the tools of Soviet propaganda. The bureau's artists could not avoid the obligatory propaganda themes: they had to create posters for Lenin, design chocolate boxes for his 100th birthday celebration, commemorate the communist October holidays or the anniversaries of the Soviet occupation. The texts embedded in advertising publications contain more obligatory propaganda signs, various rallying cries, and slogans.

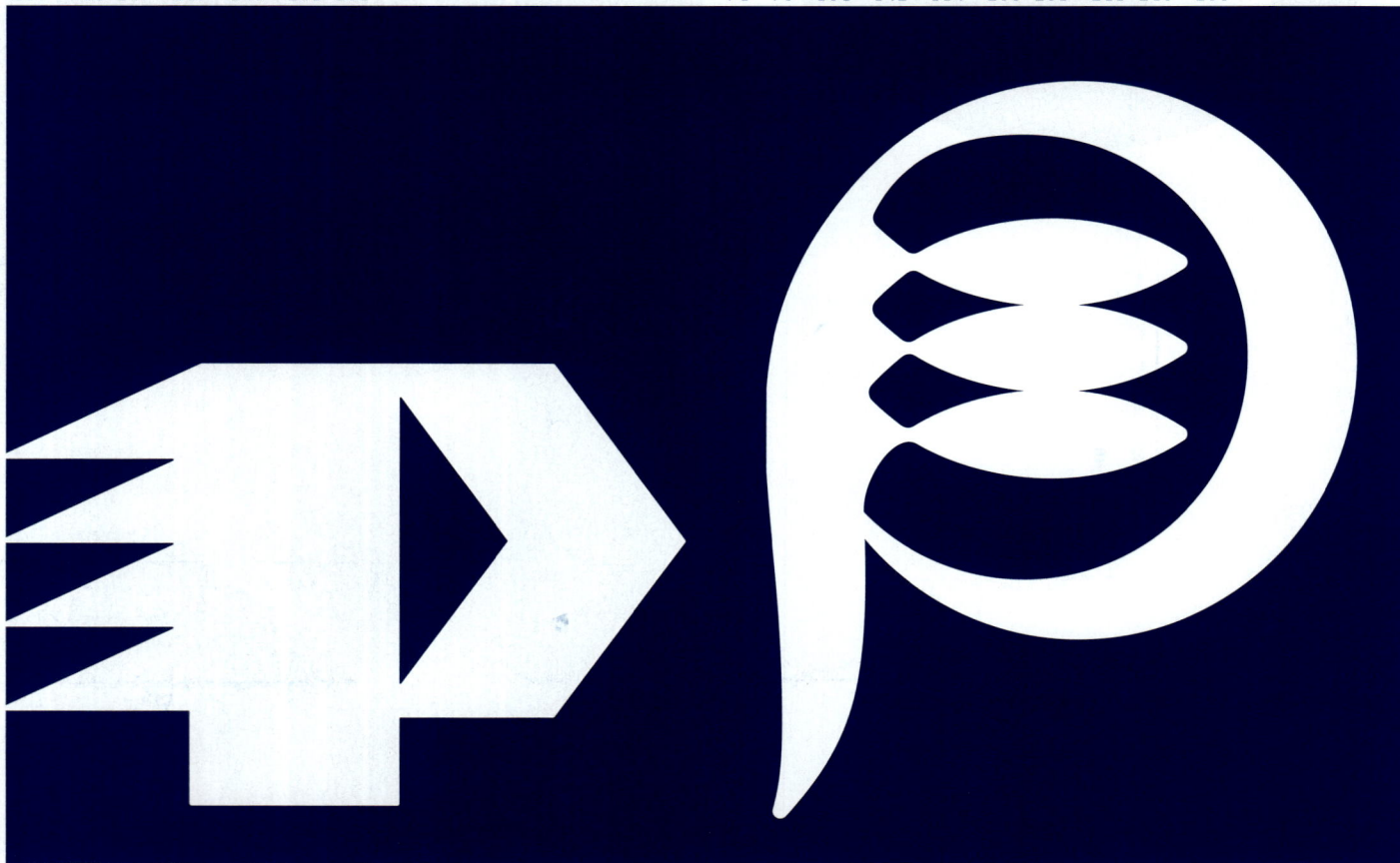

The whole Soviet system was full of non-quality: defects, clichés, out-of-placeness, and a general lack of love for people. It was, again, a paradox: when artists undertook a project they liked, they would devote a great deal of attention and effort to achieving artistic quality, only to be sorely disappointed by the constant shortage of materials, low-quality printing, wrong colours, or even an idea or composition radically changed from the original, without their knowledge.

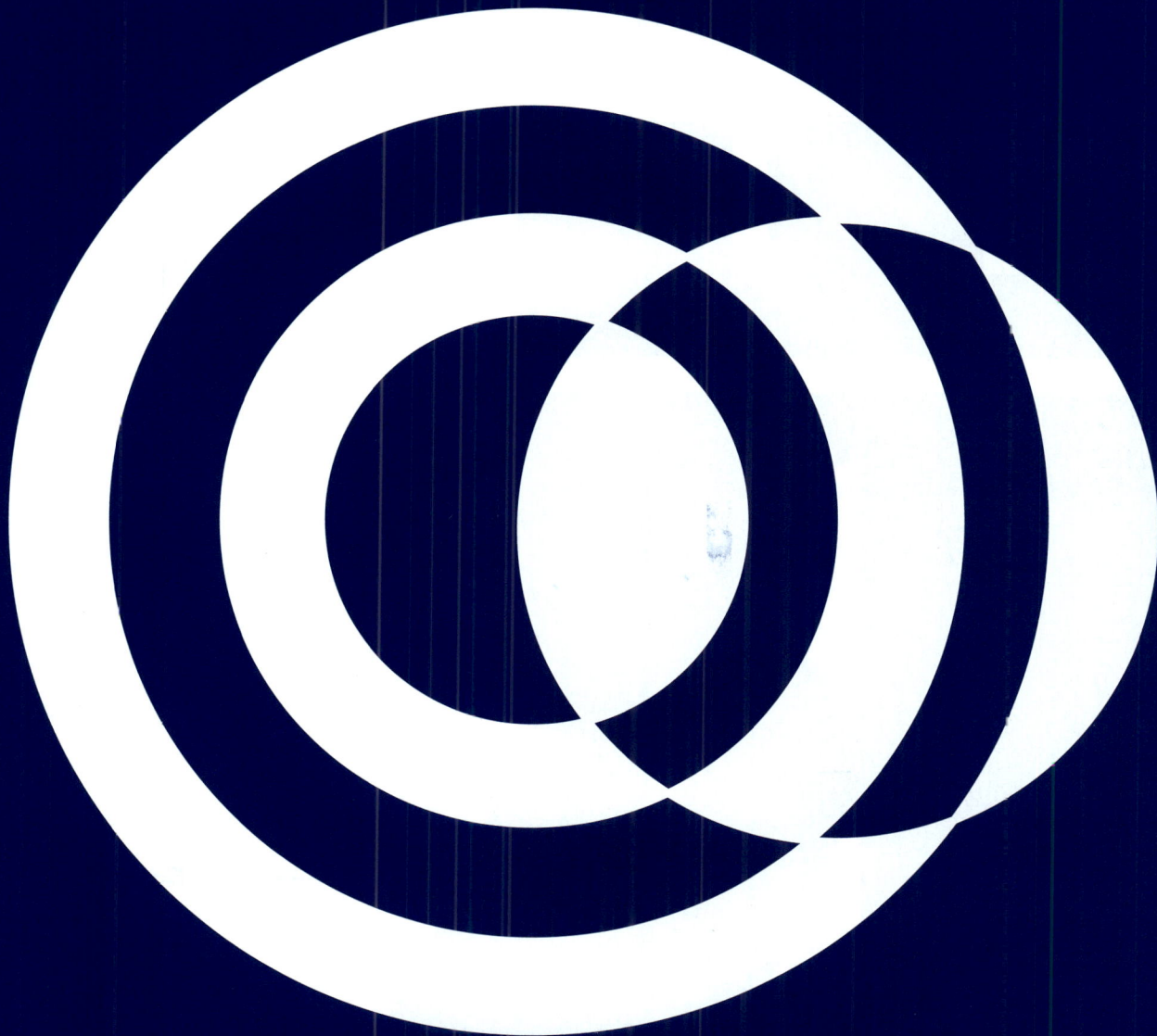

[R] is for Reklama

It is one of the key words of the time and of the Tara bureau environment, used in the Lithuanian language, but at the same time equally readable and writeable in other languages, e. g. Polish *Reklama*, Latvian *Reklāma*, Estonian *Reklaam,* in Czech *Reklama*, as well as in Russian, but in Cyrillic. The word is also associated with the bureau's specialised annual magazine *Tara. Reklama* (Packaging. Advertising), the first issues of which were published in Lithuanian, followed by a bilingual version with Russian included, until finally the last issues were published only in Russian. However, in a broader sense advertising is related to numerous paradoxes and raises questions such as whether advertising was necessary at all when the goods themselves were in short supply. In this context, an attempt was made to emphasise the more educational and enlightening function of advertising.

[S] is for slow

From a nowadays perspective, this slowness might seem like a certain privilege: artists could have a relatively long time to explore and sketch creative ideas. For instance, it was possible to spend a whole month on a single poster and to immerse oneself in the creative process. However, this slowness in other stages also had very negative consequences. Various commissions, requirements, rulings and coordination processes took very long, sometimes years, until the product itself or the promotional poster or advertising message simply became irrelevant; also, the demands from above to improve or adjust something could radically change the original creative idea.

40   43–47   78–79   116–117 244

[S] is for Soviet

There is a lot of Sovietness in Tara bureau's processes and artifacts. It manifests itself in different forms and codes. The façade of Sovietness is most easily identified through various Soviet paraphernalia and obligatory inscriptions, while the procedural Sovietness is evident in displays of power and control. The more hidden manifestations of Sovietness can be traced in more general processes such as paradoxes and absurd limitations, where so much effort was devoted for creation of a new product only for it to remain a sole exhibit (for the sake of reporting and showing). It also manifested in the constant discrepancy and wastefulness: a lot of brochures were produced, so from the outside it might have seemed that everything functioned just like in the capitalist world, but all of this was a mere illusion. So many articles were written, so many instructions were issued, but only some of them really worked. Today we understand that design is supposed to solve problems, whereas it seems that extra problems were created in order to complicate the whole process.

64   134–135   154   186   190   209   228–229   231–235 238   245   250

[T] is for typography

Typography was one of the weakest areas of graphic design. In the Soviet era there was a very poor choice of typefaces, which had to do with the control of the press. Handwritten typefaces required lots of scrupulousness. That was how the artists of the time came up with the idea of photographing alphabets, cutting and pasting them. For this, they mainly used various foreign typefaces, which they photocopied from specialised books and then pasted letter by letter, matching the Lithuanian diacritics. Everyone switched to cutting and scissor work. Even more problematic were the requirements to duplicate advertising texts in Russian. However, for some product names, the artists chose the more difficult and original way – to draw an original font. The drawn typefaces of some advertisement posters are particularly inventive and sometimes elaborate, featuring flashes of psychedelic art and popart or their influences.

62-63 66-67 76-77 92 144 148-149 154 170 248

[U] is for utopia

For the most part, graphic design remained part of a cultural façade, one of many promises ("Products will be wonderful ', "Our products must be the best in the world") that the system was never able to fulfil. The more interesting graphic design projects rarely made it into production and were instead reserved for representational purposes and only showcased abroad. However, the creators of the Tara bureau had to live in this world of utopian promises thus falling into a kind of closed world trap.

[V] is for visionary

Quite a lot of Tara bureau's projects remained unrealised, and those were usually the most interesting, the most daring, and the most experimental ideas. In some cases, the artists of the Tara bureau acted as a team of visionaries; for example, Vladas Lisaitis had created branded uniforms for different sports, but they remained only in sketches. The story of "Tariukas on the Moon" also sounds visionary: they had begun drawing cartoon characters who travel to promote Tara's projects not only around the world, but also on the Moon. On the other hand, living under surrouncing oppression required those visionary projects, immersion into which helped to make reality a little more distant.

29-33 42 106 257 258

[V] is for visitors' reviews

The Soviet system did not have the by now familiar, chain of design product development in which problem identification, user needs, and feedback play a very important role. But even in that reality, soaked in propaganda promises, Visitors' Books existed, reflecting yet another façade. It is likely that some of their records could have been staged, perhaps censored, but there still were some authentic testimonies. Now the mostly contradictory visitor responses open up new interpretations of the field allowing us to see the paradoxical aspects of graphic design.

93-97 259

[W] is for women-designers

The gender distribution among the Tara bureau's artists was more or less even. There were periods when there were more women working at the bureau, thus forming a more female-dominated team. For example, the catalogue published on the occasion of the first exhibition in 1967 presented the biographies of 22 women artists out of the 39 artists who took part in the exhibition. The interview testimonies also revealed certain stereotypical attitudes, such as the categorisation of genres or themes into more feminine or more masculine tasks. For instance, there was this notion that chocolate and confectionery packaging is a more feminine task, requiring more scrutiny and attention, and also more suitable to women because of their "sweetness and beauty".

[W] is for Western

The Cold War was a period marked by the tensions of a divided world and a competition between two different ideological systems. The enormous economic and technological backwardness of the Soviet Union turned into a constant attempt to catch up with and overtake the West. From its very foundation, the Tara bureau focused on Western models. The structure of the bureau was decided based on a case study in Finland. The Iron Curtain made it impossible for artist-constructors to travel to Western countries, it was hard to get permits even for traveling to socialist countries, so Poland to them was like a window to the West. The Tara bureau's creators highly appreciated the poster art biennials held there, and kept Polish publications such as *Projekt*, *Sztuka*, *Szpilki*, *Ty i ja* in their home libraries. They also appreciated Czech graphic design, subscribed to *Výtvarné umění*, *Domov*, *Dikobraz* or *Dievča*, and tried to get into Brno International Biennial of Graphic Design. The bureau's specialised library also offered an opportunity to learn about Western graphic design trends from French, German, Dutch or Swiss magazines. The principle of "creating the way the world did" was the artists' guiding principle, so the analyses of individual works can also reveal examples of borrowed forms or appropriation. Some of the Tara bureau's projects, advertisements and especially the minimalist logos looked very Western and non-Soviet. Here again, there was a certain trap, as this way the artists contributed to the image of the Soviet West, which was strongly promoted at export exhibitions, because it was beneficial to the Moscow regime and the local nomenclature.

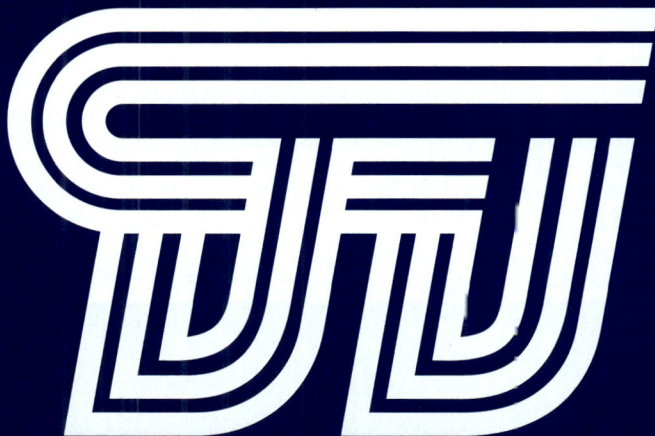

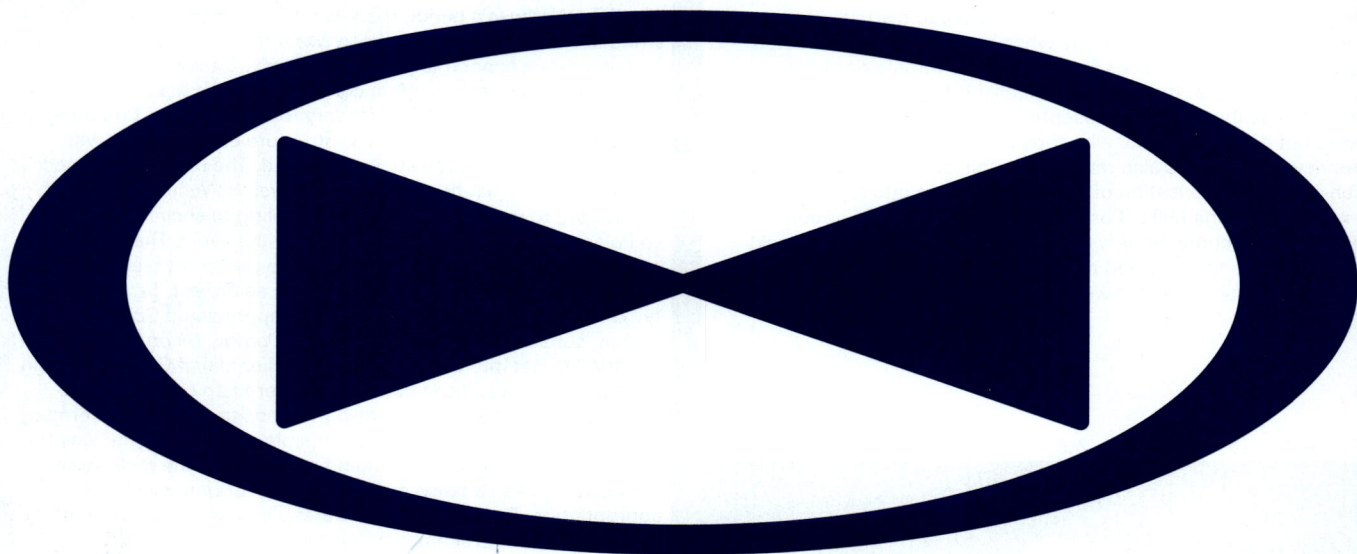

[X] is for unknown
In most cases graphic design was anonymous work, but the exhibitions and the first catalogues prepared by the Tara bureau show the artists' own desire to record authorship in this field of work by providing biographies, portrait photographs and lists of works with their titles. Therefore, one of the goals of this research was to identify the authors of the presented examples by using all possible archival sources, in addition to the interview method. However, it is necessary to admit that many names remain unknown and unsigned projects make authorship difficult or even impossible to trace back decades later.

126–129 136–139 210

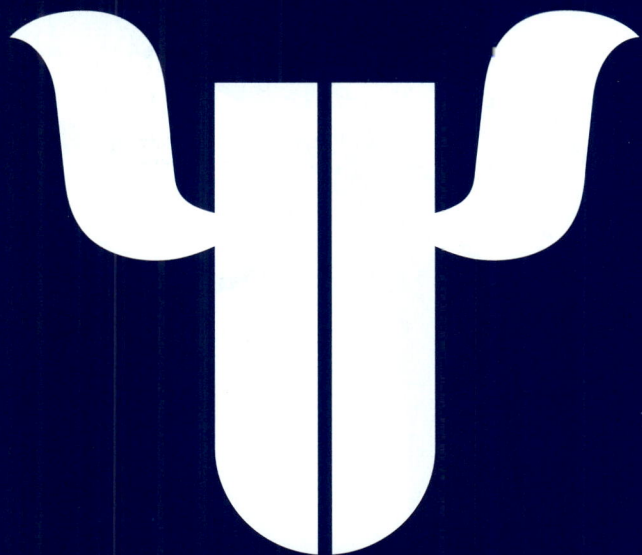

[Y] is for youth

During the Soviet era, the cult of youth was glorified and, according to the propaganda of optimistic reality, a society of hard-working, healthy, beautiful and otherwise idealised people was being created. Everything was directed towards a socialist, bright future. The themes of old age, sadness and suffering were discouraged and almost not tolerated, and any depiction of otherness, strangeness or deviation from the norm (disability, ugliness, neglect) was avoided, the same with the black colour or negativity of any kind. Another, much simpler aspect of youth, relating to the Tara bureau, is that the newly established specialised institution employed a large number of young, newly graduated artists.

151 209–212 231–235 238

[Z] is for zooming in
Zooming in was one of the main creative methods we used during this research of the Tara bureau and their artistic practices.
This encouraged us to delve deeper and immerse ourselves in personal archives, artist biographies and other case studies in order to
highlight individual details and look for overlaps, repetitions, similarities or contrasts. This method also encouraged the reproduction of
some of the works, as well as their appropriation, repetition, and the transposition of some of their individual fragments into other contexts.